C000214545

PARAS

ABOUT THE AUTHOR

William F. Buckingham was awarded his PhD on the establishment and initial development of a British airborne force. His other books include *Tobruk: The Great Siege 1941–1942, Arnhem 1944* and *D-Day: The First 72 Hours*, all published by Tempus. He lives near Glasgow.

Praise for *D-Day: The First 72 Hours*

'A compelling narrative' *The Observer*

'William F. Buckingham's iconoclastic *D-Day: The First 72 Hours* provides a refreshing antidote to the frequently anodyne 60th anniversary coverage' *BBC History Magazine*, Books of the Year 2004

Praise for *Arnhem 1944*

'Buckingham leaves the reader in no doubt that British army politics, inexperience and incompetence led to this tragedy of errors' *The Guardian*

'Startling... reveals the real reason why the daring attack failed' *The Daily Express*

'The originality of this book lies in its exploration of the long term origins of the battle as well as in its account of the fighting itself... an excellent read'
Hew Strachan, Chichele Professor of the History of War at Oxford University

PARAS

The Birth of British Airborne Forces from Churchill's Raiders to 1st Parachute Brigade

William F. Buckingham

TEMPUS

This edition first published 2008

Tempus Publishing
Cirencester Road, Chalford,
Stroud, Gloucestershire, GL6 8PE
www.tempus-publishing.com

Tempus Publishing is an imprint of The History Press Limited

British Library Cataloguing in Publication Data.
A catalogue record for this book is available from the British Library.

ISBN 978 0 7524 4594 6

Typesetting and origination by The History Press Limited
Printed in Great Britain by Ashford Colour Press Ltd

Contents

Glossary

ACAS(T) (RAF)	Assistant Chief of Air Staff (Training)
AFE	Airborne Forces Establishment
AFEE	Airborne Forces Experimental Establishment
AG (Army)	Adjutant General
ATC	Army Training Centre (Hardwick Hall)
AM	Air Ministry
AMDI (RAF)	Air Ministry Director of Intelligence
DoR (RAF)	Air Ministry Director of Research
AMSO (RAF)	Air Ministry Staff Officer
BEF	British Expeditionary Force
CAS (RAF)	Chief of Air Staff
CAS(T) (RAF)	Chief of Air Staff (Training)
CIGS (Army)	Chief of Imperial General Staff
C-in-C	Commander-in-Chief
CLE	Central Landing Establishment
CLS	Central Landing School
CoS	Chiefs of Staff
DCAS (RAF)	Deputy Chief of Air Staff
DCO	Director Combined Operations
DDCO	Deputy Director Combined Operations
DFC	Distinguished Flying Cross

DMC (RAF)	Director of Military Co-operation
DMO&P (Army)	Director Military Operations & Planning
DMT (Army)	Director Military Training
DoP (RAF)	Director/Department of Plans
DRO (Army)	Director Recruiting & Organisation
DSO	Distinguished Service Order
DZ	Drop Zone
GoC:	General Officer Commanding
GS(R)	General Staff (Research)
GTS	Glider Training School/Squadron
HALO	High Altitude Low Opening
ISTDC	Inter Service Development & Training Centre
Luftwaffe	German Air Force since 1933
LZ	Landing Zone
MAP	Ministry of Aircraft Production
MC	Military Cross
MI(R)	Military Intelligence (Research)
MTP (Army)	Military Training Pamphlet
MU (RAF)	Maintenance Unit
OTU (RAF)	Operational Training Unit
PDF (RAF)	Parachute Development Flight
PISM	Polish Institute & Sikorski Museum
PTC	Parachute Training Centre
PTS	Parachute Training School/Squadron
RAE	Royal Aircraft Establishment
RAF	Royal Air Force
RAMC	Royal Army Medical Corps
RASC (Army)	Royal Army Service Corps
RE	Royal Engineers
RFC	Royal Flying Corps
Rip-cord	manual device for deploying parachute canopy
RNAS	Royal Naval Air Service
RTR (Army)	Royal Tank Regiment
SOE	Special Operations Executive
Static-line	strap or cord linking parachute to the aircraft, permitting automatic opening
USAAF	United States Army Air Force
USMC	United States Marine Corps
WE (Army)	War Establishment
WO	War Office

Introduction

On 19 June 1998 I was privileged to attend the Aldershot parade at which the Parachute Regiment received new colours from the Prince of Wales. Conversation among Second World War Parachute Regiment veterans at the subsequent reception confirmed the findings of my research to that date. It was common knowledge that the British airborne force had been established in June 1940, that Winston Churchill was personally involved, and some knew members or had heard anecdotes about the original No.2 Commando parachute cadre. That, however, was as far as it went, a situation that mirrors the position in the published sources. There, the establishment of the British airborne force rates a few pages at best, and a few lines at worst, even in the official and semi-official histories. This is understandable, for battlefield history appears to offer more dramatic reading than the minutiae of establishments and background developments.

Be that as it may, the published accounts invariably subscribe to the same received wisdom. Prompted by the groundbreaking

German use of airborne troops in the Low Countries in May 1940, Churchill ordered the creation of a raiding force that included a parachute capability. The Army and RAF, faced with the impact of Dunkirk and seemingly imminent invasion, nonetheless applied themselves manfully to the task. This admittedly involved some minor misunderstandings and disagreements, but all concerned pulled together and Churchill's directive was duly fulfilled after an unavoidable delay and despite shortages of equipment and especially aircraft. There is of course an element of essential truth in this upbeat version of events. There is also, however, a great deal more to the matter than this rather broad-brush treatment suggests.

In addition to filling out the international backdrop to British developments, this book will challenge this received wisdom. First, it will show that British involvement in the air transportation of troops and material actually began in the period following the end of the First World War. British forces in the Empire established a world lead in the technique that became a staple, if largely unacknowledged, feature of British Imperial policing activities. The experience thus gained was to prove invaluable in the latter stages of the war in Burma, which saw the garrisons of the Admin Box, Imphal and Kohima supplied and reinforced by air, a development which totally nullified the highly mobile tactics of the British Army's Japanese opponents.

Second, and more importantly, it will show that the establishment of British airborne force in the accepted sense did not begin and end in the period June to September 1940, as is popularly claimed. In fact, it took a year and a half to field a trained parachute force on something approaching the scale Churchill had demanded in June 1940, and equipment shortages played only a comparatively minor role in this extended gestation. In reality, it was more due to the pernicious effects of inter-service rivalry, premeditated obstructionism, internal service politicking, and bureaucratic incompetence. It also involved administrative convenience, deliberate subterfuge, high-level political intervention, drastic changes in policy, and the deliberate and unacknowledged plagiarism of an ally's doctrinal and technical development work.

This work is drawn from my PhD thesis completed at the University of Glasgow in 2001, and I should like to thank the following individuals and institutions for their assistance in making it and this book possible. The late Professor John Erickson and Dr Jeremy Crang, University of Edinburgh; Mrs Edith Philips of the Scottish United Services Museum, Edinburgh; Professor M.R.D. Foot; the late General Sir John Hackett; Lieutenant-Colonel Jan Jozef Lorys (Retd); Dr Alex Marshall; Mr Simon Moody and John Edwards of The Royal Air Force Museum, Hendon; Dr John Rhodes, Curator of The Royal Engineers Museum; the staff at The National Archives, Kew; Dr James Sterrett; Mr Andrzej Suchitz, Keeper of the Archives, The Polish Institute and Sikorski Museum; all the staff, academic and clerical, at the Department of Modern History, University of Glasgow; and last but by no means least, my academic supervisor, Professor Hew Strachan, whose guidance, patience and criticism were invaluable.

William F. Buckingham
Bishopbriggs, Glasgow
March 2005

1

Developments in Transporting Troops by Air Before 1940

In common with many military ideas, that of deploying troops from the air occurred before the technology necessary to make it a reality. The earliest proponent of airborne warfare appears to have been Benjamin Franklin, one of the Founding Fathers of the United States. Being well read, a scientist and having military experience in the recent American War of Independence, Franklin immediately grasped the military potential of a hot air balloon demonstration he witnessed in Paris in 1784, as his subsequent comment clearly shows:

> Five thousand balloons, capable of raising two men each, could not cost more than five ships of the line...And where is the Prince who can afford so to cover his country with troops for its defense,

> as that ten thousand men descending from the clouds might not in many places do an infinite deal of mischief before a force could be brought together to repel them?[1]

Hot air balloons were not really a viable method of delivery, however, and the idea therefore languished for well over a century, until the imperatives of war prompted the necessary technological developments. By 1914, the aeroplane had been widely adopted for military reconnaissance, and that role was swiftly widened to encompass air-to-air combat and aerial bombing. The latter activity was initially restricted by the small carrying capacity of the available aircraft, which were almost exclusively single-engine machines with one or two crewmen.

There were, however, exceptions to this general rule from the outset, and the alternative line of development they provided marks the beginning of the path that eventually turned Franklin's vision into reality. Igor Sikorski's four-engine *Ilya Muromets* flew in the summer of 1914, as did a three-engine design by Gianni Caproni that October.[2] Because they could lift far greater payloads, machines of this size offered the prospect of striking strategic targets, and this idea was taken up in earnest by both the British and German air services. Elements within the German military and naval staffs had advocated indiscriminate aerial bombardment to break British civilian morale as early as 1912,[3] and turned to the heavy bomber when the Zeppelin airship proved too vulnerable for the job. *Kagohl 3*, nicknamed the *Englandgeschwader*,[4] was formed at the end of 1916, and carried out day and night raids against London and south-east England from a base at Ostend from mid-1917.[5]

The German effort, however, was both preceded and to some extent overshadowed by the British. The Royal Naval Air Service (RNAS), tasked to protect naval bases in the south of England,[6] liberally interpreted this brief to justify attacking the Friedrichshafen Zeppelin works by Lake Constance on 21 November 1914,[7] and a series of raids against targets in occupied Belgium in the following spring. Their relative success prompted the RNAS to canvas for more suitable bombing aircraft. The result, following a rather prophetic rejection of an early design – 'Look, Mr. Page – what I want is a bloody paralyser, not a toy!'[8] – was the Handley Page 0/100, the first of a long line of British heavy bombers that extended to the nuclear 'V Bombers' of the 1950s. The 0/100 first flew in December 1915; the first two operational machines were delivered in November 1916 and the third was accidentally gifted to the Germans by a lost delivery pilot on New Year's Day 1917.

The new type's first employment was a series of raids against industrial targets in Lorraine and the Saar, which continued until March 1917 after which they were called off, probably because the returns did not justify the effort.[9] Strategic operations were resumed in October 1917 in reprisal for the activities of *Kagohl 3*, with raids against Stuttgart, Mainz and Cologne. By June 1918 the British strategic bomber force had been expanded into the semi-autonomous Independent Force, sometimes referred to as the Independent Air Force.[10] Under the latter's auspices, 550 tons of bombs were dropped on German targets between 6 June and 10 November 1918, by which time the longer-ranged Handley Page 0/400 bomber was in service.[11] The Handley Page V1500, which was designed to reach Berlin, entered service just too late to see action.[12]

Thus by 1918 there were aircraft of sufficient size and power to make air transportation a potentially reasonable proposition. Admittedly, these machines did not appear until the latter stages of the conflict, and they were understandably deployed exclusively in the role for which they were designed. Nonetheless, there was some limited use of aircraft for transportation during the First World War. They were used regularly to deliver intelligence agents behind enemy lines, initially by landing and later by parachute, to minimise the risk to aircraft and pilot,[13] although this method appears to have been largely restricted to the delivery of individuals.[14] The most significant use of aircraft for transport was therefore related to the delivery of material rather than men.

The British pioneered this in their attempt to supply the besieged garrison of Kut in Mesopotamia, in March and April 1916. This was the first large-scale operation of its type, and was also the first to employ parachutes. The latter were used to deliver a 70lb millstone on 27 March 1916, to allow local production of flour. Initially a variety of items, including medical supplies, wireless and engine parts, mail, newspapers and money, were delivered, although it is unclear which items were free-dropped. When the siege began to bite in mid-April 1916, the focus shifted to supplying foodstuffs, following a rather optimistic request for a minimum of 5,000lb per day, including flour, chocolate, salt and ghee cooking oil. Food drops commenced on 15 April 1916 and 3,350lb was delivered on the first day. The effort was discontinued on 29 April 1916, by which time 140 flights had delivered a total of 19,000lb of supplies, 16,800lb of which was recovered by the garrison.[15]

While this did not meet the requested minimum, it does not detract from the magnitude or significance of the effort, particularly given the adverse conditions. Be that as it may, Kut proved aerial supply was viable, and the Middle East remained the proving ground, not least because it provided a convenient way of offsetting the dearth of roads and railways. In addition, the weather and terrain were generally favourable for flying operations, and there was little enemy opposition. On 22 September 1918, for example, the single Handley Page 0/400 bomber stationed in the Middle East was used as a temporary freight-carrier to deliver a ton of fuel, lubricants, spare parts and other supplies to an isolated RAF detachment.

Conditions were very different in France and Flanders, but aerial resupply was used there in direct support of ground forces on the battlefield. On 4 July 1918, twelve specially adapted RE8 aircraft from No.9 Squadron RAF delivered almost 12,000 rounds of small-arms ammunition to the 4th Australian Division. The ammunition was pre-packed in ninety-three boxes, which were dropped from 800 feet, and the ground troops were provided with white cloth letters 'N' and 'V' to signify whether they required clipped or belted ammunition. The operation lasted for around six hours, each aircraft made four thirty-minute sorties, and two were lost. Similar operations were carried out on 21 and 22 August and 1 and 2 October 1918, when 121 boxes of ammunition and a quantity of signal flares and coils of barbed wire were delivered. Subsequent drops also included food. Nos 82 and 218 Squadrons RAF delivered 15,000 individual rations, totalling thirteen tons, to isolated French and Belgian troops on 2 and 3 October 1918.[16] Ten days later No.35 Squadron delivered two tons of food in seventeen sorties to the starving population of Le Cateau, despite adverse weather conditions.[17]

Thus, by the close of hostilities in November 1918, the British at least had accepted the idea of delivering supplies to ground forces from the air, and had expanded the idea to encompass battlefield resupply. Running alongside this was at least some theoretical examination of expanding the technique to include the delivery of troops. Probably the most famous example of this was US Army Colonel William Mitchell's October 1918 scheme to capture Metz by dropping 12,000 men from the US 1st Infantry Division by parachute from Handley Page 0/400 bombers belonging to the Independent Air Force.[18] Fortunately, Mitchell's scheme was rejected, not least because there were insufficient parachutes to equip even a fraction of the projected force. The 1st Division troops were doubtless also relieved if they actually heard about the proposal, as the vast majority of them probably did not have a clue as to what a parachute was, let alone how to use it. There was rather more to creating a parachute force than dragooning men into aircraft physically large enough to carry them, as we shall see, and whether Mitchell's harebrained scheme deserves the accolades it routinely attracts is therefore open to debate.[19] Indeed, it could be argued that, in practical terms, it did little more to further the cause of airborne warfare than Franklin's musings 132 years previously.

A less well-known but rather more practical proposal appeared in October 1917, in a paper published by Winston Churchill covering a wide range of air-related matters. One proposal, which was characteristically long on theory but short on detail, was for the formation of 'flying columns' of air-transported troops for operations behind enemy lines.[20] This was not significant merely because it actually predated Mitchell's scheme by a year. In the long term Churchill's proposal shows that his sponsorship and involvement in the creation of a British airborne force from mid-1940 was not merely a knee-jerk reaction to German airborne operations in the Low Countries, as it is sometimes presented. In fact, Churchill's involvement in air matters went back virtually to the beginning. In addition to his 1917 theorising, he became Secretary of State for War and Air in January 1919, and lobbied hard for the RAF to be given an Imperial role, which resulted in the RAF being given direct responsibility for the defence of Iraq on 1 October 1922.[21] This policy, labelled Air Control, also saw the air transport role pioneered during the First World War expand into a staple of British Imperial activity across the Middle East and India in the 1920s and '30s.

Although the RAF carried it out, this expansion was by no means restricted to purely military activity. In May 1919 the Air Ministry proposed the establishment of a weekly mail service between Egypt and India, but it was abandoned after fifteen of fifty-one Handley Page 0/400s despatched to Egypt as a mobility demonstration were written off in accidents, along with several more damaged and eight fatalities.[22] A less ambitious service between Baghdad and Cairo began in June

1921, and carried over four tons of assorted mail and 120 passengers in the first twelve months.[23] Military air transport initially concentrated on casualty evacuation, the first recorded instance of which took place in the Sinai desert in February 1917. The capability was deliberately factored into the RAF's first direct foray into Imperial policing. The RAF contingent deployed to Somalia in January 1920 as part of the joint campaign against the 'Mad Mullah' fielded the world's first custom-built air ambulance. A converted DH9 nicknamed 'the hearse', the machine was developed on the recommendation of the contingent's senior Medical Officer, and the success of the concept led the Air Ministry to procure three specially modified Vickers Vimy ambulance aircraft in 1921–22.[24]

The RAF's first large-scale medical airlift was prompted by an outbreak of dysentery among troops operating in Kurdistan in April 1923. In it, 198 men were lifted the 260 miles from Girde Telleh to Baghdad, completing what would otherwise have been a six-day mule journey in a few hours.[25] By mid-May 1923, the total had risen to 255 patients, and the practice became standard in the Middle East thereafter. Between 1925 and 1935, an average of 120 patients a year were airlifted to hospitals in Egypt, Palestine and Iraq, and from April 1929 cases requiring sea repatriation to the UK were flown to Port Said and later Jaffa for embarkation. The concept was transferred to India largely as a result of the Quetta earthquake in May 1935. In the twenty-one days following the disaster, RAF aircraft delivered a fully equipped, twenty-six-strong Army medical unit, 4,300lb of clothing and 12,750lb of food and medical supplies, and evacuated 136 casualties for treatment at Karachi, Lahore and Risalpur.

By 1937 the total of Indian medical cases moved by air exceeded those of Iraq and the Middle East. This was partly due to the campaign in Waziristan, which accounted for half the 298 cases moved by air in India that year. By 1939, RAF aircraft had carried some 2,600 assorted medical cases a total of 320,000 miles.[26] This overlapped to an extent with the evacuation of officials and civilians from threatened locations. In September 1922 sixty-seven assorted evacuees were lifted from Sulaimaniya in Iraq in a six-hour operation,[27] and subsequent operations were larger and sustained. A rebellion in Afghanistan in November 1928 led to the evacuation of the British and other legations from Kabul, beginning on 23 December 1928. Despite severe winter conditions, a total of 586 passengers and 24,000lb of baggage were flown to safety in India in an operation that went on until February 1929.[28]

Purely military air transportation ran alongside this medical and humanitarian activity, and was often carried out by the same units. No.70 Squadron RAF, for example, was involved in the Sulaimaniya evacuation of 1922, the first airlift of troops in 1923, the Kabul evacuation of 1928–29, and in the pioneering battalion-sized troop lift from Egypt to Iraq in 1932. The process began on 21 September 1920 when two Handley Page 0/400 bombers successfully lifted a dismantled mountain gun, complete with crew and ammunition, from Heliopolis to Almaza in Egypt; the gun was brought into action within seven minutes of the aircraft touching down.[29] The Handley Page machines were not well adapted for carrying passengers, but the arrival of specially configured Vickers Vernon aircraft at the end of 1921 made lifting complete units of troops a practical proposition.[30] Thus in February 1923 two companies of Sikh infantry were flown into Kirkuk to stem a native insurrection, and in May the following year a company of British troops were lifted 150 miles from Baghdad to Kirkuk in response to a further outbreak of civil disorder. Thereafter, airlift became a standard crisis management measure that grew in both size and distance. In August 1929, a fifty-two-strong detachment from the South Wales Borderers was lifted by air from Egypt to Jerusalem, and on 23 October 1931 a company of the King's

Regiment was airlifted from Palestine to Cyprus. The latter was the first airlift of troops over the open sea.[31]

In June 1932, the RAF mounted its largest single air transport operation of the inter-war period, lifting 526 men of the 1st Battalion, the Northamptonshire Regiment, over 800 miles from Egypt to Iraq. Spread over 22 to 27 June, the operation involved twenty-five Vickers Victoria aircraft flying a total of thirty-six separate sorties. The lift was repeated in reverse over a less hurried twenty-five-day period between 18 July and 12 August 1932.[32] By the latter half of the 1930s, larger-scale lifts spread over longer periods were a regular feature of Imperial policing operations. During the Waziristan campaign for example, a total of 5,750 troops and 400 tons of supplies were delivered in a series of lifts between November 1936 and May 1938.[33] The practice was also extended to include routine troop movements. The 'Chitral Relief' was a twice-yearly garrison relief on the North-West Frontier that normally entailed a thirty-six-day march and the deployment of a substantial security force. The idea of carrying out the Relief by air was mooted in 1927, and by 1940 the entire Relief was being conducted by air,[34] apparently laying the foundations for the large-scale airlift operations mounted in support of operations against the Japanese in 1944.[35] The 1930s also saw the introduction of troop airlift to the UK, albeit on a more modest scale, with the RAF providing aircraft for troop acclimatisation flights at Farnborough on an annual basis. In 1938 5,250 troops took part in such flights, and included a tactical landing exercise at Catterick Barracks involving a platoon of Coldstream Guards.[36]

By 1940, therefore, air transportation by the RAF had become an accepted, regular and important feature of British military activity across the Empire and, to a lesser extent, at home. While they may have been the first to employ air transportation, however, they were by no means alone. The United States Marine Corps deployed and maintained isolated outposts and evacuated casualties by air during the Second Nicaraguan Campaign of 1925–1929, moving a total of 21,148 personnel over that period. In 1931 a US Army field artillery battery was airlifted across the Panama Canal Zone, and the exercise was repeated with a full battalion in 1933 with a full artillery battalion, and the previous year a small infantry force was air-landed during manoeuvres at Fort Du Pont, Delaware.[37] On the other side of the Atlantic, Hitler's Luftwaffe carried out a sustained airlift on behalf of Franco's Spanish Nationalist forces in 1936. Between July and September 1936, German Junkers 52 aircraft shuttled almost 9,000 troops, with their equipment, support weapons and ammunition, from Morocco to Spain.[38]

The main player besides Britain in the air-landing field for much of the inter-war period was the Red Army, however. Again, Imperial policing, in this instance in Central Asia, appears to have been the catalyst for Soviet developments. On 27 May 1928 the 8th Independent Reconnaissance Aviation Detachment carried out an 'air-landing assault' against guerrillas unit in the Turkestan Military District.[39] A contemporary account published in January 1929 that included operational conclusions and recommendations may have been referring to the same landing,[40] but at least one other operation was carried out that same year. An air-landed party was credited with driving off a band of Moslem *Basmachi* tribesmen besieging the garrison of Garm in Tadzhikistan.[41] It is unclear whether they were inspired by all this or were a separate initiative, but a series of air-landing trials was carried out in the Leningrad Military District in 1928 by future marshal M.N. Tukhachevsky. The results were used as the basis of a reinforced-company-size exercise the following year. The success of this prompted Tukhachevsky to propose the formation of '...a sample air-motorised division... for use as an operational-strategic air-landing force'.[42]

Wherever the idea came from, it marked the point where Soviet development diverged from the British policing example toward a direct role on the conventional battlefield. The chief of staff of the Red Army's air component, A.N. Lapchinsky, advocated using aircraft to deliver troops into the enemy's rear areas in significant numbers, and produced detailed plans and calculations and battalion and regimental scale missions. He also suggested these forces be used for tactical missions in support of mobile ground operations, to threaten enemy flanks, disrupt their communications and seize key terrain features like river crossings or defiles. Thus an 'aviation motorised landing detachment' of company size was formed in the Leningrad Military District in March 1931, and, beginning in January 1932, similar detachments were authorised for the Moscow, Belorussian and Ukrainian Military Districts.[43] In the event, only the Leningrad detachment became fully operational, and it was expanded to brigade size in December 1932 and re-designated the '3rd Airlanding Brigade (Special Purpose)' with three battalions and an organic, three-squadron air group. The Brigade appears to have been a success, given that similarly capable units of company and battalion size were set up and attached to corps and divisional commands across the Soviet Union from March 1933. By January 1934, these units numbered around 10,000 men, complete with representation on the Red Army staff, a dedicated training organisation and a coherent operational doctrine.[44]

The speed and scale of Soviet development was undeniably impressive, but it also marked the limit of aerial troop transportation as practised to that date. This was defined by the fact that fixed-wing aircraft were, and indeed remain, totally reliant upon suitable and secure landing grounds, conditions that were by no means easy to guarantee in a war situation, especially on or near the battlefield. The Soviet landings in Central Asia in the late 1920s did show that more aggressive tactics were possible, but these were small-scale and benefited from the element of surprise. The 1929 landing at Garm, for example, employed only three light aircraft and fifteen men including aircrew, and was mounted in a flat, desert region ideal for landing.[45] Things are likely to have rapidly taken a different turn once the *Basmachi* became familiar with the tactic and identified its limitations, as they undoubtedly would. Landing any aircraft, let alone large, heavily laden transport machines, in the face of even relatively unsophisticated opposition was an extremely hazardous and potentially costly act, as the Luftwaffe were to discover in Holland in 1940 and at Maleme on Crete the following year. The missing element was a method that would allow troops to be delivered without landing the aircraft, and for this the Soviets turned to the parachute.

Adoption of the parachute and later the glider marked the move away from using aircraft purely as transport to the development of combat-capable airborne forces in the accepted sense. Before moving on to examine this line of development, however, it is pertinent to examine why the British did not take this step until June 1940. At that point they were obliged to play catch-up under the most trying circumstances, because their initial world lead in military air transportation had been far outstripped by Soviet and German airborne progress. At first glance this was a curious turn of events, for the British appear to have possessed sufficient equipment and expertise to match these developments. Neither were they unaware of them. British officers attended the large-scale Soviet airborne exercises in the mid-1930s, while Winston Churchill hypothesised about an airborne invasion of Britain in June 1936.[46] British intelligence monitored German developments,[47] and at least one popular journal published a photo essay of German paratroopers jumping from Junkers 52 aircraft in October 1938.[48]

The reason for this lapse was a set of specifically British circumstances, perhaps the most high-profile of which was funding. The British government made clear in August 1919 that it was only prepared to sanction military spending within the 'narrow limits consistent with national safety'.[49] This policy was steadfastly maintained until the mid-1930s, when it was belatedly recognised that it had been carried to the point where the armed forces were becoming incapable of doing any such thing.[50] In practical terms this meant that there was barely sufficient funding to cover the three services' existing commitments for most of the inter-war period,[51] and the individual services had their own pet projects to fund with what surplus was available. The Army, for example, managed to lay the foundations for future mechanisation, while the RAF managed to pursue its near obsession with strategic bombing. The creation of a dedicated airborne force could have been presented as a cost-saving measure, for a properly configured and equipped force located in the Middle East could have provided a useful force multiplier for Imperial policing. Neither service appears to have been much interested in officially developing matters beyond the existing level of *ad hoc* co-operation, however, which suggests that the idea did not figure in their priorities.

In addition to this, the British Army's attitude was shaped at least in part by a shortage of manpower, particularly infantrymen, the most logical arm from which to draw the nucleus of an airborne force. The latter increased to constitute over half the Army's manpower between 1918 and 1935,[52] but this was more than offset by a parallel increase in the Army's commitments, particularly to Imperial policing duties.[53] The creation of an airborne force would therefore have imposed an additional strain upon an already hard-pressed arm. In addition, by the mid-1930s, the Army was experiencing difficulty in attracting sufficient recruits in spite of the poor economic climate, and the infantry army was also undergoing something of an identity crisis. Both topics provoked heated debate among contemporary military pundits. The recruiting crisis was attributed to a number of factors, not least of which was the disparity in Other Ranks prospects compared to non-military careers during and after service, and dissatisfaction with Reserve Service obligations. Others included the Army's concentration upon drill and turn-out, backward-looking commanders, recruiting advertising that insulted the intelligence of potential recruits and, interestingly, the perceived glamour of RAF service as a more attractive alternative.[54]

Some of these concerns overlapped with concerns over contemporary infantry training and its relevance for future warfare. Beginning in military journals,[55] the debate spilled over into the general press,[56] and subsequently drew in high-profile military theorists including Fuller and Liddell Hart.[57] The problem was also acknowledged to some extent within the Army. Future field marshal Alanbrooke, for example, set up a brigade school to remedy the poor tactical leadership skills he found, particularly at the platoon level, while commanding the 8th Infantry Brigade in 1934–35. Brooke subsequently advocated regulating and centralising infantry training via the establishment of a dedicated School of Infantry, but despite widespread support and lobbying the Director of Military Training (DMT) at the War Office in 1935, he was unsuccessful then and during his own tenure as DMT the following year.[58] In the event, the School of Infantry he advocated did not become a reality until 1942, when it formed part of a general reformation and modernisation of the Army's training practises and infrastructure.[59]

None of this necessarily precluded the Army from at least examining the airborne idea, but there were two additional reasons that militated against it too. First, the Army was fully occupied with mechanisation, a fraught process that arguably sated its appetite and capacity for innovation.[60] Second, the Army simply did not have any aircraft with which to experiment. The latter belonged to the RAF which, as the machines represented its reason for being and justification for existence as an independent entity, guarded its monopoly jealously. This might not have mattered had the RAF expressed an interest in airborne development, but it was also preoccupied with their own narrow problems and priorities.

The RAF became the world's first independent air arm on 1 April 1918 with the amalgamation of the RFC and RNAS, complete with its own Air Ministry in Whitehall and a wealth of operational experience. Between July 1916 and November 1918 – the cessation of hostilities – British aircraft flew almost a million operational hours, dropped 6,942 tons of bombs, and expended 10.5 million rounds of ammunition on ground targets. At the cessation of hostilities, RAF personnel numbered 300,000, deployed in 200 squadrons.[61] For all that, however, the RAF's overall contribution to the Allied victory was largely peripheral. The fledgling strategic bombing effort cited above yielded little for great expense in practical terms, and the new air arm's greatest contribution lay in the aerial observation and reconnaissance role for which it had been originally formed in 1914.[62] It can therefore be argued that the hugely expanded British air service ended the war roughly where it began, and as the fledgling RAF had no traditional role to fall back on, it was particularly vulnerable to post-war government cutbacks.

The RAF adroitly solved this problem by simply creating an Imperial role for itself, based on the supposed economies offered by replacing manpower with technology, augmented by some creative accounting. The RAF's first post-war foray into Imperial policing involved contributing the eight-aircraft-strong 'Z Force' to operations in Somaliland in 1919–20, at a claimed cost of £77,000; the relatively low price tag was subsequently and widely cited as justification for what was later dubbed Air Control. What was less widely cited was that this figure conveniently overlooked the Army's larger and longer-lasting involvement in the campaign, which doubled the cost to £150,000.[63] The RAF's strategy nonetheless worked, assisted by a lobbying from Churchill in his role as Secretary of State for

War and Air, and the Air Ministry was given responsibility for maintaining order in Iraq on 1 October 1922.[64]

The sheer geographical size of the RAF's new fiefdom required long-range aircraft capable of bombing or transporting materiel for smaller aircraft operating from remote locations. As we have seen, the RAF possessed a pool of large bombers which could be modified for transportation, and this dual-purpose capability became a deliberate design feature; Air Ministry specifications designated all bombers 'bomber/transports' until the mid-1930s.[65] It was thus Air Control that prompted the development of large transport aircraft and provided the conditions for their employment. Even with this capability, however, it is significant that Air Control was not considered a viable stand-alone. Churchill was then the RAF's staunchest political supporter, but he nonetheless considered that policing Iraq would require some 14,000 ground troops in addition to whatever the RAF deployed.[66]

Churchill's opinion highlighted the Achilles heel of the Air Control policy, which was the lack of a properly integrated and sufficiently large ground component to offset its limitations in the remote regions where Air Control was supposed to be most applicable.[67] The fact that the RAF was obliged to form armoured car units as a mobile ground back-up for their aerial activities suggests that they too were aware of this omission,[68] and that 'Air-and-Armour Control' was a more appropriate title for the policy, as suggested by Liddell Hart.[69] In the event, apart from the armoured car squadrons and small, locally raised units for airfield defence, the RAF did not establish any integral ground forces in the inter-war period, and for several reasons. Given the atmosphere of inter-service strife generated by the government's funding restrictions, such a move would doubtless have provoked a sharp response from the Army looking to maintain its share of funding. Besides, the RAF was subject to the same fiscal restraints as the Army, and it is difficult to see how it could have found the additional funding for a dedicated airborne force any more readily.

In addition, there was the fact that the RAF sold its Air Control policy as a means of substituting aerial technology for manpower, which in itself ruled out the establishment of a sizeable RAF ground force. The armoured car units required relatively few personnel, and could be justified as a security and rescue measure for downed aircraft and their crews. Anything larger would have been a duplication of the Army's function, assuming the Air Ministry could have obtained the requisite manpower, and more importantly an admission that Air Control was a flawed concept. It would also have undermined the RAF's carefully crafted image as a modern, high-tech force, and by extension have cast doubt upon the RAF's status as an independent service.

All this was arguably more than sufficient excuse for the RAF not pre-empting the Luftwaffe by establishing the world's first airborne force under the control of an independent air arm. The most pressing reason, however, was doctrinal. In the same way the Army was preoccupied with mechanisation, the RAF was preoccupied with aerial bombing, which had occupied a central position in its thinking since 1918. Bombing supplied the coercive element of Air Control, and widespread public fear of bombing in the 1930s provided the RAF with additional justification for independence to set alongside its Imperial policing role. This fear was largely illusory, being based largely upon a mixture of questionable extrapolations from German bombing during the First World War and sensationalised coverage of events in China and Spain, reinforced by alarmist popular writing.[70] Nonetheless, it was simultaneously encapsulated and endorsed by Prime Minister Stanley Baldwin's oft-misquoted claim that 'the bomber will always get through'.[71]

The RAF initially capitalised upon these popular fears by portraying itself as an anti-bomber force, via its theory of Strategic Interception formulated in the late 1920s, which was then gradually replaced with a home-grown offensive bombing doctrine. This doctrine, dubbed the 'Knockout Blow', had actually been drawn up in 1925 and became the RAF's guiding principle by the latter half of the 1930s. Essentially, it viewed the bomber as a war-winning weapon in its own right, capable of inflicting lethal damage to an enemy's war-making capacity.[72] This was a modification of classical airpower theory, insofar as it ignored gaining command of the air as a prerequisite for operations, and substituted an almost mystical belief in the ability of the bomber instead.[73] The unsustainable losses suffered by the unfortunate Bomber Command crews tasked to carry out daylight raids on Germany in the first few days of the Second World War rapidly and bloodily exposed the flaws in this line of thinking.[74] The point here, however, is that the RAF's chosen method of waging war had no place for the creation of an integral ground force, airborne or otherwise. Strategic bombing was intended largely as a substitute for ground operations, and the establishment of an RAF force for terrestrial operations, even ones launched from the sky, was therefore heretical at worst and irrelevant at best. As we shall see, this attitude was to exert a malign influence on the establishment of a dedicated British airborne force.

Had they been at all interested in exploring the airborne idea, the most logical course would have been for the Army and RAF to co-operate. A united front was far more likely to secure government approval and possibly additional funding; it would have permitted them to offset their respective deficiencies in means and men; and it was of course the solution eventually adopted in 1940. However, this was ruled out by inter-service rivalry of an intensity that was only partly generated by funding competition, although that would have been a not inconsiderable factor. The RAF may have possessed the necessary transport aircraft, but parachutes and all their ancillary training and storage equipment were expensive, and it is by no means clear that either Service would have been willing or indeed able to carry the additional cost. Be that as it may, inter-service rivalry focused on less exotic matters. As we have seen, the War Office resented the way the Air Ministry had impinged on its traditional Imperial domain, and was further aggrieved at the total removal of its aviation capability, a sentiment it shared with the Admiralty. For its part, the Air Ministry viewed its fellow Services with deep suspicion, merely waiting their chance to destroy the RAF's independence in order to reassert control over the assets they had lost on 1 April 1918. Like the RAF's preoccupation with bombing to the exclusion of all else, this inter-service rivalry was also to exert a malign influence over the establishment and subsequent development of British Airborne Forces.

Neither Service was blameless in the frequently childish tit-for-tat exchanges that followed across the inter-war period and beyond. The RAF, for example, only formed its armoured car units in Iraq after the Army forbade its units to continue unofficial local co-operation with their RAF opposite numbers. In that particular case at least, the Army actually shot itself in the foot. War Office reluctance to place Army units under RAF control, even temporarily, lost the Army the chance to use Imperial policing as a lever for mechanisation, in the same way as the RAF used Air Control for its survival.[75]

Nonetheless, it has to be acknowledged that this inter-service rivalry and its associated enmity was not universal within either service. This was especially the case at the operational level, and the level of hostility appears to have waned in direct relation to the distance from Whitehall. Thus in the Empire relations between Army and RAF personnel were frequently most cordial, a point illustrated in a comment by Martel in the mid-1930s: 'The Air Force is a good show out here [in India]; I wish the Army was as progressive.'[76] Martel, however, was exaggerating a little, even though his sentiment remains a popular one for critics of the British Army. The 1842 retreat from Kabul, the Crimea and both Boer Wars are recurring favourites in this theme, which invariably portrays the Army as hidebound, inflexible and generally incompetent.[77]

However, this view conveniently overlooks the fact that operations in the Empire obliged the Army to operate in extreme geographical and climatic conditions as a matter of routine, which in turn obliged adjustments in training, tactics, organisation and equipment, and bred a high level of flexibility. The creation of highly mobile Ranger light infantry units in North America from the 1740s provide a good example,[78] as does the subsequent incorporation of the idea into more conventional units as a counter to the mass tactics of Revolutionary France during the Napoleonic Wars.[79] Further examples include the creation of the all-arms Punjab Frontier Force in the mid-nineteenth century, which adapted the irregular fighting methods of the local hill tribes,[80] and the widespread introduction of mounted infantry units to enhance mobility in the vast open spaces of Egypt and South Africa.[81] These initiatives also frequently employed the latest technology. The Punjab Frontier Force, for example, was equipped with specially designed lightweight artillery pieces,[82] while the Royal Engineers deployed a traction-engine-equipped 'Steam Road Transport Company' in the Second Boer War.[83] Thus, despite being denigrated as 'merely the play of children',[84] the life-and-death reality of colonial operations demanded flexibility of a high order.

The RAF in the Empire in the inter-war period thus may well have been a flexible and progressive good show, as Martel claimed. This, however, was a direct result of the RAF being obliged, just like the Army before it, to adapt to the realities of its new operational environment. This, rather than any special qualities, explains the RAF's pioneering move into air transportation, and its *ad hoc* but nonetheless highly effective co-operation with the Army. Perhaps paradoxically, this operational flexibility was also the reason why British forces did not attempt to establish a dedicated airborne force before 1940. Although seemingly appropriate, in fact it is difficult to see what advantage such a development would have offered over the existing system of airlifting conventional troops, which required no specialist training or equipment and little more than a slight reconfiguring of personal equipment. This, in effect, was little different from travelling by road or rail, which meant it also required little or no special command and control structure or arrangements.

The only additional capability a dedicated airborne force might have offered was that of direct assault, but there was little requirement for this in Imperial policing as practised by the British. Much of this involved quelling urban unrest, and as urban terrain is highly unsuitable for landing troops from the air, a direct assault capability was of limited utility. It can also be argued that this would have been the case in the wilder hinterland of the Empire too. Tribal communities rapidly adopted deep shelters to counter Air Control bombing. They would have been no less swift in identifying the importance and characteristics of landing grounds and either avoiding or setting ambushes on them, assuming that suitable sites were available in the right locations. Forming a parachute spearhead force to secure landing grounds was one solution, but one that created further problems in addition to the matter of training and equipment. The relatively small number of aircraft capable of carrying parachutists would have restricted the size of such a force, and small parties of the latter would have been extremely vulnerable. The fate of the 'Edwards Patrol' in the Radfan Mountains in Yemen in 1964, with lightweight radios, jet aircraft and helicopters all to hand, provides a graphic illustration of the likely fate of a small force isolated in territory dominated by tribesmen.[85] The prospects for a small parachute-inserted party in the wilder reaches of the Empire during the inter-war period would have been at least as bleak.

The underlying reason why the British did not create a dedicated airborne force in the Empire is therefore simple. In practical terms such a development offered little, if any, benefit over the existing *ad hoc* system, and it was not compatible with Imperial policing as practised by the British in the inter-war period. In short, there was simply no need, and the same can be said for the creation of an airborne force in the UK, if for slightly different reasons. As we have seen, the Army and RAF had their own preoccupations when it came to conventional war-fighting, which did not include airborne warfare, although they kept abreast of developments elsewhere. An article by Major J.T. Godfrey RE published in the *Royal United Services Institute Journal* in 1935 drew heavily on contemporary Soviet military thought, and particularly the role of airborne forces within Deep Battle theory,[86] for example. Similarly, high-ranking observers attended Soviet airborne manoeuvres; both future field marshal Lord Wavell, and Lieutenant-General Sir Giffard Martel attended such exercises near Minsk in 1936.[87]

Be that as it may, there were a number of practical obstacles to establishing a British airborne force at home. As most of the RAF's transport fleet were hard at work in the Empire, there were relatively few suitable machines in the UK, and those that were remained firmly under Air Ministry control. This was an important point, for relations between the Army and RAF at home were far less flexible or cordial than in the Empire, where mutual necessity outweighed inter-service rivalry, and the RAF had no need and little need or interest in co-operation in the home environment in any case. There is also again the matter of suitability. British airborne theorising, such as it was, was based on the Soviet model, which was in turn based on large-scale offensive operations.[88] British operational need at that time was rather more restrained, being focused primarily upon defensive operations in France and Belgium. This allowed little scope for offensive airborne operations, even had the RAF possessed and been forthcoming with the necessary aircraft. The British theorists thus failed fully to appreciate the operational and fiscal realities of the British situation before 1940. Consequently, it can be argued there was even less justification for the creation of a home-based British airborne force than there had been in the Empire.

It is thus clear why, despite the seeming suitability of the airborne idea, the British did not extend their lead in air transportation and supply into the establishment of a dedicated airborne force in the inter-war period. Government parsimony played a part, as did the pernicious effects of inter-service rivalry. The overarching shortage of funding heightened the rivalry between the Army and RAF for what was available, which also precluded airborne experimentation. This was exacerbated by the RAF's independent status, which allowed it to pursue its own aims and doctrines while maintaining sole control over British military aviation. In addition, the Army was overstretched, and had difficulty attracting sufficient infantry recruits to cover its existing commitments.

Relevant as they are, however, these reasons are peripheral. The main reason why no British airborne force was established before June 1940 was simply that the British armed forces had no need of such a capability. It was of dubious utility in an Imperial policing context, and offered no real advantage over the *ad hoc* but perfectly functional Army-RAF co-operation in the Empire. British military observers kept abreast of foreign activities, while homegrown theorists provided a foundation for future development. This remained the case until the German offensive in the West in May 1940, which simultaneously delivered an object lesson in the application of the airborne idea, and transformed the British strategic situation and attitude to the creation of an airborne force out of all recognition. Before moving on to examine that, however, it will be necessary to examine how the airborne idea developed outside Britain and the Empire in the inter-war period.

2
A Feasible Method of Tactical Delivery
Enter the Parachute

Using aircraft purely for transporting troops and supplies as practised by the British in the inter-war period was a significant step simply in terms of mobility. However, the limitations of that technique were becoming apparent by the latter half of the 1920s, and the military forces that showed an interest in developing the idea began to cast around for a way of adapting air transport for a direct battlefield role. In the event, two methods were adopted and ultimately became the mainstay of airborne forces in the accepted sense: the parachute and, to a lesser extent, the glider.

Experiments with man-carrying parachutes go back at least as far as the pioneering balloon flights that inspired Benjamin

Franklin's airborne theorising. A.J. Garnerin, a French national, jumped from a hydrogen balloon over Paris in 1797 and repeated the feat over London five years later, emerging unscathed on both occasions. Garnerin used a 'rigid' parachute, which used spokes to support the shape of the parachute canopy, rather like an umbrella. While effective, such a device was clearly somewhat unwieldy, and it took the better part of a century for the more familiar unbraced or 'limp' parachute canopy to appear. This was the work of Samuel and Thomas Baldwin, who demonstrated their new invention at Golden Gate Park, San Francisco, on 30 January 1887. Within twenty-five years another American pioneer named Albert Berry used the Baldwins' invention to make the first successful parachute jump from a powered aircraft over Jefferson Army Barracks, Missouri on 28 February 1912.[1]

These developments might well have remained little more than carnival curiosities had the First World War not provided the impetus for more systematic development. The British were early users of parachutes for a variety of purposes. Everard Calthorpe's 'Guardian Angel' device was adopted for use by observation balloon crews,[2] and parachutes were also used for intelligence purposes, specifically the delivery agents and carrier pigeons behind enemy lines on the Western Front and in Italy.[3] The primary British use of parachutes was for aerial resupply, however. As we have seen, this began as part of the effort to supply Kut in 1916 and was later utilised for battlefield resupply on the Western Front in 1918, and the practice was carried over into the Empire after 1918.

British troops in Kurdistan in 1923 were supplied with a wide variety of material by parachute, including 1,000 pairs of boots and 3,000 pairs of socks.[4] The technique was not always an unqualified success or without risk to the recipients, however:

> A great quantity of the stores fell on ground from which they could not be recovered; sacks of flour and grain were dropped

> only to split open on the ground; a mule was knocked over; a bag of horse shoes brought down a tent; while a rain of boots caused many soldiers to run about with a left or right boot in their hand, looking for its mate. Finally, when a party of officers had almost suffered the fate of the mule, the dropping of further consignments was stopped by an order communicated by wireless.[5]

Thereafter, parachute resupply became a routine part of British Imperial policing. In September 1930, the Chitral Relief column, consisting of 1,400 troops and their animals, was supplied for two days solely by air, which involved dropping around six tons of rations and forage at pre-arranged night stopping points. Air supply also played a vital part in the Waziristan campaign of 1936–38, particularly in the period October 1936 to January 1937, when heavy rains rendered road transport impossible for troops operating in the Khaisora Valley.[6]

The first to use parachutes as a means of delivering troops rather than materiel were the Italians, using their home-developed and produced 'Salvatori' static-line parachute. Broadly speaking, parachutes can be broadly grouped into two types, static-line and rip-cord, the terms referring to the precise method by which the opening sequence of the parachute canopy is initiated. The rip-cord parachute can be deployed at a time of the parachutist's choosing, by pulling a strap or handle called the rip-cord. This method is commonly used by civilian parachutists and specially trained military personnel. The latter are usually Special Forces troops, utilising specialist techniques such as HALO (High Altitude Low Opening) to avoid detection from the ground. In contrast, the static-line parachute performs the action of deploying the parachute canopy automatically, via a strap or cord called the static-line that links the parachute to a suitable strongpoint in the aircraft. All the parachutist has to do is attach the static-line prior to leaving the aircraft and gravity does the rest.

The static-line method has a number of advantages in a military context. Minimising individual input reduces the possibility of human error, and permits parachuting skills to be concentrated into a minimal number of set drills that can be learned by rote. It also leaves the military parachutist free to concentrate on getting himself and his equipment to and through the aircraft exit as quickly as possible. This was and remains no mean feat, given the unsuitability of some of the early transport aircraft for their task, and the very heavy loads routinely carried by paratroopers in addition to their parachutes under operational conditions, when the aircraft may be taking evasive action, and possibly in the dark. Exit speed is also important because military parachuting usually involves jumping as a group or 'stick', rather than as individuals. A fast and compact group exit minimises dispersal of the stick between leaving the aircraft and reaching the ground, which in turn reduces the time necessary for post-jump reorganisation, an important consideration in the early days when it was common to drop personal weapons and equipment in containers. Consequently, static-line jumping is the standard military parachuting technique employed worldwide.

Parachute pioneers like Garnerin, the Baldwin brothers and Albert Berry used both methods, usually depending on how the parachute was carried. It was common to mount early parachutes on the aircraft or balloon rather than on the parachutist's body, in order to offset their relative weight and bulk. This was an important factor in the early days of aviation, which partially justified the oft-quoted reluctance of the British authorities to issue combat pilots with parachutes during the First World War. Models tested by the Air Board for use by pilots in January 1917 weighed up to forty pounds, a considerable burden for contemporary aircraft.[7] The parachute, or more specifically its method of carriage, thus underwent further refinement, with the first modern rip-cord-type parachute being demonstrated by American entrepreneur Leslie Irvin to officers of the US Army Air Service in April 1919.

The Italian Salvatori parachute was based upon a static-line model designed by American carnival parachutist Charles Broadwick. This placed the parachute canopy and suspension lines in a bag stitched to the back of a modified jacket. The parachute canopy was also linked to a wing strut by a cord, and Broadwick successfully tested his static-line system just before the First World War.[8] Thus equipped, the Italians set up the world's first formal military parachute-training course in 1927, catering for around 250 trainees, and graduates of the course performed the world's first collective parachute drop by fully equipped troops at Cinisello airfield near Milan that same November. Development thereafter was less spectacular, possibly due to the death of the new arm's commander in a parachuting accident in 1928. Nonetheless, by the end of the 1930s Italian forces fielded several parachute battalions. These participated in manoeuvres in Libya in 1937 and 1938,[9] and in the seizure of the Greek island of Cephalonia in April 1941. The Italian parachute force was expanded into the *Folgore* Division, with two 2,500-strong parachute regiments, the following year.[10]

The airborne lead thus passed to the Red Army, which by 1930 had embraced the parachute as an alternative to small-scale tactical air landings. Following trials in August 1930 at Voronezh, an eleven-strong parachute detachment participated in local manoeuvres, and further tactical parachute jumps performed near Leningrad in August and September 1931 appear to have confirmed the utility of the idea. The Leningrad 'Aviation Motorized Landing Detachment' was subsequently augmented with a forty-six-strong parachute spearhead, tasked to secure landing areas in the enemy rear,[11] and the Detachment was expanded to brigade size with a full parachute battalion in December 1932.[12] Thereafter, parachute and air-landing units were set up in Military Districts across the Soviet Union and battalion and brigade operations became a matter of routine. The 1935 manoeuvres in the Kiev Military District involved a mechanised corps attack over the River Dnieper. This was spearheaded by 1,188 paratroopers who seized landing grounds for a further 1,765 air-landed troops. The latter came equipped with armoured cars, light tanks and artillery, and it was claimed an additional 2,500 troops were air-landed within a forty-minute period.[13]

Parachute troops played an even larger role in the Moscow Military District manoeuvres near Minsk the following year. On 22 September 1936, 2,200 paratroopers were dropped into the 'enemy' rear areas to spread confusion and seize a number of water crossings. They were followed an hour later by a further 3,000 paratroopers who seized an airfield forty kilometres away, into which an entire infantry division was air landed.[14] Impressive as this was, it appears to have been merely the tip of the Soviet airborne iceberg. According to the Soviet Commissar of Defence, Kliment Voroshilov, the Red Army possessed over 15,000 trained parachutists, and it was planned to double that number in 1937.[15] Such numbers were perfectly feasible given the popularity of sport parachuting in the Soviet Union at that time, sponsored by the *Komsomol* (Communist Union of Youth) and *Osoaviakhim* (Society for the Promotion of Defence and the Furthering of Aviation and of the Chemical Industry of the USSR). These organisations provided parachute-training towers in every major town in the Soviet Union,[16] and one contemporary writer claimed that 2 million individuals had undergone basic parachute training by 1939.[17] According to Soviet sources, in May 1941 the Red Army possessed fifteen airborne brigades grouped into five airborne corps, totalling approximately 100,000 men.[18]

The Soviets wasted no time in co-opting the spectacular nature of their new airborne arm for propaganda purposes. Film of the 1935 Kiev manoeuvres was screened to an invited audience at the Soviet Embassy in London early the following year, and the footage was subsequently included in newsreel films screened across the world.[19] Foreign military officers, whom the Soviets invited to observe their manoeuvres in large numbers, provided more objective analysis. The British delegation to the 1936 Minsk manoeuvres, for example, was led by future field marshal Lord Wavell and included the armoured expert Sir Giffard Martel. Both men were impressed, Martel especially so by the noticeable lack of parachuting casualties as he was driven around the drop zone. However, both also noted flaws in the Soviet method, including the paratroopers being dropped separately from their weapons, their dispersion and the amount of time it took for them to assemble. Martel estimated the latter took the better part of an hour, while Wavell judged the process still incomplete after ninety minutes and expressed reservations over the tactical value of the technique as a result.[20] Wavell's observations in particular are typically quoted piecemeal as evidence of reactionary and obstructionist British Army thinking, but this conveniently overlooks the general tone of his remarks in full, and the fact that Wavell was one of the most enthusiastic proponents of a British airborne force in 1940 and 1941. This strongly suggests that both officers were commenting on the flaws of the airborne method as implemented by the Soviets, rather than the airborne idea *per se*.

Be that as it may, the Soviets underpinned their practical developments with a properly thought-out doctrine based originally on Tukhachevsky's 1928 trials in the Leningrad Military District.[21] I.E. Tatarchenko, the Chief of Airborne Service of the Red Army Air Force Staff, expanded upon Tukhachevsky's ideas in his 'Technical, Organisational, and Operational Questions of Air Assault Forces'. This advocated large-scale airborne insertion into enemy rear areas, using multiple landing sites, darkness and poor weather to hinder enemy reactions. Small pathfinder teams were to locate suitable landing sites, which would then be seized by parachute troops.

An air-landed vanguard force tasked to defend the landing area would then reinforce the paratroopers, followed by the main force complete with light armour, vehicles and artillery. The whole force would then commence offensive operations in concert with mechanised ground forces.[22]

Tatarchenko's ideas were integrated into the Red Army's 1932 'Temporary Regulation on the Organisation of Deep Battle' and subsequently the 1936 Field Service Regulations which formalised the new Soviet mechanised doctrine of Deep Battle.[23] The airborne role within the Deep Battle framework was defined in Article 7 of the 1936 FSR:

> Parachute landing units are the effective means... [of]... disorganizing the command and rear services of the enemy. In coordination with forces attacking along the front, parachute landing units can go a long way toward producing a complete rout of the enemy on a given axis.[24]

Airborne units were thus involved in some way in virtually all subsequent Soviet operations. The 212th Airborne Brigade was deployed to the Khalkin Gol on the Mongolian-Manchurian border in summer 1939, although the rapid success of the Soviet armoured formations rendered parachute insertion superfluous and the Brigade fought in the ground role.[25] A number of small reconnaissance and diversionary parachute operations were carried out during the Winter War against Finland, though the prevailing conditions reduced the scope for larger operations, and the 201st, 204th and 214th Airborne Brigades carried out several drops during the Soviet occupation of Bessarabia in June 1940. Two of these were full brigade jumps, and Soviet parachute troops also occupied the cities of Bolgrad, Kagul and Izmail ahead of Soviet mechanised forces.[26]

By June 1941, Soviet airborne forces consisted of five corps, one independent brigade and a host of smaller units. These were supported by an independent administration linked directly to the Soviet Ministry of Defence, and an updated doctrine in Article 28 of the 1941 Field Service Regulations.[27] This was a creditable achievement in less than a decade, but the process was far from complete and the Soviet airborne arm went to war lacking a good deal of equipment, not least suitable transport aircraft and radios. Circumstances immediately following the German invasion obliged most Soviet airborne troops to be employed as conventional infantry, but a number of small diversionary parachute operations were carried out. These began with a company raid against a German vehicle concentration near Gorki on 14 July 1941, and later were often carried out in conjunction with partisan groups. Subsequently, larger operations were carried out in support of ground operations. These included drops to shield Moscow in December 1941 and January 1942, and in support of ground offensives in the regions of Viaz'ma during January and February 1942, at Demiansk in the period February to April 1942, and as part of the Dnieper crossing in September 1943. Although little known, these operations were comparable in size and scope with Western airborne operations, and the heavy losses they entailed raised similar doubts over the utility of large-scale airborne operations.[28]

Be that as it may, Soviet airborne activity in the inter-war period inspired widespread investigation and imitation. The 1936 Minsk manoeuvres inspired the French to establish an experimental two-company force of *Infanterie de l'Air* with an attached transport squadron; the force was disbanded in 1939.[29] The Spanish Republicans set up a parachute school at La Rosas using Soviet staff and equipment, and an ambitious plan to wipe out the Nationalist Legion Condor on the ground at its base at Barbastro in April 1938 was only stymied by a lack of suitable parachuting aircraft.[30] Perhaps the closest imitators of the Soviet system were the Poles. The Polish

LOPP (League for National Air Defence) mirrored the Soviet *Komsomol* and *Osoaviakhim* in promoting sport parachuting and gliding, and provided similar facilities. The first Polish public parachuting tower was erected in Warsaw in 1936; by 1939 a further seventeen had been erected across the country, and Polish Boy Scouts gave a parachuting demonstration at the 5th International Scouting Jamboree in August 1937.[31] High-profile as it was, Polish imitation of the Soviet method seems to have been unofficial. There does not appear to have been any Soviet input, presumably due to traditional Polish-Russian antipathy, and the Poles thus appear to have adopted the idea by what one contemporary Polish witness called osmosis.[32] The practical details were probably provided by the Polish intelligence services, and some of the military material they gathered also appears to have been channelled to the British embassy in Warsaw.

In the summer of 1935 the journal of the Royal United Services Institute published an article by the British military attaché in Warsaw, Major J.T. Godfrey R.E.[33] Entitled 'Winged Armies', Godfrey's paper examined the relevance of airborne developments in the British context and in the process picked up a trick missed in the wider-known mechanised theorising by Fuller and Liddell Hart. Godfrey recommended the formation of a joint Army/RAF mechanised air brigade equipped with 360 machine-gun and anti-tank gun carriers and a dedicated air transport wing of 120 aircraft each capable of carrying three vehicles each. The brigade was to be delivered to a nodal point 50 to 100 miles behind enemy lines, where it was to undertake operations like a mobile 'tumour on the enemies arteries' for a period of several days. The article contained a good deal of operational detail including logistic calculations, and closed with the recommendation that the method be adopted and a British strategic reserve be established in the Sinai for rapid despatch across the Empire via a chain of specially constructed airfields. This was noteworthy as the first and most comprehensive British discussion of the airborne method in the inter-war period, but nonetheless bears more than a passing resemblance to contemporary Soviet theorising. Indeed, the author admitted being inspired by the Communist political practice of placing a cell at the heart of the enemy camp.[34]

For their part, the Polish military initially used parachuting as a character-building exercise for trainee officers, with parachute towers being constructed at officer cadet schools at Bydgoscz and Legionovo, and at the Infantry School at Komorovo. Voluntary parachute courses were offered to cadets in their final year of training, along with sport gliding, rock climbing and hill walking. The course lasted four weeks, during which trainees were taught parachute packing – individuals were responsible for packing their own equipment – and underwent pre-jump ground training. This was followed by two or three jumps from a captive balloon, and three jumps from an aircraft, all using rip-cord parachutes. These required a high degree of judgement, and one trainee recalled the near-demise of a fellow cadet during a balloon jump at Komorovo. Trainees were taught to operate their rip-cords as they passed the cable tethering the balloon to the ground, but the cadet in question closed his eyes on jumping and consequently missed his cue. The assembled trainees and instructors watched in horror as he plummeted earthward, but fortunately he realised his error in the nick of time; his canopy had barely deployed when he touched down. On completion of the course, candidates were awarded a small enamelled parachute badge that was permitted on military uniform.[35]

In September 1937 the Poles formalised their interest in military parachuting by forming a dedicated sabotage and diversion force. This appears to have encouraged further expansion of the Polish airborne infrastructure, with the establishment of the Military Parachuting Centre at Bydgoscz in May 1939. The

Centre was tasked to deal with research and development work as well as training, with the latter courses being open to volunteers of all ranks. The first training course graduated in June 1939, but the second was cut short by the German invasion on 1 September 1939. The Military Parachuting Centre was destroyed in the fighting, which also effectively dispersed the graduates and staff.[36] As we shall see, some of these men, with their invaluable expertise and doctrinal theorising, eventually wound up in Britain after the debacles in France and Norway. This in turn proved extremely fortuitous for the British in the early stages of establishing their own airborne force.[37]

While noteworthy, all this was relatively small-scale stuff, and the main inter-war proponent of airborne warfare besides the Soviets was Hitler's Germany, although the source of its inspiration is unclear. According to one source Hermann Göring and Kurt Student, future heads of the Luftwaffe and its airborne arm respectively, attended a Soviet tactical parachute demonstration in 1931.[38] This is problematic, however, for Göring was not a serving officer at that time, and it is therefore difficult to see why he would be participating in the highly secret liaison between the *Reichswehr* and the Red Army under the Rapallo Treaty of 1922. Student's presence is also questionable, for while he was involved in the aerial side of this Soviet-German liaison,[39] his involvement ceased in December 1928 when he was posted to an infantry unit in East Prussia.[40] On the other hand, future *Panzer* expert Erich von Manstein does appear to have observed a parachute exercise in the Trans-Caucasian Military District in September 1932.[41] It is therefore logical to assume that the German military picked up the airborne idea from the Soviets during their secret co-operation prior to Hitler assuming power in 1933, and that Göring and Student's involvement may have come somewhat later.

Whether or not this was the case, Göring was certainly responsible for setting up the first German parachute unit, the *Polizei Gruppe Wecke*, in February 1933.[42] This was a paramilitary Prussian police unit, which was subsequently integrated into the Luftwaffe in March 1935 as part of the Hermann Göring Regiment. One battalion of the regiment was to be parachute-trained, and 600 volunteers came forward despite a less than inspiring parachute demonstration on 1 October 1935, which left the sole participant injured and unconscious.[43] German Airborne Forces in the accepted sense were born at the beginning of the following year, with a call for volunteers for parachute training in the Luftwaffe Order of the Day for 29 January 1936, and training commenced on 11 May 1936 at the Luftwaffe parachute-training school at Stendahl.[44] At around the same time the *Heer* set up its own parachute company, which was expanded to a battalion in June 1938.[45] The *Heer*'s interest appears to have been prompted as much by inter-service rivalry as any faith in the potential of airborne forces, although a lack of facilities obliged the *Heer* to send its men to Stendahl for training. A platoon of Luftwaffe paratroopers participated in manoeuvres in Saxony in October 1936, and a larger detachment made up of Luftwaffe and *Heer* paratroopers carried out a demonstration before Hitler in the spring of 1937.

The future of the new arm remained unclear until 1 June 1938, when it was tasked to attack fixed defences around Freundenthal as part of the planned invasion of Czechoslovakia. Student was given command of the venture, with the proviso that all planning and preparation be complete by 15 September 1938, and an umbrella organisation for the operation called 7th *Flieger* Division was established on 1 July 1938. Student reported his new command combat ready on 1 September 1938, although the prospective operation was rendered superfluous by the Munich Agreement. This was probably just as well, given that the *Heer* refused to provide the number of troops Student requested, and that the shortfall had to be made up with virtually untrained personnel from the *Sturmabteilung*.

To add insult to injury, the *Heer* also removed its parachute battalion and other troops from Student's control immediately after the Munich Crisis.[46]

Inter-service rivalry undoubtedly played a part in this, but there was also genuine disagreement over the size and employment of the new force. The original Luftwaffe concept was to employ parachutists as saboteurs, using small teams to strike targets inaccessible to bomber aircraft, whereas the *Heer* leaned toward Soviet practice and saw parachute troops as a spearhead for large-scale air-landing operations in support of ground forces.[47] A third and more radical alternative was put forward by Student, who recommended the formation of a self-sufficient airborne force with integral transport aircraft, close air support and artillery.[48] This force was to operate under a tactical doctrine he labelled the 'drops of oil' technique, which advocated the simultaneous seizure of multiple landing sites behind enemy lines. These were to be developed into air-supplied pockets, which would then expand and link up, first with each other and then with advancing ground forces.[49]

Student's ideas were radical, but they may have been less original than they are usually portrayed. They bore an uncanny resemblance to the proposals put forward by Tatarchenko in 1932,[50] and to the French colonial 'strategy of the oil patch' formulated by Marshal Lyautey before the First World War.[51] Be that as it may, German airborne doctrine eventually became a compromise between these three views, and Student succeeded in bringing all airborne matters under his personal control with some astute political manoeuvring. This began with a carefully stage-managed air-landing exercise during the occupation of the Sudetenland in October 1938, involving 242 transport aircraft. The demonstration impressed Göring, and his support proved crucial in the bureaucratic tussle that followed the *Heer*'s withdrawal from the airborne project after the Munich Crisis. By January 1939, Student was Inspector General of Airborne Forces, and the Luftwaffe had absorbed the *Heer* parachute battalion. He had also gained operational control of the *Heer's* specially configured 22nd *Luftlande* (Air-landing) Division,[53] and his oil-drop theory had been incorporated into the official airborne doctrine drawn up by *Oberkommando der Wehrmacht*, the German High Command.

The nature of the Nazi regime, to say nothing of the fact that the original German parachute cadre was drawn from a Nazi-oriented paramilitary police unit and enjoyed the support of high-ranking Nazis, made a political dimension to the new force inevitable. Hitler's 'Ten Commandments' for the *Fallschirmjäger* (literally 'parachute hunters') set the tone by urging them to fight to the death, consider battle to be a fulfilment and to be '...as agile as a greyhound, as tough as leather, as hard as Krupp steel... and [thus] be the German warrior incarnate'.[54] Nazi propaganda chief Josef Goebbels took a similar line and personally encouraged his Propaganda Ministry staff and family, including his stepson, to volunteer for the new arm. Nazi propaganda thus exploited the rigorous *Fallschirmjäger* selection procedures (which initially at least accepted only one candidate in four) and their intense physical training to the full for home and foreign consumption. A photo essay of German paratroopers making a training jump appeared in the *United Services Review* in October 1938, for example.[55] In a similar vein, much was made of the presence of the famous boxer Max Schmeling among the ranks of the *Fallschirmjäger*, with a similar photo spread on the boxer appearing in the January 1941 edition of the Luftwaffe's in-house magazine *Der Adler* (The Eagle).

In the event, Schmeling proved to be a less than useful or co-operative propaganda tool. The boxer was initially reported missing and then shot while trying to escape Allied captivity during the battle to secure Crete in May 1941. Goebbels assumed the British had deliberately executed him due to his high profile, which fitted neatly with the tales of British atrocities on Crete which the Propaganda Ministry was running at the time. Schmeling upset this convenient tale by turning up in a German military hospital, very much alive and unperforated, but suffering from dysentery. He then added insult to injury by refuting tales of British atrocity and sending greetings to all his US fans in an interview with an American reporter. There was little if any truth to the lurid Nazi tales, which appear to have been deliberately formulated to offset a number of documented atrocities against Cretan civilians by Schmeling's *Fallschirmjäger* comrades. Some German airborne soldiers, including Student, were tried and found guilty of these crimes after the war, although in the latter's case at least the sentence was never confirmed. The evidence therefore suggests that the *Fallschirmjäger* carried their political attitudes onto the battlefield, their popular portrayal as a hard-fighting but chivalrous foe notwithstanding.[56]

Be that as it may, being an integral part of the Luftwaffe brought with it a number of advantages and peculiarities for the German airborne arm. This arrangement simplified training and operational control, as it allowed the *Fallschirmjäger* to remain under Luftwaffe control. This principle was reinforced by the Luftwaffe's airborne doctrine, which only authorised outside control for a brief period immediately following relief by ground forces. On a more practical level, it permitted unrestricted access to suitable aircraft. The Luftwaffe possessed a substantial number of three-engine Junkers 52 bombers, and their airliner origins and obsolescence in that role coincided neatly with the new requirement for large numbers of parachute transport aircraft. As we shall see, the British approached things rather differently, and the results were to dog British airborne development and operations throughout the Second World War.

German airborne doctrine and propaganda may have mimicked Soviet practice, but they also added an innovation that was to be copied by their Soviet forebears and imitators alike. While the Soviet and Polish governments were subsidising sport parachuting through *Oasviakhim* and the LOPP, the German state was sponsoring sport gliding by funding talented individuals, and training via the *Hitler Jugend* youth organisation. The Treaty of Versailles placed tight restrictions on powered flying in Germany, and sport gliding provided a convenient means of circumventing them, so successfully that by 1930 German pilots dominated the sport worldwide. Student was involved in covertly funnelling military funds to the German gliding community in the early 1920s, and was seriously injured in a gliding accident in 1923. Thereafter, recognising the potential for delivering troops with precision and in cohesive groups, he took a personal interest in adding a glider capability to his fledgling airborne force. He personally test flew the prototype DFS 230 machine that became the standard Luftwaffe assault glider in the summer of 1938, and subsequently added a glider assault regiment, intended to be the elite of the Luftwaffe's airborne arm, to 7th *Flieger* Division's order of battle.[57] The Soviets followed Student's lead in this instance, and included 'Glider Groups' in their Airborne Brigade organisations from 1940, although the degree to which this was implemented is unclear.[58]

It was under this organisation and doctrine that Student's new airborne force went to war in 1940. Hitler unilaterally decided to give 7th *Flieger* Division a leading role in his planned attack in the West on the grounds that '...parachute and air-landing troops were a new and unknown weapon, capable of dealing a knock-out blow if used with strength and boldness at a decisive point'.[59] Student was informed on 27 October 1939 that his force was to lead a thrust into neutral Holland and Belgium with a multifaceted operation that was to both make history in May 1940, and prompt Churchill to order the formation of a British force with similar capabilities

3

Catalyst and Example

German Airborne Operations in the Low Countries and the Allied Defeat in France, May–June 1940

The outbreak of war in September 1939 did not change the British attitude to airborne forces, not least because of the defensive nature of their continental commitment. All that changed with the German offensive of 10 May 1940, which in the space of a mere twenty-four days saw Holland and Belgium overrun, the Anglo-French Armies split, and the bulk of the British Expeditionary Force (BEF) evacuated in an *ad hoc* operation from Calais and Dunkirk. The remainder of the BEF, accompanied by a variety of Allied military personnel and civilians, was lifted from the north and western French seaboard by 20 June 1940.[1] British military circumstances thus changed out of all recognition at a stroke, and with them the British attitude to airborne forces. Before examining this shift, however, it will be necessary to briefly examine the German operation to place subsequent developments in their proper context.

At Hitler's personal insistence, the German assault upon the Low Countries was spearheaded by a series of special operations, some of which were relatively small in scale and assigned to the *Brandenburger* Special Service Regiment. The remainder was entrusted to Student's 7th *Flieger* Division and the 22nd *Luftlande* Division.[2] Although the Low Countries attack was to be their debut *en masse*, Student's airborne force already had some limited operational experience. While the parachute units were held back for a series of aborted airborne operations during the Polish campaign, one of 22nd *Luftlande*'s infantry regiments fought in the closing stages of the campaign. Some *Fallschirmjäger* had their baptism of fire in Scandinavia in April 1940 via a series of small drops to seize airfields at Aalborg and the bridge linking Copenhagen with the Gedser ferry terminal in Denmark, and the Oslo-Fornebu and Stavanger-Sola airfields in Norway. All were successful, although not without some confusion, particularly at Oslo-Fornebu. An operation to prevent Norwegian and British troops linking up at Dombas failed when bad weather prevented resupply or reinforcement; the survivors were captured after fighting alone for ten days.[3] While this was going on Student expanded his force with an experimental glider unit in November 1939, codenamed 'Test Section Friedrichshafen'. Intended to test the utility of the glider as transport for assault engineers attacking fixed defences, the unit was subsequently formally established as 'Assault Battalion Koch', after its commander, *Hauptmann* Walter Koch.[4]

Student divided his force into three parts for the Low Countries assault, each with a specific set of objectives. Assault

Battalion Koch was tasked to neutralise the fortress of Eben Emael and seize three nearby bridges across the Albert Canal, for which it was subdivided into Groups 'Granite', 'Concrete', 'Iron' and 'Steel'.[5] Group North, consisting of 22nd *Luftlande* Division with an attached parachute spearhead, was to strike at the heart of 'Fortress Holland' by vertically outflanking two Dutch defence lines by securing airfields at Valkenburg, Ockenburg and Ypenburg. This would permit the seizure of the Dutch government, Royal family and military leadership in the nearby Dutch capital of Den Haag, and would also deny the RAF a base from which to bomb Germany.[6] Last but not least came Group South, made up of 7th *Flieger*'s parachute units and elements of 22nd *Luftlande* Division. Their task was to seize road and rail bridges at Moerdijk, Dordrecht and Rotterdam, and Waalhaven airfield near Rotterdam. The latter was to be a conduit for resupply and reinforcement, and the seizure of the Rotterdam bridges involved twelve Heinkel He 59 seaplanes delivering troops directly onto their objective.[7] The overall objective was to provide German ground forces with an avenue of attack into Western Belgium and the Channel ports.

As we have seen, there were three major strands to German airborne thinking at this time. These were the original Luftwaffe concept of a small airborne sabotage force, the *Heer*'s view of parachute forces as a spearhead for air-landing operations, and Student's more radical concept of an independent, all-arms airborne force to operate in support of major ground operations. The German plan contained all three strands and was thus something of a mixed bag. The same can be said for the results achieved, for in the event Assault Detachment Koch and Group South achieved almost total success while Group North's efforts ended in costly failure.

The success of Assault Battalion Koch was due in no small part to surprise, being the combat debut of the troop-carrying glider. This was bolstered with meticulous planning and painstaking training carried out with live ammunition on ex-Czech fixed defences; the latter led to the development of special shaped charges to penetrate Eben Emael's armoured gun cupolas.[8] Group Granite was so well prepared that it carried through the initial phase of the assault on the Eben Emael fortress without its commander. *Leutnant* Witzig's glider force-landed in Germany after a near-collision in the pre-dawn darkness. Undaunted, he organised a replacement tug aircraft and landed atop the objective in broad daylight and before the fortress was fully subdued.[9] Groups Concrete and Steel seized their allotted bridges over the Albert Canal, and Group Iron managed to establish a bridgehead after the defenders demolished their target as they approached. All three objectives were held until relief by ground forces on the afternoon of 10 May 1940. Group Granite was reinforced by *Heer* engineers at around 0700 hours on 11 May 1940, and the fortress and its garrison of 1,200 men surrendered at 1315 hours the same day.[10]

Surprise also played a crucial part in the success of Group South. The bridges at Moerdijk, Dordrecht and Rotterdam were seized intact, and Waalhaven airfield was secured with an imaginative parallel assault. This began by delivering *Fallschirmjäger* along the edges of the airfield to distract the defenders and seize the runways, swiftly followed by waves of transport aircraft. Several aircraft crash-landed after being hit by defending fire, but within minutes the attackers had an entire infantry battalion on the ground and the airfield was rapidly secured. The plan went awry when troops from Waalhaven moved to relieve the elements holding the bridges in Rotterdam proper. The former became embroiled in street fighting which continued until the arrival of the 9th *Panzer* Division on 13 May 1940.[11] Student had opted to jump in with Group South and played a prominent role in the Rotterdam fighting, but was severely wounded by members of the SS

Leibstandarte Adolf Hitler in the closing stages of the battle. His fate highlights the very real dangers associated with leading from the front and placing airborne troops in front of advancing ground forces.

Despite this, Assault Battalion Koch and Group South both achieved their primary aim of enabling German ground forces '...to burst through a defence system which could not have been overcome so quickly by traditional means'.[12] Group North, however, was less successful. The Dutch had reinforced their defences at the target airfields and obstructed the runways in anticipation of an airborne attack, and this was exacerbated by a combination of flawed operating procedures and plain bad luck. Despite using the tactics that worked at Waalhaven, things went seriously awry at Ockenburg and Ypenburg. The perimeter parachute drops were scattered and the *Fallschirmjäger* were unable to recover their weapons, which were dropped separately in containers, before the transport aircraft arrived.[13] The defenders shot up the first wave of aircraft on their final approach to the unsecured runways, obliging those following to land instead on roads, fields and beaches across the surrounding area. The *Fallschirmjäger* spearhead at Valkenburg secured the landing area, but the grass strip proved too soft to support a fully laden Junker 52, and the field was rapidly blocked by bogged aircraft; the last wave was diverted to Waalhaven. Group North's survivors were thus obliged to abandon their mission, and instead moved toward friendly forces at Rotterdam, where they arrived on the night of 12–13 May 1940.[14]

The cost of this failure was severe. Two-thirds of the 430 aircraft employed were either destroyed or rendered irreparable, with the Group North contingent losing ninety per cent of its assigned aircraft.[15] The human cost was also heavy, with the 22nd *Luftlande* Division losing forty per cent of its officers and twenty-eight per cent of its other ranks killed.[16] Little of this was apparent to the Allies at the time, however, and the impact of the German operations was considerable. This was exacerbated by the pronouncements of contemporary observers, which ranged from understandable misunderstanding to wild exaggerations of German airborne capabilities.[17] The British official airborne history, for example, referred to Assault Battalion Koch arriving atop Eben Emael by parachute as late as 1950.[18] German disinformation also played a part; Assault Battalion Koch's glider tugs also dropped dummy paratroops equipped with pyrotechnic gunfire simulators, which caused considerable confusion among the local Belgian garrison.[19]

Even so, the British were able to gain valuable information to guide their own initial airborne effort. A good deal of this came from the 1,600 Germans captured in Holland, some of whom were shipped to Britain for incarceration. These included Luftwaffe *Fallschirmjäger* and *Heer* air-landing soldiers; pictures of both appeared in *The Times* on 20 May and 21 June 1940.[20] Thus the original British parachute cadre used step-in cotton duck jump smocks and high-leg, side-laced boots modelled closely on German equipment for a time.[21] The British also copied German operational techniques. The Eben Emael attack and a subsequent glider *coup de main* against crossings over the Corinth Canal in 1941 inspired the British seizure of the Orne River and Canal bridges to seal the eastern flank of the D-Day invasion beaches in 1944, for example.[22] The British were also quick to identify the flaws in German operating procedures. Despite events at Ockenburg and Ypenburg, *Fallschirmjäger* continued to drop separately from their weapons throughout the war, although this was due in part to the limitations of their parachutes and aircraft.[23] The British quickly developed a variety of special weapon sleeves and valises that allowed their paratroopers to jump with all their personal weapons to hand.[24]

All this, however, lay far in the future from the dark perspective of May and June 1940. Events undoubtedly had the heaviest impact upon the Army, which lost all but a fraction of the equipment and supplies it deployed to France with the BEF. Only 322 of the 2,794 assorted artillery pieces were evacuated back to the UK, as were 4,739 of 68,618 vehicles, 32,303 of 109,000 tons of ammunition, 33,060 of 449,000 tons of other stores and supplies, and 1,071 of 166,000 tons of fuel. Arguably more importantly, the BEF left 68,111 of its personnel in France, killed, missing or as POWs.[25] This clearly amounted to a comprehensive defeat, and appears to justify Major-General Montgomery's typically forthright opinion that the British Army was totally unfit to fight a first-class European war in 1939.[26]

However, the matter was somewhat less black and white than this would suggest. At least some effort had been made to rectify the failings in infantry training identified in the mid-1930s. A new Military Training Pamphlet (MTP) issued in March 1940 coincided with a reorganisation of the infantry platoon structure, in which the eight-man rifle section was subdivided into a rifle group and a two- or three-man gun group equipped with a Bren Light Machine Gun. This in turn had the effect of turning the corporals commanding rifle sections into tactical commanders in their own right with two tactical components under their direct control, a system that remained in use until the early 1980s.[27] Neither does there appear to have been much wrong with the Army's basic raw material. The SS *Leibstandarte Adolf Hitler*, for example, classified the British infantry they met near Dunkirk as the most severe opposition they had encountered to date, and assumed that they were elite troops.[28] The fact that they had encountered Territorial rather than Regular soldiers surely proves the qualitative point, especially as territorial units were considered to be handicapped by a shortage of training and experience.[29]

It is also perhaps worth noting that the BEF represented only around a tenth of the combined Anglo-French strength, and was therefore subject to constraints arising from its subordinate position. The French insistence on radio silence, for example, precluded Command Post Exercises from practising communications and control,[30] and there was little the BEF could do to challenge French insistence that a German assault through the Ardennes was impossible, or their faith in the impregnability of the Maginot Line.[31] Neither was there much the BEF could do about the flaws in the 'Plan D' which required it to advance into Belgium and occupy a defensive line along the River Dyle, but only at the specific invitation of the Belgian government. The invitation was late in coming, given the Belgians' understandable wish to avoid provoking the Germans, and this was exacerbated by their similarly motivated failure to actually prepare the defensive positions the BEF were supposed to occupy.[32]

Not that the BEF's masters in London were blameless. Some BEF units were reallocated for Churchill's abortive scheme to aid Finland against the Soviet Union; an entire division was removed to create a 'War Office Reserve' in April 1940; and still more units and equipment were diverted for the ill-fated Norway expedition.[33] None of this excuses the fact that the BEF suffered a shattering and comprehensive defeat ending in its ignominious ejection from the continent, but it does suggest that there were some mitigating factors alongside inflexibility and incompetence.

It would also be inaccurate to claim that the cost of defeat was borne solely by the Army. The RAF's Advanced Air Striking Force (AASF) and BEF Air Component suffered losses proportionately as heavy as those of the Army, if not more so.[34] RAF casualties during the Battle of France totalled 931 aircraft and 1,526 killed, missing or captured, the majority of which were aircrew.[35] Squadrons equipped with the Fairey Battle bomber were particularly hard hit, suffering a fifty-six per cent casualty rate attacking bridges over the Meuse at

Sedan.[36] Like the Army, the RAF suffered from conflicting priorities. Until July 1939 the Air Ministry planning was based upon the premise that the Luftwaffe would be operating from bases inside Germany.[37] However, the rapid German advance into France and the Low Countries obliged the RAF to adjust its priorities, for it simply did not possess the resources to support the BEF *and* defend British airspace. Fighter procurement for Home Defence had been a pre-war bone of contention,[38] and assigning machines to the AASF and BEF Air Component eroded the minimum figure considered necessary by both the Air Ministry and Fighter Command.[39] By 15 May 1940 demand for fighter support reached unsustainable levels, and the War Cabinet was obliged to stop the despatch of fighters to France in the interests of maintaining home defence capabilities. Thereafter, what air cover could be spared for the BEF was deployed from bases in the south of England.[40]

The result was a growing, widespread but largely inaccurate perception within the Army that it had been let down, which led to a further souring of Army-RAF relations, which were frequently far from cordial to begin with. The Army perspective was based on the all too visible depredations of the Luftwaffe, in contrast with the apparent absence of the RAF. Alanbrooke, for example, claimed in his diary that he practically never saw an RAF fighter during his time in France, and made numerous references to unopposed German air attacks upon the BEF.[41] The BEF's lower echelons were less circumspect. One RAF pilot claimed that an Army officer informed a pilot seeking evacuation at Dunkirk that any available boats were reserved for Army use and not for the RAF,[42] and another recalled being roundly abused by newly evacuated soldiers at London's Victoria station.[43]

Army reactions may have been understandable, but they were unfair because RAF fighter aircraft, frequently outnumbered, were indeed present over France. According to a participant pilot, this was because air fighting moved from 7,000 to 20,000 feet in a matter of days once hostilities commenced, which of course meant it moved out of sight of Army observers on the ground.[44] It is also likely that the misunderstanding was exacerbated by poor Army aircraft recognition. A forced-landed RAF pilot was present at an Army brigade headquarters near Dunkirk during an air-raid alarm. To the surprise of his hosts, including the brigadier, the pilot was able to categorically identify the aircraft that sparked the alert as RAF machines because their undersides were painted black and white as a ground recognition measure. On hearing this, the brigade staff admitted to having seen similarly marked aircraft quite frequently, but had not realised they were RAF machines because they were unaware of the significance of the markings. The pilot concerned understandably and correctly considered this to be a serious and major intelligence failure, especially at a brigade level formation.[45]

Unjustly maligned as it was, the RAF nonetheless has to shoulder a share of the blame for the breakdown of inter-service relations. The Air Ministry had made it abundantly clear that it viewed air support for ground forces as a 'gross misuse' of air power,[46] and the costly RAF actions in France as an unwelcome distraction delivering a 'knock-out blow' to Germany's war-making capacity. This attitude came clearly to the fore during the War Cabinet crisis meeting on 15 May 1940.[47] Faced by Army appeals for the RAF to emulate the Luftwaffe by attacking the forward communication centres feeding the German advance, the Air Staff stated that the best way to halt the German advance was to unleash a long-planned strategic air offensive against targets in the Ruhr.[48] The fact that Dowding supported this proposal despite having fought hard against the bomber lobby to establish an effective Fighter Command underlines the extent to which bombing dogma permeated the RAF.[49]

The Air Staff's attitude was further undermined by the fact that it lacked the means to carry out a strategic bombing offensive. In September 1940, Bomber Command consisted of forty operational squadrons,[50] classified as 'medium' or 'heavy medium' bombers.[51] These fielded Bristol Blenheim, Handley Page Hampden, Armstrong Whitworth Whitley and Vickers Wellington aircraft, which collectively lacked the speed, range, defensive armament and payload for strategic bombing. The four-engine Short Stirling heavy bomber was in the pipeline, but it did not enter squadron service until August 1940, was not operational until the following February, and even then suffered from an 'unimpressive bomb-load' and poor service ceiling.[52] Neither did Bomber Command possess the necessary operating procedures and tactics. The fifty per cent casualty rate suffered in daylight raids during 1939 showed that despite pre-war dogma, bombers were unable to defend themselves effectively,[53] and shifting to night bombing merely threw up another set of problems. Not least of these was the rather important matter of locating the target which Bomber Command's first night raid, against a German seaplane base at Hörnum in the Friesian Islands on 19 March 1940, showed was far from straightforward. The raid involved fifty aircraft, but succeeded only in wounding three Germans already ensconced in the base sick bay and inflicting minor damage on a handful of aircraft; the British after-action reports considered night bombing to be ineffective with then-current navigation skills and equipment.[54] There was clearly some work to be done before Bomber Command would be capable of meeting the Air Ministry's strategic bombing pretensions.

Given all this, it is unsurprising that establishing a dedicated airborne force was not high on the priorities of the Air Ministry or the War Office, whatever intelligence or equipment had been gleaned from the German airborne operations in the Low Countries. The Army had its hands full attempting to repair the damage incurred at Dunkirk and preparing for seemingly imminent German invasion, the same was largely true for the RAF, and relations between the two services were at an all-time low. Nonetheless, a low-key and small-scale investigation into airborne matters was underway, but this was a long way from sanctioning a formal establishment, and there the matter would most likely have ended without intervention from outside Whitehall.

That intervention came from Prime Minister Winston Churchill, who ordered the formation of a parachute force in a series of directives from the beginning of June 1940. The first of these, addressed to the Military Secretary to the Cabinet General Sir Hastings Ismay, appeared on 3 June 1940. Among other things, Churchill expressed concern about possible German air and sea landings on British soil, strongly recommended acquiring similar capabilities to those recently demonstrated by the Germans, and specifically demanded the formation of at least ten self-contained, 1,000-strong raiding units.[55] In another minute issued on 5 June 1940, Churchill demanded action on his earlier recommendations and added practical details on the make-up of the raiding units. He suggested that the latter be formed from Australian troops en route to the UK, and that they be rapidly employed in raiding operations to create a 'reign of terror' all along the coast of German-occupied Europe. The minute ended with a numbered list of five specific measures for immediate action. Number one demanded detailed proposals for organising the raiding units; number four ordered the 'deployment of parachute troops on a scale equal to 5,000'.[56]

Churchill's directives led directly to the formation of the Commandos, and subsequently a host of smaller, more specialised units such as the Special Boat Section and Combined Operations Assault Pilotage Parties.[57] They have also attracted a good deal of attention from critics for allegedly diverting high-quality manpower away from conventional units for the sole purpose of prosecuting a 'vigorous, enterprising and ceaseless offensive against the whole German-occupied coastline [of Europe]'[58]. This critical focus on small-scale raiding is largely Churchill's own fault, for it arose directly from his habit of framing broad concepts in dramatic language and leaving the details for others, thereby providing ammunition for his detractors. One possible explanation may be that formulating aggressive schemes provided Churchill with a psychological safety valve. His directives of 3 and 5 June 1940, for example, coincided with the critical end-phase of the Dunkirk evacuation, and another minute specifically relating to parachute troops on 22 June 1940 followed the final Allied evacuation from the French Atlantic seaboard.[59] Be that as it may, Churchill was certainly labouring under formidable pressure for a man of his years, even one equipped with his mental resilience and capacity for work; he made a habit of working from his bed into the small hours of the morning, for example.[60] He also exhibited an impressive grasp of detail which, possibly exacerbated by stress and pressure of time, appears to have been a two-edged sword. On occasion it led him to expend energy on relative trivia that found its way into his directives, and thus obscured his underlying point.

This would certainly appear to be the case in this instance, for the content of Churchill's various pronouncements clearly points to a larger purpose than small-scale nuisance raiding. Leaving aside that a combined force of 15,000 men appears to have been somewhat excessive for that purpose, his references to employing Australian, New Zealand and Canadian troops in the new raiding units provides an important clue. Australian and other Commonwealth troops were routinely employed in the assault role during the First World War, and comments he made at a Defence Committee meeting on 19 June 1940 show that he also viewed German airborne troops as a more up-to-date version of First World War stormtroops.[61] This strongly suggests that Churchill's underlying intent was to equip the British military with something it lacked. This was a dedicated, formally established shock force capable of spearheading full-scale invasions, and it is exactly what the British military got via the creation of the Commandos, Combined Operations HQ and Airborne Forces.

The initial focus on small-scale nuisance raiding was therefore an acknowledgement of reality rather than a statement of long-term intent, and even this provided useful operational research and experience. The raid against the Norwegian port of Vaagsö on Boxing Day 1941, for example, involved co-ordinating an Army landing force, Royal Navy landing vessels and a naval covering force that included a cruiser and a submarine, and air cover and close support from the RAF.[62] The same was true of the operation mounted against the French port of Dieppe eight months later, on 19 August 1942. Involving over 6,000 troops, tanks, 252 assorted landing vessels, a flotilla of minesweepers and sixty-nine air squadrons, Operation JUBILEE was a temporary invasion in all but name.[63] Despite its cost and attendant controversy, the operation yielded lessons that proved invaluable to the success of the Normandy invasion in June 1944, not least the decision to dispense with seizing a port and initially supply the invasion forces over the beach via specially constructed temporary harbours. Indeed, the Normandy invasion can be seen as the ultimate endorsement of Churchill's initiative, given the crucial spearhead role played by shock troops from the 1st and 4th Special Service Brigades and the 6th Airborne Division.

Be all that as it may, Churchill's demand for a parachute force was not solely prompted by events in the Low Countries. In fact he had a long-standing interest in airborne matters, dating back to 1917 when he first hypothesised about the deployment of troops from the air.[64] He warned against airborne landings in the English north-west in a 1936 paper entitled 'Invasion by Air', which he reissued on 16 June 1940 as part of a demand to the Home Defence authorities to keep him informed of measures to repulse such an event.[65] He had already raised this concern in his minute of 3 June 1940, which explicitly referred to the possibility of German invasion in spite of British sea power,[66] a clear reference to German airborne capability. This was followed by his specific requirement for a British parachute force on 5 June 1940, and then by a letter to Ismay on 22 June 1940 that is sometimes claimed to be his first pronouncement on the matter:

> We ought to have a corps of at least 5,000 parachute troops, including a proportion of Canadians, Australians and New Zealanders, together with trustworthy Norwegians and Frenchmen... I hear something is being done already to form such a corps but only, I believe, on a very small scale. Advantage must be taken of the summer to train these forces, who can none the less play their part meanwhile as shock troops in home defence. Pray let me have a note from the War Office on the subject.[67]

This then was the shape of Churchill's intervention that placed the British airborne ball centre stage, and firmly in the Air Ministry and War Office court. Their reactions provide the next stage of the story.

4

Immediate Reactions

Churchill's Directives, the Army and the RAF, 4 June–15 July 1940

Perhaps unsurprisingly, War Office and Air Ministry reactions to Churchill's directives varied considerably. The War Office accepted both the raiding and parachute directives more positively than the Army's straitened circumstances might have suggested. In part this was because it had a pre-existing interest in irregular operations dating from the mid-1930s and the establishment of the small General Staff (Research) (GS(R)) section. The section's second commander, Major J.C.F. Holland RE, had personal experience of irregular operations from service in the First World War and Ireland, and he initiated an investigation into the future relevance of guerrilla operations in 1938 in light of events in China and

Spain. This paralleled similar moves by the Foreign Office, which established departments codenamed EH and Section D in 1939 with a remit to investigate methods of attacking potential enemies in ways other than conventional military operations.[1]

In 1939 GS(R) was expanded, notably with the arrival of Major Colin Gubbins MC in April, and renamed Military Intelligence (Research) (MI(R)). MI(R) was tasked to lay the groundwork for future guerrilla operations, including the production of training manuals and research and development facilities for special arms and equipment.[2] Gubbins, who also had a background in irregular operations, produced three pamphlets – *The Art of Guerrilla Warfare*, *How to Use High Explosives* and *The Partisan Leader's Handbook* – and carried out covert reconnaissance missions in Rumania, Poland and the Baltic States.[3] With the outbreak of war in September 1939, MI(R) was involved in an abortive scheme to aid the Finns in their Winter War against the Soviets, and in the despatch of irregular units to Norway following the German invasion in April 1940.[4] Ten 'Independent Companies' were formed, largely from Territorial Army volunteers, and five saw action in Norway before being evacuated back to Scotland in early June 1940.[5]

The Army was also well used to working in co-operation with its sibling services, with the RAF in the Empire between the wars and even longer with the Royal Navy. Co-operation with the latter was largely *ad hoc* until the First World War, when the Gallipoli landings prompted more formalised arrangements.[6] Post-war developments were handicapped by a divergence between amphibious theory and practice, funding limitations and a perceived lack of need for a coherent amphibious strategy. Nonetheless there was some low-level contingency planning, leading to the issue of a Combined Operations manual in 1925, and annual if small-scale amphibious exercises were held from 1924. In 1930 an invasion exercise was held on the Isle of Wight, for example, and in 1934 the 5th Division carried out landings on the Yorkshire coast that included tanks, motor landing craft and smokescreens.[7] Revision of the Combined Operations manual in 1936 led to the establishment of a Deputy Chiefs of Staff Committee on Inter-Service Training (DCOS(IT)) and the Inter-Service Training and Development Centre (ISTDC) for research and development the following year. These and the revised manual were supposed to cover all inter-service co-operation, but thanks to Admiralty pressure focused almost exclusively on amphibious matters, despite complaints from the Air Ministry and War Office.[8]

Interestingly in light of future events, the Air Ministry tried to include airborne matters within the ISTDC remit. The DCOS(IT) issued at least one memo on the matter, and it was also suggested that the ISTDC commandant should attend French parachute trials in 1939.[9] Interest appears to have lapsed after the French disbanded their experimental parachute unit later that year.[10] Given their preoccupation with bombing and subsequent behaviour, it is doubtful that the Air Ministry was interested in the creation of a large-scale airborne force in the accepted sense. It is rather more likely its interest lay in the creation of a small parachute sabotage force to augment the capabilities of Bomber Command, like the original Luftwaffe concept cited above.

Whatever the Air Ministry's motives, it and the War Office continued to monitor German airborne developments closely,[11] to the extent that German airborne landings in the UK were considered a possibility from September 1939.[12] As press releases show, the intelligence was very accurate. An article in *The Times* of 15 May 1940, for example, correctly detailed German operational jumping heights and stressed the need for paratroops to be well drilled for a compact jump pattern.[13] *The Times* also published an accurate drawing of a fully equipped German paratrooper on 8 June 1940,[14] which was probably based on examination of equipment taken from the 1,600

German airborne soldiers captured in Holland.[15] A detailed précis of the material thus gathered was presented at an Air Ministry conference on 10 June 1940.[16]

The War Office also pre-empted Churchill's parachute directive, albeit by a much narrower margin. The driver appears to have been public interest in the spectacular events in the Low Countries, which caught the British public imagination. Every issue of *The Times* between 11 and 22 May 1940 referred to the matter in some way, from fairly accurate reporting of events to erroneous reports of German paratroopers wearing British uniforms.[17] It also inspired an editorial that entreated 'country gentlemen' to refrain from taking 'flying or running shots at... missionaries of Hitlerism dropping from the skies',[18] and optimistic claims that the new threat had been successfully mastered.[19] With the press confusing *Fallschirmjäger* with Fifth Columnists disguised as '...nuns, Red Cross nurses, monks, tram car conductors, policemen and postmen',[20] it is unsurprising that public perceptions were muddled, and neither was the resultant paranoia a uniquely British phenomenon. A contemporary Czech writer claimed first-hand evidence of three 'paratroops' disguised as a nun, a policeman and a schoolboy being captured at Lowicz in Poland on 4 September 1939. They were allegedly betrayed by bruises from their parachute harnesses, and the nun apparently compounded her error by wearing silk underwear.[21] It is virtually impossible to verify such accounts, but the British public clearly thought the threat sufficiently acute to respond enthusiastically to the Secretary of State for War Eden's call for volunteers for Local Defence units on 15 May 1940.[22]

War Office interest was prompted specifically by questions in the House of Commons. On 4 June 1940 Mr Frederick Cocks, MP for Nottingham Broxtowe, asked the Secretary of State for War whether he intended to organise a corps of parachutists and gliders. Eden's evasive response, which invoked the National Interest in an attempt to stymie further discussion, prompted Mr George Garro Jones, MP for Aberdeen North, to cut to the heart of the matter:

> Mr Garro Jones: 'Is the right Honourable Gentleman not aware that operations of this kind have been in process of experiment in other countries for many years; and is this the first time that they have come under the study of the British War Office?'
> Mr Eden: 'I never said that.'
> Mr Garro Jones: 'I am asking the right Honourable Gentleman whether this form of warfare, which has been experimented on by foreign armies over the last three years, has been equally studied by the British War Office.'
> Mr Eden: 'The reply which I made referred to recent operations and it is those recent operations, which are a new development of a method practised before, which are now being studied'.[23]

Eden was saved further embarrassment by an outbreak of heckling, which avoided him having to admit that the short answers to Mr Garro Jones' questions were no, yes and no.

The War Office was fully aware of this, having formulated Eden's evasive response to Mr Cocks, probably on 3 June 1940,[24] and having issued an internal minute entitled 'Creation of a Parachute Corps' on 4 June 1940:

> This idea [the formation of a parachute force] has real possibilities at the present time. The objection will come from the RAF e.g. provision of special equipment and troop carrying aircraft. Will you make a short preliminary investigation into the possibilities of putting it into effect?[25]

Given the timing and wording – both referred to a 'corps' – it is reasonable to assume that the Parliamentary question was the driver for the War Office instruction. Whether or not this was the case, it nonetheless appears that the War Office was ahead of

Churchill, albeit probably only by a matter of hours. It is therefore possible that it was the War Office activity that prompted Churchill to include the parachute requirement to his eclectic list of offensive measures on 5 June 1940. If so, it casts a slightly different light on the received wisdom that the establishment of a British airborne force was a purely Churchillian initiative.[26]

It can therefore be argued that the War Office reacted positively to Churchill's early June directives because they were already working towards that end. However, it would be unwise to push the prescience argument too far, as the War Office also had less praiseworthy reasons to embrace the directives. Its newfound enthusiasm for parachute forces coincided conveniently with public and political interest in the matter, and Mr Garro Jones' hostile questioning made it clear that a perceived omission had not gone unnoticed. Perhaps more pertinently, the War Office must have been looking to restore the Army's badly sullied reputation, especially with the RAF taking centre stage against seemingly imminent German invasion. The RAF had long sold itself as a modern, high-tech force, and forming a parachute unit would permit the Army to portray itself in a similar manner, prepared to learn from past mistakes by adopting the latest military techniques. It would also enable the Army to capitalise on public fear as the RAF had done with the fear over aerial bombing in the 1930s to support its strategic bombing pretensions.

Be that as it may, the first practical response to Churchill's directives came from the War Office. A Chiefs of Staff meeting was held to discuss the matter on 6 June 1940, and included a scheme for raising a raiding force by Lieutenant-Colonel Dudley Clarke. This also suggested naming the projected 1,000-strong units 'Commandos' in honour of their Boer forebears. Clarke's scheme was approved two days later, with the proviso that it did not divert resources from Home Defence.[27] On 9 June 1940 the Director of Recruiting and Organisation (DRO) ordered Northern and Southern to forward the names of forty officers and 1,000 Other Ranks for short-term service. Six of the former were to be of up to lieutenant-colonel rank and considered capable of leading a Commando. Commando service was to be a temporary detachment from units of origin, and volunteers were fit, active service veterans, immune to seasickness and preferably able to swim. Driver and sapper training was considered an advantage; NCOs were explicitly required to be capable of keeping their men under control without commissioned supervision. Other Rank volunteers were to be intelligent, of independent character and respectful of private property; given that the latter point was mentioned several times, the author of the order appears to have equated independent mobile operations with opportunities for looting. All volunteers were to be selected via blind interview, and were free to withdraw once the terms of service were revealed.[28]

The volunteer requirement was refined in two further memos from the Director of Military Operations and Planning (DMO&P), Major-General R.H. Dewing, on 12 and 13 June 1940. The first recommended extending the call for special service volunteers to all Home Commands,[29] while the second dealt with organisation, administration and employment.[30] A target of 200 officers and 5,000 men was suggested, with Commando officers selecting their immediate subordinates in an establishment of ten fifty-strong troops, each including one or two officers. Equipment was to be issued from a central pool for specific operations and no accommodation was provided. Instead, all ranks were to be given cash to make their own arrangements, all in an effort to keep the Commando administrative tail to an absolute minimum and avoid diverting resources from Home Defence. The intent was to create a flexible force of specially trained soldiers capable of organising themselves to meet the specific requirements of whatever irregular operation they were assigned.[31]

The Army Council accepted these recommendations on 17 June 1940,[32] and the call for volunteers was extended to all Home Commands the same day.[33] Only the 3rd Division, which was earmarked for home defence, was exempt.[34] Commando organisation was formalised by the War Office on 20 June 1940,[35] and a memo with suggested organisation, ranks and appointments was circulated to all Home Commands the same day. Twelve Commandos were to be formed under War Office control but administered by their local Home Commands. Southern and Western Commands were to raise three each, Northern and Eastern Commands two each, and Scottish and Northern Ireland Commands one apiece. The exact size of each Commando was to be determined by the Command GOC according to the number of suitable volunteers,[36] and all nominated Commando leaders were to assemble at the War Office on 24 June 1940.[37]

The War Office end was handled by AG 17, a department within the Adjutant General's department also code-named 'Forcedly Seventeen'. The bureaucratic status of the Commando volunteers was fixed in a DRO memo on 26 June 1940, which formalised the selection procedure and their conditions of service. Volunteers could be returned to their original units at the discretion of their Commando OC, and were free to follow this course themselves at the end of any active operation.[38] A daily allowance of thirteen shillings and four pence for officers and six shillings and eight pence for other ranks was paid to cover food, accommodation, heating fuel and lighting, which the individual was expected to obtain locally.[39] This was in addition to normal pay, including any trade or proficiency rates, and the allowance was also payable during leave or sickness until October 1940.[40]

A number of flaws rapidly became apparent in these arrangements. Western Command requested and was refused additional administrative personnel for No.2 Commando on 29 June

1940.[41] The DRO then ordered all Home Commands to provide HQ administrative personnel for each Commando supernumerary to volunteer establishment,[42] although similar requests and complaints continued through July 1940.[43] Pay problems were especially rife, thanks to a cumbersome arrangement that had the relevant Home Command provide normal pay and Commando allowances, while the volunteer's parent unit dealt with family and dependants' allowances and allotments.[44] This meant maintaining two sets of pay records at widely separated and frequently shifting locations for each volunteer, with all the scope for error that entailed. Obtaining accommodation and especially food also proved problematic when Commandos moved to poorly resourced areas, which brought the War Office into conflict with the Ministry of Food.[45]

Even so, sufficient volunteers were ultimately found to form and maintain ten and a half Commandos of the projected twelve, each with a strength of 500, all ranks.[46] It is safe to assume that the total of volunteers outnumbered those selected, given that it is unlikely that all met the required standard, and the precision of the DRO's instructions was probably instrumental in forestalling the traditional response to such calls of sending handy undesirables. Selection by interview, however rudimentary, provided a further safeguard.[47] However, enthusiasm for the Commando policy does not appear to have been universal. At least one harried staff officer complained about Churchill's 'harping on',[48] and it is doubtful that unit commanders were pleased at the removal of their best and most aggressive personnel, even temporarily.[49] Some Commands were also noticeably tardy in implementing their instructions, although it is unclear whether this was deliberate obstruction or inefficient administration. Eastern Command, for example, did not transmit the order to release selected volunteers from 52, 18 and 55 Divisions until AG 17 demanded immediate compliance on 22 October 1940.[50]

Overt opposition may have been offset by the stated temporary and short-term nature of Commando service, but parent units soon began agitating for the return of their volunteers. GOC Northern Command was relaying such enquiries by the end of July 1940, with a personal rider about the deleterious effects of removing high-quality personnel from existing units.[51] Such concerns were not restricted to critics of the Commando initiative. The CIGS, General Sir John Dill, was a supporter but nonetheless raised the same concerns with the War Cabinet Chiefs of Staff Committee on 6 August 1940, and recommended that volunteers be returned to their units unless operational employment was imminent.[52] GOC Southern Command did the same in October 1940,[53] as did Western Command, which also complained the issue was affecting parent unit and volunteer alike.[54] Matters were not helped by uncertainty at the top. Volunteer recruiting was suspended for a month from 22 August 1940 for a rethink of the raiding requirement,[55] which severely disrupted progress.[56] There was further confusion when the suspension was lifted on 1 October 1940 and the order was passed down the chain of command. The CIGS ordered all Commandos to be brought up to strength within a week;[57] AG 17 transformed this into 'forthwith',[58] but Home Forces HQ merely informed all Home Commands GOCs that the matter was at their discretion.[59] Southern Command promptly refused to denude existing units of more men to bring Nos 7 and 8 Commandos up to strength, and suggested that volunteers be drawn from Infantry Training Centres (ITCs) instead. AG 17 then invoked the CIGS to force compliance against Southern Command and Home Forces HQ when it supported its subordinate.[60]

The first specific War Office response to Churchill's parachute directive appeared on 10 June 1940, with a request to the Chiefs of Staff for permission to establish a 'parachute division at Home'.[61] On 12 June 1940 the DMO&P recommended that this be folded into the Commando recruiting effort, on the assumption that the parachute unit was intended for the same purpose.[62] An Army Council conference endorsed this assumption on 17 June 1940, and instructions for all Home Commands to compile a separate list of parachute volunteers alongside the Commando candidates were issued the same day.[63] The War Office formalised the arrangement by authorising the establishment of a 500-strong parachute cadre on 20 June 1940; the temporary reduced establishment was justified by the lack of RAF training facilities.[64] No.2 Commando was redesignated for this purpose, and was to be manned by fifty-strong lettered troops raised by the various Home Commands. Northern Command was to A and B Troops, Southern Command C and D and a suitable Commando leader, Eastern Command E and F, and Western Command G and a proportion of H. Northern Ireland Command was to raise the remainder of H Troop, and Scottish Command J Troop.[65]

Southern Command supplied AG 17 with the names of six officers interviewing parachute volunteers for 'number 2 Commander' on 26 June 1940.[66] These were ordered to report to Major C.J. Jackson RTR at 54 Training Regiment, Perham Down on 1 July 1940; Jackson was to report when his force was ready to move, tentatively, to Manchester.[67] The Air Ministry had selected RAF Ringway, formerly Manchester Airport, as the location for its new parachute training facility, with effect from 1 July 1940.[68] Major Jackson formally assumed command of No.2 Commando at Ringway on 3 July 1940, and the volunteers were billeted in the nearby village of Knutsford.[69] It is unclear what proportion of No.2 Commando was actually present. One troop may have actually arrived at Ringway before Jackson, on 27 June 1940,[70] and the operational records specifically refer to two more troops being present by 9 July 1940.[71] It was certainly some time before the unit was up to strength. On 14 July 1940 Northern Ireland Command was instructed not to concentrate its parachute volunteers because the RAF training facilities were not ready,[72] and Scottish Command was being chivvied to complete its contribution as late as 9 September 1940.[73]

These delays may have been partly due to the general revision of Commando recruiting criteria that occurred on 14 July 1940,[74] and to the tighter physical profile for parachute selection issued by the DRO on 30 June 1940. This specified that parachute volunteers had to weigh a maximum of 250lb with clothing and light equipment, should be able to pass through a three-foot diameter hole wearing a parachute, and should be free from physical imperfections including thin skulls and weak ankles.[75] The revision must have obliged some interesting improvisations as there was an acute shortage of parachutes at the time,[76] and it does not appear to have solved the problem of unsuitable volunteers. Only 342 of the original 500 volunteers had been assessed suitable to undergo formal parachute training by 21 September 1940.[77] In an effort to make up the shortfall, newly promoted Lieutenant-Colonel Jackson was authorised to tour all Home Commands on 21 October 1940,[78] but AG 17 was still chasing volunteers for the under-strength No.2 Commando in November 1940.[79] Be that as it may, such teething problems were arguably inevitable, and they do not alter the fact that the War Office had moved with impressive speed given the prevailing circumstances. A proportion of the new force was ready to commence parachute training by 3 July 1940, less than a month after the instruction to launch a preliminary investigation, and within thirteen days of the new force being formally authorised. This, however, was only half the story and it will now be necessary to examine the RAF's side of the matter.

The Air Ministry's first inkling about a parachute force appears to have been Churchill's 5 June 1940 directive, and its reactions once appraised were almost as swift as the War Office. On 8 June 1940 the Air Ministry's Director of Plans, Air

Commodore Sir John Slessor, issued a preliminary note on 8 June 1940, in preparation for a conference two days later. Entitled 'Development of Parachute Troops', this began by outlining Churchill's directive, that the Chiefs of Staff had agreed in principle and passed the matter to the General and Air Staffs, and that a Parachute Training Centre (PTC) was to be set up as quickly as possible. It then recommended lowering parachute provision to 1,000, with one recipient suggesting that this be reduced again to 500, and stressed the importance of agreeing a united front before even approaching the General Staff to discuss organisation and training requirements. Only when all this was settled to Air Ministry satisfaction were matters to be passed to the Air Ministry Staff Office (AMSO) and Assistant Chief of Air Staff (Training) (ACAS(T)) to oversee formal establishment.

The note then listed specific points for consideration. These included the location of the PTC and where the necessary aircraft, crews and parachutes were to come from. As existing parachutes were likely to be unsuitable, it was suggested that the Air Ministry's Director of Intelligence (DI) be approached for advice on German developments. It was also specifically assumed that the Army would be responsible for providing the troops while the RAF provided the specialist training, equipment and transport. There was to be no question of the RAF providing anything more. Transport was to be a secondary role for bombers, as producing dedicated transport aircraft was 'uneconomic', but without disrupting bomber operations. An investigation into which type was most suitable for 'decanting' parachutists was recommended.[80]

This was markedly different to the reaction of the War Office, and the 10 June 1940 conference minutes make it clear this was collective Air Ministry opinion rather than just that of Slessor. The conference began by questioning the future relevance of parachute troops without novelty value, and placing responsibility for finding the requisite manpower firmly on the War Office; Air Ministry involvement was to be restricted to providing parachutes, ground training and cargo-dropping equipment and suitable aircraft. Adapting existing bombers was considered the best option because producing dedicated transport aircraft would place additional strain on aircraft production facilities, and using twin-engine trainer and civilian machines was suggested as a temporary expedient until the most suitable bomber had been selected and modified. This, however, came with the strict proviso that these modifications were not to interfere with the operational employment or availability of the bombers in any way. Rapid establishment of an experimental parachute unit in Canada or South Africa was recommended, using presumably captured German examples as a starting template. Consideration was then given to a number of vaguely operational provisions for parachute troops including body armour, portable flame-throwers, anti-tank scatter bombs and portable bicycles mounting small mortars. The conference then closed on a rather upbeat note given the overall tone:

> However fantastic an idea may seem at first let us not discard without due thought and ad hoc [original emphasis] research and trial. We laughed at the whole idea of parachute troops until recently and now the enemy has made us divert much of our energy to guard against the threat. If he never uses them against this country he has nevertheless gained something by the threat.[81]

The Air Ministry was thus not just less enthusiastic than the War Office about Churchill's parachute directive: it was openly hostile. The Air Ministry clearly meant to keep its involvement in what was clearly regarded as an irrelevant and unwarranted waste of resources to an absolute minimum. The emphasis was almost exclusively on pointing out difficulties, and virtually every measure and recommendation appears calculated to obstruct or delay, albeit with ostensibly reasonable and varied justifications. RAF involvement was viewed implicitly as very temporary, open to interpretation and unilateral modification. While somewhat negative and lacking in compliance, this was a perfectly legitimate position for the Air Ministry to take in readiness to openly argue its corner. This, however, does not appear to have been the Air Ministry's motive, for the conclusions of the meeting released for external consumption toned down or simply omitted the more contentious elements.

This document, which was also dated 10 June 1940 and again originated from Director of Plans Slessor, was a model of dutiful compliance.[82] It began by pointing out that there were insufficient aircraft available to lift 5,000 parachutists, and suggested an upper drop limit of 700–800, with larger forces being moved in multiple lifts. Again it was made absolutely clear that there was no prospect of the RAF supplying the manpower for the parachute force. Shortages of aircraft and aircrew, rather than overstretching the aircraft industry, were cited as justification for not forming dedicated transport units, and for making such tasks an alternative role for bombers. Of all the types in service, only the Armstrong Whitworth Whitley was deemed suitable, being capable of carrying ten or twelve parachutists and 1,000lb of equipment. However, adding a sliding door was recommended, although it is unclear whether this referred to a new entrance or modifying the existing door in the port rear fuselage. With regard to parachutes, the existing RAF rip-cord training model was selected because its larger-diameter canopy could carry greater loads, subject to modification for static-line operation. This was necessary to allow safe use at the recommended jump height of 500 feet. A production rate of 100 units per week was claimed to be achievable with three weeks' notice.

The conclusions then went on to advocate setting up a dedicated PTC as quickly as possible, the head of the RAF's Parachute Development Flight (PDF) at Henlow being recommended as commander. No location was suggested, but somewhere close to the trainee's billets with 'synthetic' ground training and parachute packing facilities was the preferred option; trainees were to pack and maintain their own parachutes as a confidence-building measure. Alternatively, these facilities were to be provided at the trainee's barracks to maximise training time, and it was also suggested that at least one Army officer be attached to the PTC to assist with liaison and research and development. The PTC's eventual air complement was to be twenty-one Whitleys, to allow 200 drops per day, and a Whitley fuselage was also to be issued as a synthetic training aid. The possibility of using gliders to carry parachutists was suggested, using large numbers of glider pilots thought to be serving in the RAF. The conclusions closed by requesting permission from the AMSO to initiate discussions with the General Staff, to establish a PTC, select six Whitleys for parachute modification, and to place an order for 10,000 training parachutes. An attached list instructed the Air Ministry Director of Research (DoR) to oversee the Whitley modifications, to investigate the possibility of modifying new machines on the production line, and to investigate the glider option.

This was very different in tone and detail to what had gone before. The principle of restricting RAF involvement to supplying transport, ancillary equipment and training was firmly stated, but there was no overt criticism of the parachute concept, nor mention of reducing the size of the projected parachute force to a mere 500. The idea of locating the PTC or associated research and development overseas was omitted, as was the proposal to substitute training or civilian aircraft for bombers, and any suggestion of sidelining the project until resources were more plentiful. The grounds on which the Whitley was selected with such certainty as the only suitable option, or how its parachuting capacity was established, are also unclear, given that the conference recommended an investigation to ascertain that same information. The disparity is therefore curious, although it is possible that the Air Ministry had a collective change of heart in the period between the end of the 10 June conference and the drafting of the external conclusions. Alternatively, the pre-conference note and subsequent conference reflected the Air Ministry's real opinion, and the external conclusions were deliberately toned down for external consumption to buy the authors time to find ways to evade involvement or even stymie the airborne project altogether. Subsequent events would prove which was nearer the mark.

Practical measures to implement these recommendations began four days later, via a joint executive memo from the Air Ministry Department of Plans and Department of Operations issued on 14 June 1940. Among other things, this ordered a formal table of organisation to be compiled, authorised selection of the six Whitleys for modification, requested that the appropriate departments ascertain the exact number of parachutes available and whether this was sufficient, and requested the proposal of a suitable date for formal establishment of the PTC. Recipients were also asked to propose a suitable location once the Air Ministry's Director of Military Co-operation (DMC) ascertained where the Army intended to concentrate its parachute personnel.[83] This was followed on 17 June 1940 by a Secret Organisation Memo that informed all RAF Commands that:

> 1. The Parachute Training Centre will form at [RAF] Ringway on 21th [*sic*] June 1940
> 2. It will form to Establishment No.WAR/AC/102 and will be placed in No.22 Group for administration
> 3. It will be under the operational control of the Director of Plans, Air Ministry
> 4. The aircraft establishment will be 4 + 2 Whitleys.[84]

A 'Table of War Establishment for Parachute Training Centre' was attached to the memo, which assigned the PTC six Officers and six Other Ranks under command of Squadron Leader D.R. Shore.[85] It is unclear whether the latter was the head of the PDF at RAF Henlow as recommended in the 10 June conference conclusions, but subsequent developments suggest he was not.[86] A margin note requesting eight additional NCO instructors was subsequently refused.[87] Shortly thereafter the new establishment was renamed the Central Landing School (CLS),[88] which caused some confusion. At least one official communication to Ringway was addressed to the 'Central Laundering Service', and an Army parachute trainee received a redirected letter addressed to the 'Central Sunday School'. This caused some amusement among the CLS staff, which at one point rendered its telegraph address as 'Droppings, Ringway'.[89]

The CLS was thus established on paper with effect from 21 June 1940, but the reality was less straightforward largely due to Squadron Leader Shore breaking his leg in a parachute accident at RAF Henlow.[90] By 24 June 1940 a number of personnel had congregated at RAF Ringway, including at least six RAF pilots, and possibly Captain J.F. Rock RE, the official War Office representative, who arrived between 24 and 27 June.[91] The new arrivals had only the sketchiest idea, if any, of why they had been posted to Ringway, as did the station staff, and this mutual ignorance prevailed until 28 June 1940, when one of the pilots took matters into his own hands. Pilot Officer Louis Strange DSO, MC, DFC and Bar, borrowed an aircraft and flew to London to clarify matters. There he sought out an old friend serving as Deputy Director of Combined Operations (Air), learned of Squadron Leader Shore's mishap and returned to Ringway as commander of the CLS with the rank of squadron leader, with official effect from 1 July 1940.[92]

Strange had joined the RFC before the First World War, and earned his decorations and the rank of Lieutenant-Colonel during the conflict. His war service was eventful, and included hanging upside down by the fingertips from his aircraft after the machine inverted and his seatbelt gave way as he tried to clear a jammed gun. Somehow Strange managed to regain control of the aircraft and return safely to base. He was recalled for service in December 1939 with the rank of acting pilot officer and served with No.24 Squadron, flying a transport shuttle service to France. During the latter stages of the Dunkirk evacuation Strange was ambushed by German fighters while flying an unarmed Hurricane fighter to RAF Manston. Although he had never flown this or any other high-performance type before, Strange avoided his pursuers with a near-suicidal display of low flying and landed his badly shot-up machine safely at Manston, for which he was awarded the Bar to his DFC.

Strange's appointment to command the CLS was thus whimsical and serendipitous, as he was an extremely capable military maverick with a long-standing habit of bending or simply ignoring rules and regulations if he thought it necessary. His attitude is summed up by his alleged response to accusations that he had no respect for procedure: 'I have if it proceeds'.[93] Normally such an attitude would have been a liability, but it was exactly what was required in the extraordinary circumstances of June 1940. Strange was the right man in the right place at the right time for the establishment of a British airborne force, and he swiftly embarked upon his new task in his own inimitable style, beginning with the matter of parachutes.

There was more to this than the Air Ministry had assumed, not least because, according to the survey of RAF parachute holdings requested on 14 June 1940, there were only fourteen unissued training parachutes in the whole of the UK, three of which were unserviceable. The survey also revealed that the observer-type harnesses ordered for use with the 10,000 training parachutes was incompatible with that type of parachute without modification, and that production of the harnesses was being delayed by a shortage of buckles and quick-release mechanisms. In addition, the training parachute production target was only achievable in less than five months if aircrew parachute production ceased, but such a cessation would interfere with flying training under the Empire Training Scheme. Unsurprisingly, the RAF departments involved were soon calling for guidance, and before the CLS was officially established.[94]

Strange resolved the problem by personally appropriating the entire stock of training parachutes held at the PDF at RAF Henlow on 29 June 1940, including some already modified for static-line operation. He also acquired the NCO parachute instructors refused by the Air Ministry on 21 June,[95] by simply addressing the Henlow staff with their commander's blessing and calling for volunteers; this suggests that Squadron Leader Shore was not the commander of the PDF. Ten came forward and more were acquired by drafting in Army Physical Training Instructors (PTIs), six of which arrived at Ringway on 1 July 1940.[96] Three days later Strange had enough commissioned officers to draw up a preliminary training syllabus and delineate responsibilities,[97] and by 8 July the CLS staff numbered eleven. These were Strange, his adjutant, an intelligence officer, a chief flying instructor and three pilots, a chief and assistant chief landing instructor, a chief PT instructor and Major Rock RE.[98] The latter, as the official War Office representative, had been promoted to match Strange's elevation to squadron leader.[99]

The CLS also required aircraft, and some of the six assigned Whitleys must have arrived at Ringway before 5 July 1940, given that the operational records show that the unqualified pilots assigned to the CLS had received the necessary remedial training in-house by that date.[100] Despite the Air Ministry recommendation that the Whitleys assigned to Ringway should have side-doors, all but one were standard machines. The exception was an *ad hoc* modification by the PDF that replaced the tail gun turret with a small platform for 'pull-off' jumps, and removed the ventral gun mounting to create a circular aperture in the floor of the aircraft.[101] The pull-off method was the then-standard RAF training technique, and required trainees to deploy their parachutes and let the developing canopy yank them from the aircraft.[102] The aperture was a new method, which was successfully tested by Strange's PDF volunteers on 30 June 1940. Strange then sidestepped official channels again and persuaded Armstrong Whitworth to modify four more of his aircraft at their works. This appears to have been completed by 9 July 1940, when the CLS pilots began drop training using sandbag dummies.[103]

The aperture modification became the operational standard for parachute-assigned Whitleys, and the side-door idea seems to have been allowed to quietly lapse. The Air Ministry later claimed that this was because the existing door was too small, and enlarging it would have compromised the aircraft's structural integrity.[104] Nevertheless, the first Polish Special Operations Executive operatives delivered to Poland on the night of 15-16 February 1941 claim to have dropped from a Whitley side-door; all three complained they had been trained to jump from the aperture, although the drop was completed without mishap.[105] It is logical to assume that this Whitley had been modified, as it is unlikely that the PDF and CLS staff failed to check the suitability of the existing side-door before going to the trouble of creating the floor aperture. However, no such aircraft is mentioned in the operational records, official documentation or other accounts, as it surely would have been had the CLS been aware of it, given that the Whitley's suitability was shortly to become a matter of serious dispute between the Air Ministry and War Office.

Quite why the aircraft was not assigned to the CLS is therefore a mystery. It may simply have been misdirected within the RAF administration system, or possibly considered surplus to CLS requirements and issued elsewhere once the aperture exit became standardised. On the other hand, given the Air Ministry's schizophrenic reaction to the parachute directive, it is not impossible that the machine was deliberately 'lost' to hamper development of the CLS and thus limit RAF involvement in the parachute project. This may appear far-fetched, but such a bureaucratic ploy would have been in perfect accord with clearly expressed Air Ministry sentiment and, as we shall see, the latter were to play equally duplicitous tricks subsequently. If the intent was to obstruct and delay establishment of the CLS, it is ironic that it was overturned by an RAF officer, for Strange's unilateral and highly irregular action ensured that at least one Whitley capable of dropping parachutists was available at Ringway virtually from the outset.

The CLS thus had aircraft, instructors and parachutes, but still lacked somewhere to use the latter. Ringway had been chosen because it lay well away from RAF operational areas,[106] but a fully functioning airfield was obviously unsuitable for parachuting. A large and uncluttered landing area was needed, and Strange set about locating one with his customary directness and speed on 6 July 1940.[107] Tatton Hall Park, just five miles south-west of Ringway, recommended itself immediately. Strange promptly requested that the site be photographed from the air to assess its suitability,[108] and approached the owner. Lord Egerton duly granted permission,[109] and Strange then applied to the Air Ministry for official clearance to use Tatton Hall Park as a permanent parachute landing area on 7 July 1940. The application included the relevant map sheet and grid references, requested a two-mile air exclusion zone around the Park, and clearly stated that the owner had given permission.[110] Clearance was granted the next day, provided there was no cost to the Air Ministry and the owner's permission was confirmed,[111] and obstruction of the Park to comply with local anti-invasion measures was halted.[112]

Then, in mid-July 1940, someone from No.22 Group or the CLS suggested setting up a landing facility for powered aircraft at Tatton Park,[113] prompting Lord Egerton to contact the

Under-Secretary of State for Air, Captain Harold Harrington-Balfour, regarding compensation for loss of grazing land.[114] The idea was not finally abandoned until January 1941, after a long-winded process involving Lord Egerton and his estate staff, the Air Ministry, the CLS, No.22 Group, several Air Ministry Works departments, GHQ Home Forces, and the Cheshire War Agriculture Executive Committee.[115] The only bright spots in this sorry saga were that Lord Egerton did not withdraw permission to use his land, and that the bureaucratic wrangling did not interfere with CLS business. The first drop onto the park, using sandbag dummies, took place on 11 July 1940.[116] Tatton Park was not a perfect landing zone as it contained several lakes, which came to be viewed with trepidation by Ringway trainees. This inspired some wag on the training staff to pen a ditty entitled 'Mind the Lake' to the tune of 'Bless 'em All',[117] and the lakes were later used to train SOE operatives in water-jumping techniques.[118]

The final obstacle facing the CLS was the dearth of facilities at Ringway itself, and there was little even Strange could do to alleviate this in the short term. As we have seen, No.2 Commando were obliged to obtain civilian billets in nearby Knutsford, many of the RAF NCOs were billeted a mile or more from Ringway, and the Army PTIs drafted in by Strange had to be housed in the station gymnasium. The CLS allocation of two hangars for training, maintenance and storage was rapidly proved inadequate, and in the middle of July the CLS had to ask permission to use the Airmen's Dining Room for parachute packing between 1800 and 2200 hours.[119]

Matters were complicated by the arrival of the first parachute volunteers from 3 July 1940.[120] Two troops of No.2 Commando began ground training and took air experience flights from 9 July, concurrent with equipment modification and testing.[121] The latter was delayed by inclement weather, as the local conditions confirmed Manchester's reputation for the vilest climate in England.[122] Nonetheless, the dummy drops at Tatton Park were followed by live jumps performed by the CLS staff on 13 July 1940, witnessed by a large crowd of civilian onlookers despite supposed secrecy.[123] Two pull-offs and six aperture jumps were carried out and the parachutists included Strange himself, making his first descent; all but one of the aperture jumps used the static-line modified parachutes obtained from Henlow.[124] A further fourteen descents were carried out on 14 July, with six soldiers including Major Rock using the pull-off method while RAF instructors carried out more test exits through the aperture. The first Army aperture descents, by selected PTIs, were carried out without mishap on 15 July,[125] and Air Marshal Sir William Mitchell inspected the CLS the following day. Mitchell was treated to a ground training display followed by a demonstration drop by eight RAF and six Army instructors. The Commando volunteers were also assembled to see the latter, although the confidence-building value of the demonstration was somewhat undermined by one of the RAF instructors injuring himself in a landing accident.[126]

The CLS was thus ready to begin training military parachutists twenty-one days after its paper establishment, an achievement that compared favourably with the Army's reaction to Churchill's parachute directive. The crucial difference is that the RAF progress was almost entirely due to the unorthodox and unauthorised efforts of Squadron Leader Strange to secure the necessary personnel, equipment and facilities. Had matters been left to proceed via normal RAF channels as the Air Ministry clearly intended, this would have taken a great deal longer. Certainly there was a noticeable lack of application in the RAF implementation of the Air Ministry's orders, which mirrored the hostile opinions expressed in the latter's internal deliberations. This is clearly apparent in the indifferent treatment of those posted to Ringway, and the fact that Strange was finally enlightened by an acquaintance on the Combined Operations staff at the Admiralty after drawing a total blank at the Air Ministry emphasises the point.[127] This does not suggest a venture enjoying high-level support, an impression reinforced by the refusal to provide a mere eight additional NCO instructors and the posting of pilots unqualified on the Whitley to Ringway. The latter point is especially curious, given the Air Ministry's insistence that the Whitley was the only available aircraft suitable for parachuting.

This was all in marked contrast to the Army side of the matter. The War Office did unilaterally fold the parachute project into the Commando recruiting effort, apparently for administrative convenience, and it also tacitly accepted reducing the initial parachute commitment to 500 rather than 5,000 although the latter modification was prompted by the dearth of RAF training facilities. However, the essential point is that the War Office not only disseminated its policy decision in a manner which brooked no argument, it also swiftly assembled the necessary administrative machinery, gave it sufficient authority for enforcement, and lent additional support when necessary. As we have seen, AG 17 wasted no time before invoking the authority of the CIGS when faced with objections or obstructionism, real or assumed.[128]

Of course, the RAF lapses could have been coincidental, the result of administrative errors, incompetence, or the pressure of circumstances. On the other hand, it is not beyond the bounds of possibility that Strange's single-minded approach upset a subtle RAF scheme to slow or even stymie compliance with Churchill's parachute directive, using red tape camouflaged behind a show of acceptance. At this stage of the story there is insufficient evidence to render a verdict one way or the other. What can be said is that there was a marked dichotomy in the attitude and effort displayed by the War Office and Air Ministry, and the latter's behaviour was the beginning of a consistent pattern that was to become increasingly apparent over time.

5
Laying the Groundwork
The Development of a British Airborne Infrastructure, July 1940–April 1941

It took just over five weeks from Churchill issuing his parachute directive to the newly formed Central Landing School carrying out its first parachute descent. In that time the War Office had provided an initial batch of trainees via its Commando recruiting effort, and the Air Ministry had provided aircraft, training personnel and facilities at RAF Ringway. The latter's contribution was hastened and augmented by Squadron Leader Louis Strange, who adroitly circumvented official RAF channels to obtain the ancillary equipment and facilities necessary to turn the CLS into a functioning concern. This was just the beginning of his problems, however, for the CLS and its trainees then had to contend with the *ad hoc* and largely untried nature of the equipment.

The descents onto Tatton Park on 13 July 1940 were the first regular use of the modified Irvin training parachutes obtained from RAF Henlow, and of the Whitley floor aperture.[1] Over the next eight days the CLS staff made a number of drops, including Major Rock and others that lacked parachuting experience,[2] and trainee descents began at 0500 hours on 22 July 1940, to take advantage of clear early morning weather. The CLS was thus combining training with operational testing, and initially all went well. Five officers and six other ranks had been successfully dropped by 0800 hours on the first day,[3] a further seventy-two descents were carried out on 23 July 1940, most from the floor aperture, and other trainees were given air experience flights when the weather became unsuitable for parachuting.[4] No parachuting took place on 24 July 1940, and twenty-one successful descents had been made from Whitley K7230 on 25 July when 175282 Driver Evans RASC was killed by a parachute malfunction at 08:00 hours. Parachute training was prohibited with effect from 1645 hours the same day.[5]

The cause of Driver Evans' death was the *ad hoc* modification of the Irvin training parachute for static-line operation. In practical terms this consisted of permanently attaching a length of woven tape to the manual rip-cord handle with a clip at the other end.[6] The clip was to be attached to a strongpoint in the aircraft, so the parachute was automatically deployed as the parachutist fell away from the aircraft. The problem was that the Irvin system was designed to allow the parachute canopy to emerge from the pack before the rigging lines linking it to the parachutist's harness. This was not an issue in free fall or pull-off jumps because the parachutist's speed or aircraft slipstream would inflate the canopy before the rigging lines emerged. However, the opening sequence occurred at much slower speed in static-line drops, resulting in the rigging lines emerging from the pack before the parachute canopy was fully deployed. The rigging lines could thus become entangled with the canopy and prevent it from opening properly, a mishap that became known as a 'Roman Candle', a macabre reference to the semi-collapsed parachute streaming out behind the unfortunate victim. If the parachutist did not exit the aircraft cleanly in the prescribed posture there was also a possibility of his limbs becoming entangled in the rigging lines, with the same result.[7] It was one or both of these circumstances which killed Driver Evans.

It is impossible to know what difference, if any, it might have made, but Driver Evans was not equipped with a reserve parachute. The official view set out by Group Captain Maurice Newnham, head of parachute training at Ringway from April 1941, was that such provision represented an unwarranted drain on fiscal, material and labour resources for little practical benefit. The operational drop height of 500-600 feet was too low to deploy a reserve parachute in an emergency, especially in darkness with no visual reference, and there was also a risk of the reserve becoming entangled with the failed main canopy.[8] This was reasonable enough, although the Soviets used reserves from at least 1931,[9] and US paratroopers were equipped with them from the outset.[10] Neither appears to have encountered such problems, and the RAF's reluctance may well have been prompted by the additional bulk and weight, a critical factor given the cramped interior and limited weight-lifting capacity of the Whitley. Whatever the reason, British airborne soldiers were not issued with reserve parachutes until the 1950s, in line with NATO regulations. Even then, the last large-scale British jump, by the 3rd Battalion, The Parachute Regiment into Suez in November 1956, was carried out without reserves, due to weight restrictions and because the 700-foot drop height was too low to make it worthwhile.[11]

It rapidly became apparent that a systematic fault rather than an isolated malfunction had killed Driver Evans. The Director of Combined Operations (DCO) visited Ringway on 26 July 1940, and while the parachute training ban prevented a planned training drop, a group of instructors stood in using rip-cord parachutes while the Whitley aperture was demonstrated using eight sandbag dummies. Three of these suffered the same malfunctions that killed Driver Evans.[12] The modified Irvin training parachute was thus removed from service on 29 July 1940, and as no alternative was available, No.2 Commando was despatched for two weeks' tactical training.[13]

An officer had been despatched to RAF Henlow to test modifications suggested by the CLS staff on 26 July 1940, and Strange visited the PDF the following day to select the most suitable for delivery to Ringway by 29 July.[14] At some point the CLS also called in Raymond Quilter and James Gregory of the GQ Parachute Company.[15] Quilter redesigned the parachute pack to reverse the opening sequence so that the rigging lines were fully extended before the parachute emerged from the pack. The parachutist was thus twenty feet clear of the aircraft before a final tie attaching the apex of the canopy to the pack separated, leaving the pack and static-line attached to the aircraft. This was a simpler system with a much less severe opening shock, and a much lower probability of the rigging lines fouling the canopy.[16]

Quilter's modifications were tested with sandbag dummies on 30 July 1940 and functioned perfectly, even when dropped as low as 100 feet.[17] Following a post-test conference with Strange and the CLS staff, Quilter was authorised to produce 500 redesigned parachutes at a rate of 100 per week. The existing stock of Irvin training canopies was to be despatched in batches to the GQ works at Brookland for modification, and Strange stipulated that the new equipment be put through 500 dummy drops before being accepted for training.[18] Quilter's modified parachute was later mounted on an improved Irvin harness which incorporated the latter's patent quick-release box; according to one source Irvin modified the harness while Quilter and Gregory were working on the deployment system.[19] Christened the X-type, this parachute remained in British airborne service until the 1960s.[20] On 2 August 1940, 150 factory-modified parachutes were delivered to Ringway,[21] and the 500 test drops with Quilter's initial prototypes were successfully completed by 7 August 1940. Strange thus informed No.2 Commando that parachute training would recommence on 8 August 1940.[22]

Raymond Quilter's work was swift and praiseworthy, but it is unclear why he was brought in, given that Driver Evans was killed using an Irvin product. Irvin had attended a Ringway conference on 23 July 1940,[23] possibly because he had misgivings about the modifications to his training parachute,[24] and it is possible he may have declined further involvement or been sidelined as a result. Quilter may therefore have been involved before his first appearance in the official records on 30 July, and possibly with the modifications tested at Henlow on 26 July. Certainly Quilter was more intimately involved thereafter than Irvin appears to have been previously. He was on the scene immediately when another trainee, Trooper Watts, was killed by a parachute malfunction on 27 August 1940.[25] Quilter identified a fault in the way the parachute was secured within the pack, formulated a remedy the same day and had it incorporated into the GQ production line within two days.

The speed with which Quilter produced his modified deployment system suggests that development was underway prior to Driver Evans' death, possibly due to the CLS conference of 23 July 1940 attended by Irvin. Bringing Quilter in may therefore have been a Whitehall ploy to avoid placing an extremely lucrative parachute monopoly in the hands of a neutral foreign national, Irvin being a US citizen. Mating the Irvin canopy with Quilter's redesigned pack guaranteed the latter a half share in future sales, and the old-boy network may have been involved too, given that Quilter was a former Guards officer.[26] It may also have been a reflection of the pre-war Air Ministry practice of dividing equipment production between manufacturers. Originally intended to keep the latter afloat and preserve their production facilities, this also had the useful side effect of stimulating competition and driving down prices. Be that as it may, the important point is that the CLS overcame an unforeseen problem with commendable speed. This, however, merely revealed equally serious problems with the aircraft allotted to the CLS.

As we have seen, the Air Ministry decided that the Armstrong Whitworth Whitley bomber was the only suitable machine for use at Ringway on 10 June 1940.[27] Quite what this choice was based on is unclear, and as there is no reference in the official records to the machine even being examined prior to nomination, it appears to have been a purely paper choice. Whatever the Air Ministry's reasoning, the Whitley was highly unsuitable for parachuting, as Director of Combined Operations Sir Roger Keyes pointed out to Churchill after his visit to Ringway:

> ...the Whitley machines are thoroughly unsatisfactory. They can carry only eight men, who would have to sit throughout the passage overseas, huddled up in the bomb tube in great discomfort, and then drop through the middle of a small hole, with no margin whatever for error in poise. Conditions which are calculated to damp the light-hearted enthusiasm with which these young men volunteer for a hazardous adventure.[28]

Keyes cited the Bristol Bombay was a possible alternative, although the Air Ministry claimed there was a shortage of engines for these machines. He therefore recommended that Douglas DC aircraft be obtained from the US, and suggested Churchill use his influence to acquire six such machines belonging to the Dutch airline KLM located in the UK.[29]

Subsequent events proved far less straightforward than Keyes can have envisaged. The Air Ministry promptly despatched an officer to the US and contacted the Dutch Foreign Ministry about the KLM machines. The latter responded on 2 August 1940 by declining to approach KLM without details of what the aircraft were required for and provision for replacement in the event of loss or damage.[30] The next day Sir Arthur Street at the Air Ministry informed the Military Secretary to the Cabinet, General Sir Hastings Ismay, that contact with the relevant Dutch official had been lost, and that the matter could not therefore be pursued further.[31] On 5 August 1940 Ismay received a further letter from either Keyes or the Foreign Office informing him that another Air Ministry department was trying to acquire the KLM aircraft.[32] It also accused the Air Ministry of failing to consider other civil aircraft for parachuting, suggested the De Havilland Frobisher as a candidate, and expressed the intention of seeking clarification from Street in person.[33] What, if anything, became of all this is unclear, but Ismay penned a curious letter to Mr van Kleffens on 9 August 1940, informing him the KLM aircraft were no longer required for the original purpose but that the Air Ministry was still attempting to secure them for another project.[34] Van Kleffens replied three days later with a cryptic reference to the KLM aircraft being turned to 'another good purpose for the Allied cause'.[35]

The good purpose was probably service in Africa, as an Air Ministry paper dated 12 August 1940 referred to the machines being tropicalised and thus ideal for such employment.[36] Wherever the KLM machines went, it was not to Ringway, despite Churchill's personal support; on 10 August he asked Ismay whether they were to be allotted to Combined Operations and offered to intercede personally with the Dutch authorities.[37] Ismay replied that it was no longer possible to acquire them for Keyes and that the Frobisher was under investigation as a possible alternative.[38] In spite of acknowledging their suitability for parachuting,[39] the Air Ministry thus appear to have assigned them elsewhere. This might have been a bureaucratic mix-up, given that Churchill himself had previously described the Air Ministry as 'a most cumbrous and ill-working administrative machine'.[40] At best, the episode therefore further illustrates the low esteem in which the Air Ministry held the parachute project. At worst, it was a calculated piece of bureaucratic deception, designed to hamper the parachute project by blocking CLS access to more suitable aircraft than the Whitley.

Ironically, the Whitley was originally intended to be a bomber-transport in line with RAF inter-war policy, but was modified to meet the pure bombing specification B.3/34, issued in July 1934.[41] The CLS staff shared Keyes' low opinion of the Whitley, and considered it a major factor in the high wastage rate among early trainees. Strange claimed its dark and gloomy interior was bad for trainees' nerves and felt this was exacerbated by the high probability of facial injury from the side of the aperture exit.[42] This was echoed by an RAF parachute instructor:

> And that Whitley was diabolical!... The fuselage... was never made for passengers, let alone ones with bulky parachutes on their backs. It was merely a dark, narrow tunnel designed to join the nose to the tail. Into this sewer-like passageway one crawled on hands and knees to take a seat on the cold floor, five men forward of the hole and five aft if there was a full stick of ten jumpers. Being on the forward side was much preferred. From aft, there was a tendency for the legs to be blasted backwards as they entered the slipstream and, as the body pivoted, for the face to be smashed against the forward edge of the hole. 'Ringing the bell' it was called.[43]

It is thus hardly surprising that Polish parachute trainees at Ringway in 1941 composed a song that began 'The Whitley soars through the clouds like a tomb... Inside are ten paratroopers as if they were dead...'.[44]

Confidence in the Whitley was undermined further on 31 July 1940, when the bar for securing the static-lines came adrift, allowing sandbag dummies and unopened parachutes to fall to the ground, almost taking a crewman with them.[45] A day or so later a Whitley making dummy drops almost crashed when excessive slipstream caused a parachute to become entangled with the aircraft's tail-wheel. Thereafter Whitleys were only permitted to drop in a tail-high attitude, with the engines throttled back to a maximum airspeed of ninety miles per hour.[46] Whitleys posted to the CLS were subsequently fitted with tail-wheel fairings, after a similar mishap in September 1940.[47]

By the time Strange announced the resumption of parachute training on 7 August 1940 the damage was done, and Major Rock refused to allow Army personnel to use the Whitley without a direct order from Keyes or the War Office.[48] Strange responded by pointing out that '...it was not customary in the RAF to suspend training just because a man got killed',[49] and on 8 August led a demonstration drop by CLS instructors.[50] Despite this, Rock remained adamant, and relayed his decision to the War Office with a request that the Whitley be replaced with the Bristol Bombay. The War Office backed Rock, and the Air Ministry responded by hosting a joint conference on 12 August 1940, the conclusions of which were distributed to the Chiefs of Staff, Churchill and the War Office. The Army was bluntly informed it was the Whitley or nothing, and told to '...accept the current casualty rate or give up for the time being the idea of parachute troops'.[51] As it lacked the means or expertise to challenge this ultimatum, the War Office was therefore obliged to lift its ban on 14 August 1940,[52] and parachute training recommenced the following day.[53]

As the Air Ministry's assertions from the 12 August conference have become accepted as fact, the conference conclusions warrant close scrutiny. The document began by restating that parachuting had to be a secondary task for bombers as transport production was unfeasible, and that the Whitley was the only option. That only six of the promised twenty-one Whitleys had actually appeared at Ringway was justified with the circular argument that '...all the commandos [*sic*] were not yet available or trained'. This sidestepped the issue of exactly how long it would take to train 500 parachutists with so few aircraft concurrent with operational development work, to say nothing of the time necessary to modify them for parachuting.

The Whitley's limitations were acknowledged, but justified by comparison with possible alternatives. The Frobisher was rejected because its door was mounted too far aft, which risked parachutists striking the tail on exit, and the door on the De Havilland Flamingo, a small-production-run airliner dubbed the Hertfordshire by the RAF, was too small.[54] The Bristol Bombay's door was acceptable, but all except three of the twenty-one machines available lacked engines, which were claimed to be in short supply.[55] The type was deemed additionally unsuitable because it was unarmed,[56] and because all the available machines were required for vital communication work, including ferrying replacement pilots to Fighter Command.[57] Douglas DC airliners were also deemed suitable, but the five tropicalised KLM machines in the UK were considered best employed in Africa, and the possibility of obtaining more from the US as previously suggested was now considered remote. Finally, the new Short Stirling heavy bomber was suggested as a possible long-term alternative, pending investigation of door modifications.[58]

The problem with this impressive analysis is that it appears to be based almost entirely on unsupported opinion and speculation. The only establishment anything like qualified to make such assessments was the CLS, and there is no evidence that it examined any of these aircraft before 12 August

1940. The operational records show the CLS did not see a Stirling or a Flamingo/Hertfordshire until January and April 1941 respectively,[59] and the Frobisher does not figure at all. Line drawings of the latter do show the door a significant distance from the tailplane, however.[60] The grounds for rejecting the Bombay were equally thin. The Bristol Pegasus engine was still in production and widely used on RAF aircraft.[61] A mere half-dozen would have permitted replacement of all Ringway's Whitleys, and thirty-six would have restored the entire UK Bombay fleet. The problem was more likely that the Vickers Wellington bomber was a notable user of the Pegasus, given the Air Ministry's bombing fixation. It is unclear why the Bombay's lack of armament mattered, for although the UK-based examples may have been faired over, the aircraft was originally equipped with two gun turrets,[62] and in any case the same objection should have ruled out the Frobisher, Flamingo/Hertfordshire and Douglas machines.

Neither does the claim that the available Bombays were fully occupied hold water, for one from No.271 Squadron was posted to Ringway for parachuting tests from 6 August 1940.[63] This was the only parachute-capable aircraft there during the War Office ban on the Whitley, and was modified by removing the door and fitting a static-line attachment point. One trainee noted that the attachment point became noticeably loose after the first few exits, but this was pointedly ignored as no one wished to be labelled a 'jibber'.[64] Seventy-seven successful jumps were carried out on 12 August 1940,[65] twenty-two the following day and a further thirty-four on the day the Bombay left Ringway, 14 August 1940.[66] It is unclear who authorised the attachment, although it followed an information-gathering visit by the commander of No.271 Squadron on 9 August 1940.[67] This suggests its presence was Air Ministry-sanctioned rather than due to one of Strange's personal initiatives, possibly to deflect criticism during the Whitley ban. This would certainly explain its prompt disappearance the day the ban was lifted. Whatever the situation, the machine spent nine days at Ringway, thereby contradicting the claim that all airworthy Bombays were fully engaged in vital communications work.

These inconsistencies cast serious doubt on the Air Ministry's insistent assertions, but the most serious flaw in the RAF position does not appear to have been mentioned at the 12 August conference conclusions at all. The Handley Page Harrow was designed in 1935 to meet Air Ministry specification B.29/35 for a bomber-transport,[68] and 100 examples were in service by December 1937.[69] When the squadrons using them were re-equipped in 1939 the machines were withdrawn to No.19 Maintenance Unit at Kemble, which began reconfiguring some as transports in March 1940. At least ten of these, nicknamed 'Sparrows', were in service with No.271 Squadron by May 1940.[70] The machine could lift twenty fully-equipped troops or 9,500lb of cargo; it had a starboard side-door;[71] and it was originally equipped with gun turrets, some of which were faired over on the modified examples.[72] The Harrow served in Europe until April 1945,[73] some examples being fitted out for casualty evacuation after D-Day. Ironically, these carried 1st Airborne Division casualties from Arnhem back to the UK in September 1944.[74]

The Harrow transport was thus in squadron service *before* Churchill's parachute directive; it was available in roughly the same numbers as the Whitley; it was suitable for parachuting; and the type was serving with the squadron that supplied the Bombay to Ringway in August 1940. Quite why the Harrow did not figure in the 12 August conference minutes, or why the Air Ministry failed to recommend it hitherto is unclear. The Air Ministry cannot have been unaware of the type's existence, and it is also curious that it escaped Strange's attention but there is no mention of the Harrow in the primary or secondary material apart from one reference to a single machine serving at Ringway at an undetermined time.[75] There is no reference to this in the CLS operational records, however. It is therefore difficult to avoid concluding that the Harrow did not figure because it did not suit the Air Ministry's purpose to acknowledge its existence.

The question is therefore why this was the case, given that the Air Ministry was opposed to involvement with an airborne force because it meant diverting resources from strategic bombing. The existence of the Harrow ought to have been a cause for rejoicing, and the key to why it was not appears to lie in the Air Ministry's seemingly illogical insistence that parachuting had to be an alternative role for bombers. This makes perfect sense if the Air Ministry was looking to use the parachute project as a front to gather additional resources for Bomber Command. Under this logic the Frobisher, Flamingo/Hertfordshire and Bombay had to be found wanting, and the Harrow's existence concealed, to avoid having bomber production capacity diverted to their manufacture. Acknowledging the suitability of the Douglas aircraft ran no such risk because they were produced in the US, although the KLM machines had to be diverted away from Ringway to keep the progress of the parachute project within acceptably low bounds. Assigning the obsolescent Whitley to parachuting duty reinforced this objective, and allowed the Air Ministry to argue for their replacement in the inventory with more modern machines. The discovery that the new Short Stirling might be suitable for parachuting on 12 August is therefore probably not coincidental.

It can therefore also be argued that the Air Ministry failure to supply Ringway with sufficient aircraft was deliberate, and was intended to hamstring the project and draw out development until Churchill lost interest. In the meantime, maintaining a show of co-operation deflected criticism and allowed the Air Ministry to try and turn the situation to its own advantage. This is of course speculation, but speculation that is very firmly supported by the evidence, and it is difficult to see any other explanation for much of the Air Ministry's behaviour. It therefore appears that the same motivation underlay Air Ministry advocacy of another seemingly reasonable step, the development of military gliders.

The Air Ministry first referred to gliders on 10 June 1940, and expanded on the theme on 12 August 1940 to support its assertion that parachuting was clumsy, obsolescent and probably tactically and operationally redundant. Gliders were felt to offer a better avenue for development, and it was claimed that a troop-carrying example was available and ready for rapid and economic production.[76] The theme was reinforced in another Air Ministry paper on 31 August 1940, which extolled the safety of gliders and their ability to deliver fully equipped troops into restricted landing areas in compact groups. Gliders were also claimed to be more efficient as they allowed more troops to be carried per sortie, and their wooden construction would put less strain on aircraft production.[77]

Practical measures in this regard were already in place at Ringway by this time. No.22 Group had ordered the CLS to include a glider section on 30 July 1940,[78] using No.2 Special Flight at Christchurch, which had been testing the radar profile of gliders as part of the anti-invasion effort.[79] Pilot Officer P.B.N. Davis thus arrived at Ringway on 7 August 1940 with his small band,[80] and was promptly arrested by Strange even though Ringway had been warned of their arrival on 3 August 1940.[81] This was Strange's standard response when matters required clarification, and he allegedly had an understanding with Major Rock that one should place the other under arrest to avoid complying with unhelpful Air Ministry or War Office directives.[82] Wing Commander G.M. Buxton visited Ringway on 9 August to arrange further glider experiments,[83] and Strange raised the formation of a dedicated glider sub-organisation with the Air Ministry on 11 August 1940.[84] A CLS Glider Flight was authorised on 13 August 1940,[85] and Wing Commander Buxton was assigned to oversee its establishment on 23 August 1940.[86]

This was swift work but it did not really add up to much in practical terms, certainly not as much as the Air Ministry's assertions inferred, and the latter once again do not stand up to close scrutiny. The confident dismissal of the future utility of the parachutes was of course proved wildly inaccurate by subsequent events, and it also contradicted the frenzied measures being enacted across the South of England to repel German parachute landings, in which the RAF was fully involved.[87] Air Ministry scepticism thus appears to have been motivated more by reluctance to provide the necessary transportation than concern over tactical efficacy. It is also unclear which glider the Air Ministry had ready for production. Specification 10/40 for the RAF's first glider, the eight-seat General Aircraft Hotspur Mk.1, was issued in June 1940, and made its maiden flight on 5 November 1940.[88] It is therefore unlikely that the machine was ready for production in mid-August 1940, and the Air Ministry was probably once again being economical with the truth.

Gliders ultimately proved to be a crucial addition to the nascent British airborne force. Glider soldiers were to make up a third of the standard British airborne division's infantry strength, and virtually all the division's support elements, including signals, artillery, anti-tank and field ambulance units, were also delivered by that means.[89] Most used the twenty-five-seat Airspeed Horsa gliders, with heavier items including specially designed light tanks being carried in the General Aircraft Hamilcar which, with a payload of seven tons, was the largest and heaviest Allied glider used in the Second World War. Both machines came from specifications issued in September 1940, and made their maiden flights in September 1941 and

March 1942 respectively.[90] The Horsa's first combat use came in November 1942, when a handful were despatched and lost in the ill-fated raid upon the German heavy water plant at Vermork in Norway; the type was not available in numbers until the following year, being employed in Sicily in mid-1943.[91] The Hamilcar did not make its operational debut until the Normandy invasion in June 1944.

The glider idea therefore proved to be a good one, but whether the Air Ministry deserves the credit is arguable. There is certainly a disparity between the Air Ministry's paper enthusiasm and the resources it actually allocated to the matter. The CLS Glider Flight consisted initially of two First World War vintage Avro 504 biplanes, four ground-crew NCOs, one civilian sport glider and a Ford motor car.[92] This was later augmented with five single-seat and one two-seat sport sailplanes commandeered from civilian owners,[93] two Westland Lysander co-operation aircraft and at least one Tiger Moth biplane. The powered machines may also have been assigned to Ringway for general duties, rather than purely as glider tugs,[94] and the complement of venerable Avro 504s was reduced to one when the other was written off in a ground accident.[95]

To be fair, this handful of civilian sailplanes were the only gliders in existence in the UK, and even the application of military livery proved problematic. Issue camouflage paint refused to adhere to the glider's highly varnished finish, and the CLS had to seek assistance from civilian experts.[96] A proposal to use the airframes of powered aircraft as makeshift gliders for research purposes came to nothing,[97] so until the Hotspur appeared the Glider Flight was obliged to make the best of the motley and inadequate means at its disposal, just like the rest of the CLS.[98] The Flight's personnel rose admirably and ingeniously to the challenge, but practical limitations severely limited the scope and value of their work, to the extent that it is legitimate to question why the Air Ministry bothered. It would surely have made more sense to set up the necessary administrative arrangements and await the arrival of the production gliders, rather than cluttering up the already inadequate facilities at Ringway. This seems to have been the point, however, for the glider initiative appears to have been another ploy to hamstring the CLS by expanding its responsibilities while reducing the requirement for parachute aircraft and looking to secure additional resources for Bomber Command. It is therefore no surprise that the 12 August conference conclusion suggested that gliders could also be employed as additional fuel tanks for bombers, or to carry additional bombs.[99]

Interestingly, these suspicions were shared at the time by Churchill, who had been monitoring progress at Ringway and was not impressed with what he saw. He responded to being informed by the Chiefs of Staff that 500 parachutists were undergoing training on 6 August 1940 by scrawling 'I said 5000' on the report,[100] and he requested clarification from Ismay four days later.[101] This came via the Air Ministry conference of 12 August, a detailed minute from the Director of Combined Operations dated 24 August 1940,[102] and another Air Ministry paper from 31 August; Ismay's synthesised report appeared the same day.[103] Thus Churchill was aware of the Air Ministry's new enthusiasm for gliders, and his response to Ismay clearly illustrated his suspicions:

> Of course if the Glider scheme is better than parachutes, we should pursue it, but is it being seriously taken up? Are we not in danger of being fobbed off with one doubtful and experimental policy and losing the other which has already been proved? Let me have a full report of what has been done about the Gliders.[104]

Ismay relayed this sceptical reaction to the Chief of the Air Staff,[105] and a response from the Vice-Chief of Air Staff and the Air Ministry's Department of Plans appeared on 5 September

1940.[106] This reiterated activity to date, claimed that twelve eight-seat gliders were under construction, and that the design of an eight-ton tank-carrying glider was in progress. It also reported a preliminary investigation into a forty-seat design, and referred to a joint conference scheduled for 5 September 1940, to formulate a unified airborne policy with the War Office and the Director of Combined Operations.[107] It is doubtful whether this satisfied Churchill, given his jaundiced view of the Air Ministry, but he had little option but to await the outcome of the 5 September conference.

Back at Ringway, parachute training progressed despite the added complications of the new Glider Flight. By September 1940 at least 464 parachute descents had been made,[108] integrated into three overlapping courses running between 9 July and 3 September, and a ten-week training syllabus had been drawn up. This envisaged trainees spending their first four weeks undergoing fitness, weapons, sabotage and map-reading training before moving on to Ringway for a three-week parachuting course. Week one consisted of ground training and a single jump from 800 feet, and week two included two more jumps, this time in pairs from 500 feet. Week three required two further jumps, with equipment and weapons containers in a stick of four and then eight. Trainees were then to spend a further three weeks on tactical training at Tatton Park, which was to include at least one group descent, after which they were to be considered a fully-fledged parachutist. Thereafter provision was to be made for troop drops or larger at locations other than Tatton Park.[109]

Work was also underway to reconfigure the CLS for its expanded responsibilities, and to rationalise its position in the chain of command. Strange suggested transferring the CLS to the Air Ministry's Director of Technical Organisation (DTO), and setting up separate glider and development sub-sections within the CLS on 11 August,[110] and conferred with Keyes at

Combined Operations the next day before reporting back to the Air Ministry.[111] The CLS was granted administrative control of the Glider Flight on 13 August 1940,[112] and Strange's proposals prompted a series of meetings beginning with a conference at the Air Ministry on 19 August 1940. Representatives of the latter and Combined Operations visited Ringway on 26 August,[113] and another conference was held the day No.22 Group assumed responsibility for the CLS, 31 August 1940. Those attending included Air Vice-Marshal Blount, Air Officer Commanding (AOC) No.22 Group, Strange and Captain Lindsay, War Office GSO3. Lindsay was deputising for Rock, who had been hospitalised by a parachute accident on 22 August.[114] The meeting appears to have been preparation for a formal joint meeting scheduled for 4 September 1940,[115] for which Strange attended further discussions at the Air Ministry on 3 September 1940.[116] The joint conference finally went ahead on 5 September 1940,[117] and authorised No.22 Group to appoint Squadron Leader Benham and Major Rock Flying and Ground Air Staff Officers (ASOs) respectively with effect from 6 September 1940.[118] No.22 Group was also instructed to draw up detailed proposals for subdividing the CLS, which was done following a conference at Ringway on 12 September 1940.[119]

The upshot of all this was officially implemented on 1 October 1940.[120] The CLS was renamed the Central Landing Establishment (CLE), and gained a dedicated headquarters element tasked to oversee the existing Parachute Training Squadron (PTS) and Glider Training Squadron (GTS), and a new Development Unit (DU) (see Fig. 1). No.22 Group informed the Air Ministry of the changes on 6 October,[121] a progress meeting was held at the Air Ministry on 18-19 October 1940,[122] details of which were passed to Churchill on 8 November 1940.[123] The CLE also received a new commander, Group Captain L.G. Harvey, posted in from the Air Ministry's

Directorate of Repair and Servicing on the not unreasonable grounds that Ringway's work was largely technical in nature.[124] Strange retained command of the PTS, and his cavalier attitude to bureaucratic niceties was likely a major factor in his sidelining. Ironically, the evidence suggests that Strange had set the reorganisation in motion before receiving official sanction, and Harvey appears to have been involved in this, having actually arrived at Ringway on 18 September 1940.[125] He was joined the following day by Wing Commander Nigel Norman, who was to serve as Harvey's Senior Air Staff Officer (SASO) alongside Major Rock in his capacity as attached War Office GSO1.[126]

Personnel to fill the appointments created by the new organisation arrived at Ringway through September and into October 1940. Wing Commander Buxton assumed command of the DU on 21 September, and Captain W.B.P. Bradish was appointed Instructor of Infantry Tactics and as liaison between the CLE and No.2 Commando. Flying Officer Tim Hervey MC took over the GTS on 3 October, and Squadron Leader Maurice Newnham DFC, who later commanded the PTS, took up an administrative post in CLE headquarters the following day.[127] A steady flow of non-commissioned specialist personnel also reported over the same period, and the arrival of RAF Sergeant Page for duty as 'Flight Sergeant, Disciplinary' on 23 September 1940 arguably marks the point when the CLE became properly regularised.[128] Harvey formally inspected his new command on 7 October 1940.[129]

The reorganisation at Ringway was undoubtedly necessary, and replacing an abrasive and unorthodox squadron leader with a suave and well-connected group captain cannot have harmed the new establishment's standing with the Air Ministry. The new establishment continued to profit from Strange's unconventional activities, however. On 11 September, for example, he obtained two surplus Whitley fuselages from the Armstrong

Whitworth works at Coventry for use as ground training aids,[130] and he also recruited three men who had been stunt parachutists with Cobham's Flying Circus in the 1930s. Bruce Williams was an Air Gunner with a Boulton Paul Defiant squadron,[131] and was recruited by Strange after being shot down over the English Channel.[132] Harry Ward was serving with Coastal Command, and Bill Hire was tempted from his job as a dance-hall manager by the prospect of a commission.[133] Williams was at Ringway by 27 July 1940 and was involved in the parachute tests at Henlow following the death of Driver Evans. According to one source he was also responsible for inventing much of the apparatus used for ground training, including jump platforms for landing practice and suspended parachute harnesses for teaching trainees how to manipulate the lift webs correctly. He may also have been behind Strange's acquisition of the surplus Whitley fuselages for teaching exit drills.[134] Hire was posted to the PTS on 31 October, and Ward was serving there by 27 November.[135] Strange also brought in a former Cobham's pilot, Flight Lieutenant Earl B. Fielden, from No.24 Squadron on 5 August 1940.[136]

However, Strange's greatest legacy was probably the use of captive balloons for parachute training. He examined an airship mooring mast and an 'R' Type observation balloon at the RAF's Balloon Development Establishment at Cardington on 1 August 1940. A number of test drops with sandbags were carried out by a warrant officer from Henlow the next day, and an order was then placed for a large passenger cage for attachment to the standard R-type balloon.[137] Strange may have been inspired by the issue of parachutes to observation balloon crewmen during the First World War,[138] or he may have picked up the idea from Polish servicemen at Ringway.[139] The Poles used the technique in their own parachute training courses in the late 1930s.[140] Wherever the idea came from, Harry Ward made the first descent from the prototype balloon cage on

27 November 1940.[141] He was impressed, not least because the lack of slipstream significantly reduced the chance of twisted ringing lines and the likelihood of ringing the bell on exit, and allowed the instructor to monitor the trainee's performance and offer advice while the jump was in progress.[142] For this reason balloon jumping became an integral part of British military parachute training, and remained so until the early 1990s.[143]

The major difference between a balloon and aircraft jump was the four-second delay before the parachute canopy deployed. During this time the parachutist fell approximately 200 feet in silent dead air, and opinion on the experience was mixed. The Air Ministry, doubtless buoyed by the prospect of balloons cutting the CLE's aircraft requirement, supported Ward's assessment and claimed the delay provided an additional thrill.[144] On the other hand an Army officer who tested the new method with Ward claimed it was the most terrifying experience of his life,[145] an opinion shared by Williams after he jumped from the first operational parachuting balloon on 8 April 1941.[146] Williams had advocated constructing a Soviet-style parachuting tower, but the Air Ministry demurred after an engineering firm quoted £30,000 for a 350ft structure.[147]

The balloon was located at Tatton Park, but only after a rerun of the bureaucratic wrangling that followed the attempt to establish an aircraft landing ground within the park boundaries in 1940. The players again included Lord Egerton, various Air Ministry departments, the Ministry of Works and the Cheshire War Agriculture Executive Committee.[148] All this took two months, which partly explains the four-month delay between the Cardington tests and the balloon's operational debut. A shortage of materials, caused by priority being given to barrage balloon production, may also have played a part.[149] Nonetheless, Williams' descent came four days before the local Ministry of Works received permission to construct a balloon installation and eight days before the Air Ministry approved the idea.[150]

The GTS initially continued the research work it had been engaged in before integration, with the assistance of the DU. A moonlight landing test using four gliders was carried out at Tatton Park on the night of 29-30 September, although only one was able to locate the landing zone due to cloud.[151] A week later a daylight test proved the feasibility of double towing and the ability of gliders to locate their landing point after a free flight of fourteen miles.[152] The DU also discovered that gliders could not be launched 'hands off' on 14 October, when a Minimoa sport glider overtook its tug during take-off.[153] These tests were followed by a series of operational exercises, with the sport gliders standing in for troop carriers and the troops being deployed by road. A two-glider demonstration was held for the Duke of Kent at Tatton Park on 26 September 1940, and another exercise on 26 October deployed two gliders as part of a mock attack on a rail viaduct near Macclesfield for the benefit of War Office observers.[154] At least one exercise involved parachutists and gliders. On 13 December 1940 five gliders and two sticks of eight paratroopers attacked a target in Tatton Park for the benefit of CIGS Sir John Dill and other Air Ministry and War Office observers. The gliders and paratroopers landed successfully in under a minute within 200 yards of the target; the CIGS was suitably impressed.[155]

Spectacular demonstrations were the exception rather than rule, however, and much of the DU's work was more prosaic if no less vital. On 19 November 1940 Corporal Carter was killed when the snap-hook connecting his static-line to the aircraft snagged on the edge of the aperture; this disconnected the parachute and prevented it from opening.[156] The DU began an investigation immediately and by 27 November had designed and tested a locking safety pin for the snap-hook,[157] which was officially accepted by the CLE three days later.[158] Experiments with different methods of dropping equipment containers were carried out and the results passed to Armstrong

Whitworth for further development,[159] and tail-wheel spats to prevent parachutes fouling the Whitley's tail-wheel were tested and fitted in-house at Ringway.[160] Attempts to design seats for the Whitley's passengers were less successful, presumably due to the cramped dimensions of the aircraft's fuselage, and issue mattresses were used instead.[161]

Similar research and development work was carried out for the GTS, which sometimes required makeshift solutions to overcome a lack of basic equipment. Perhaps the most alarming expedient involved using Swallow light aircraft as makeshift gliders, with ground crew being pressed into service as human counter-weights.[162] Less hazardous was the fabrication of the 'sector light' for night towing tested on 6 November 1940. This consisted of a lamp fitted to the tail of the tug with three shrouded filters. Red indicated the glider was flying higher than the tug, amber below and green indicated correct alignment.[163] While the device worked, it was useless in cloud and was thus superseded by an electrical device that indicated the 'angle of the dangle' between glider and tug on a dial face, which was designed and tested in December 1940.[164] The glider idea was so new that tests had to be carried out to ascertain even basic information such as the optimum length for towlines.[165] A standardised terminology was coined, referred to as 'glider patter', along with a number of new and specific duties connected to glider operations.[166] A detailed ground training syllabus was drawn up to reflect the experience gained, which included training in interpreting aerial photographs when these proved more useful than maps for navigation.[167]

Perhaps inevitably, a considerable amount of time and effort was wasted testing projects that turned out to be of limited utility. The Rotachute, invented by a German national called Hafner, consisted of '...a man sitting in a cradle suspended from a propeller, which resembled and acted in a similar manner to a falling leaf'.[168] The device was suggested as a substitute for parachutes *and* gliders at the joint conference on 5 September 1940, and further investigation was authorised despite the reservations of the Assistant Chief of Air Staff (Technical).[169] Hafner had to be released from internment as an enemy alien, but a scaled-down Rotachute was tested on 5 November 1940.[170] A larger model with a three-foot rotor span weighing 4.5lb was tested on 11 November, and a full-scale example weighing 300lb was ready for test-dropping from a balloon the same day.[171] Detailed drawings for a model with a ten-foot span were completed on 24 November,[172] and successfully tested at Tatton Park on 14 and 18 March 1941.[173] Thereafter the device appears to have been recognised as a blind alley and abandoned.

Similar effort was expended investigating the utility of gliders for parachuting. The idea was first mooted by Flight Lieutenant Hodges from the CLE in a memo to No.22 Group on 12 September 1940. Hodges suggested that side-doors for this purpose be included in the design of the forty-seat glider then being drawn up.[174] No.22 Group requested Ringway give the matter additional consideration on 19 September 1940,[175] and informed the Air Ministry of developments the same day.[176] Combined Operations HQ and the War Office were drawn into the discussions over the next four days.[177] The upshot was the integration of a parachuting capability into the Airspeed Horsa, with doors on either side of the fuselage to allow simultaneous exits, means to despatch supply panniers from within the aircraft and six under-wing cells for supply containers. None of this appears to have been used operationally, however, and the idea appears to have been effectively abandoned by the time production Horsas appeared in June 1942.[178]

While the GTS was short of gliders, there was no concomitant lack of pilots as the CLS had gathered a number of service personnel with civilian gliding experience. Squadron Leader Tim Hervey, commander of the GTS, had been chief instructor at the Dunstable Gliding Club in the 1930s, for example.[179] The real problem was the shortage of facilities, for the GTS required weatherproof storage for its gliders and the CLE had only been allotted two hangars. One of these was occupied by the PTS and the other was divided between the DU and aircraft maintenance, although the latter frequently spilled over into both hangars.[180] Using motor cars to launch gliders was also a hazard on an operational airfield, and the obvious solution was to relocate the GTS to an airfield of its own. An official request was lodged on 8 October 1941,[181] and airfields at Ratcliffe and Rearsby near Leicester were suggested.[182] Ringway was informed on 16 October,[183] and Newnham and Hervey visited both locations two days later.[184] However, the airfields had also been earmarked as bombing ranges, leading to a strong protest from Bomber Command on 23 October 1940,[185] and in any case both were already occupied by the Ministry of Aircraft Production, which was disinclined to move out for anyone.[186]

Undaunted, Wing Commander Norman found another suitable airfield at Side Hill near Newmarket. The CLE staff inspected it on 13 November, and the results of a detailed survey confirming its suitability were relayed to the Air Ministry on 18 November,[187] although permission to use the new site had been granted the previous day.[188] The CLE issued a movement order on 20 November 1940, an advance party was despatched the next day and flying at Ringway was suspended on 22 November in preparation for the move.[189] Things then went awry on 24 November 1940 with complaints about the change of use from the Jockey Club and Bomber Command. The latter used Side Hill as an emergency landing site, and although local bomber units were reportedly unconcerned,[190] the move was cancelled and the advance party returned to Ringway on 6 December 1940.[191] Hervey had by then begun a systematic survey,[192] and within a week had located seven suitable sites.[193]

These were narrowed down to two at an Air Ministry conference on 11 December 1940, with an airfield at Haddenham near Aylesbury being the CLE's preferred option.[194] The Air Ministry sanctioned the latter on 20 December 1940, the CLE issued a movement order ten days later and another advance party left Ringway on New Year's Eve.[195]

Haddenham was a far from inviting prospect. The runway was littered with wheel-less cars as an anti-invasion measure, although these were cleared for Hervey's powered aircraft to fly in on 1 January 1940; the gliders arrived by road.[196] The station also lacked a surfaced access road and accommodation for aircraft and personnel. Temporary arrangements were made for the latter, the officers being lodged nearby with a Colonel Sedgewick and the Other Ranks in a barn leased from a Mr Purser for three pounds per week plus rates.[197] The aircraft were housed in twelve-bay Bessoneau-type hangars, which the local Works department began to erect on 2 January.[198] The GTS began flying the next day, and had logged thirteen hours of glider time by the official commencement date of 5 January.[199] The GTS therefore faced the New Year with the location, if not the means, to fulfil its primary function.[200] In the meantime GTS gliders participated in tests to ascertain their vulnerability to attack by fighter aircraft at the Air Fighting Development Unit (AFDU) at RAF Duxford,[201] and March 1941 saw two notable firsts. Corporal Weston made the first 'prang' in the history of Army gliding by crashing a Kite glider through the roof of the Sergeants' Mess,[202] and Sergeant Strathdee made the Army's first solo glider flight.[203] The following month the GTS was renamed No.1 Glider Training School, Haddenham was renamed RAF Thame, and the first General Aircraft Hotspur glider arrived from the factory.[204]

While all this was going on, the parachute side of matters was undergoing its own trials and tribulations. On 2 October 1940, for example, a consignment of faulty under-carriage jacks grounded all Ringway's Whitleys for nine days,[205] and on the night of 22–23 December German bombs intended for Manchester damaged one of the CLE's hangars and several aircraft within it.[206] The most serious brake on progress, however, was the unavoidable practice of carrying out training and research and development work simultaneously, which required No.2 Commando to maintain a detachment on standby from 10 September 1940.[207] The DU began using this detachment for operational exercises from 26 September 1940, and research work soon expanded to include demonstrations for high-ranking observers. On 3 December 1940 Montgomery requested the inclusion of a platoon-sized drop in an exercise on Salisbury Plain, during which the Commandos commandeered the car of Crown Prince Olaf of Norway. The Prince was so impressed by this display of 'Airborne Initiative' that he treated them to a round of drinks from a nearby public house when reunited with his vehicle.[208] The Commandos also carried out the combined parachute and glider assault for the CIGS at Tatton Park on 13 December 1940,[209] and similar exercises at Camberley in Surrey and Salisbury Plain for the Commander Home Forces and Dill and Alan Brooke on 6 January and 19 February 1941 respectively.[210]

Such exercises provided good publicity for the new force, but at the cost of disrupting individual and unit-based training. 11 Special Air Service (SAS) Battalion, as No.2 Commando was redesignated on 21 November 1940, was scheduled to complete advanced group parachute training by February 1941, but it took until Christmas Eve 1940 for all ranks to complete the basic individual course. The need to train non-infantry volunteers in basic infantry skills complicated matters too. In practice it took five months to train 176 men to a level corresponding with section training in an infantry battalion,[211] leading Major Rock to recommend in July 1941 that fighting airborne troops be drawn exclusively from the infantry.[212]

The situation was exacerbated further by the fact that 11 SAS Battalion spent much of its time in a state of organisational flux. The original ten-strong Commando sections were re-organised into sections of eight on arrival at Ringway, and then back into tens in December 1940 to fit the supposed capacity of the Whitley, for example. Deployment on demonstrations and as enemy for conventional formations probably had some training value, but it is unlikely this equalled the value of a more systematic training regime.

However, the most disruptive activity in this period was arguably Operation COLOSSUS, the first British parachute operation in history.[213] Launched in February 1941, COLOSSUS absorbed almost all of Ringway's resources for the better part of a month,[214] and the CLE's commander personally oversaw the operation from Malta.[215] This hands-on involvement was not accidental, for the period December 1940 to January 1941 saw a serious difference of opinion between the Air Ministry and War Office over the future of airborne project. Ringway therefore needed a successful airborne operation to demonstrate that the airborne idea merited further development, and the gloomy strategic background badly needed a propaganda success for domestic and international consumption, to show that Britain remained a force to be reckoned with.[216] COLOSSUS was intended to disrupt the flow of fresh water to the ports of Bari, Brindisi and Taranto by destroying the Tragino aqueduct in Southern Italy; supplies and reinforcements were being funnelled through those ports to Italian forces in Albania and North Africa.

The aqueduct was pointed out to the Air Ministry by a British civil engineering involved in its construction, and was passed to Combined Operations after investigation in early December 1940 showed it was too difficult a target for aerial bombing. As the target was sixty miles from the coast, it was decided to insert the attackers via a night parachute drop, and once the operation was approved on 11 January 1941 it was passed to Ringway for execution.[217] The PTS staff carried out a night jump on 13 January to test the feasibility of moonlight jumps and the utility of specially fabricated lights to aid post-jump reorganisation.[218] 11 SAS Battalion volunteered for the mission in its entirety and seven officers and thirty-nine men were selected, including two interpreters of Italian origin. This group, christened 'X Troop', immediately embarked on an intensive training programme. A scale model of the Tragino aqueduct and surrounding area was housed in Harvey's office, and a full size mock-up was constructed at Tatton Park. Parachute drops in sticks began on the night of 14 January 1941,[219] and were a hazardous undertaking in themselves. Lance-Sergeant Dennis was drowned when high winds blew him into one of Tatton's lakes on the night of 22 January,[220] and Knutsford Fire Brigade had to be called in on 1 February when several volunteers became hung up in trees.[221] X Troop and a number of the CLE staff including Group Captain Harvey left RAF Mildenhall for Malta six days later.[222]

The operation was launched on the night of 10-11 February. After demolishing the aqueduct, X Troop were to withdraw to the mouth of the River Sele where they would be picked up by the submarine *Triumph*, which would be laying off the coast on the nights of 15-16 and 17-18 February. The aqueduct was demolished as planned, but the entire force was intercepted and captured traversing the sixty mountainous miles to the coast, although this spared them discovering that the *Triumph* had been ordered to abandon the rendezvous on 13 February. A Whitley bomber engaged in a diversionary attack for the raid force-landed in the same area and transmitted a rescue request, and the Admiralty, not unreasonably, decided that the COLOSSUS rendezvous was compromised and recalled the *Triumph*.[223]

This decision, while distasteful, was the correct one given that the Admiralty's first priority was the preservation of the submarine. Allegations that X Troop were deliberately written off have surfaced nonetheless, but do not really hold water.[224] The volunteers can certainly have entertained few illusions. The CO of 11 SAS Battalion explicitly warned them that survivors should not expect any special extraction arrangements, and a member of the CLE staff involved in planning the operation insisted that any plan that did not offer participants a sporting chance would not have been entertained.[225] What constitutes a sporting chance is open to conjecture, but the calibre of the decision-makers involved and the fact that the *Triumph* was despatched at all make it unlikely that X Troop was written off beforehand.

Whichever, X Troop may have demolished the aqueduct, but the predicted disruption to drinking water supplies did not materialise. Operation COLOSSUS did, however, come as an unwelcome shock and the Italian authorities were obliged to divert troops and resources to guard against a repeat. The raid thus at least partially fulfilled its primary aim while demonstrating that Britain was still a force to be reckoned with. It also proved that airborne operations were feasible and revealed flaws in existing operating procedures. The revelation the day the raid was scheduled for launch that there were actually two aqueducts highlighted the need for up-to-date reconnaissance and intelligence, as did X Troop's subsequent discovery that the support pillars were brick rather than concrete. The raid also showed that Ringway's night-dropping techniques required further refinement, and uncovered a previously undetected electrical fault in the container release mechanism that resulted in some containers failing to drop. The latter were specially fabricated metal items produced when it was discovered that the existing soft pattern sagged so much when fully loaded that the Whitley bomb-bay doors could not be closed. These in turn provided the pattern for the containers used in huge numbers in subsequent large-scale airborne operations.[226]

The Tragino raid was the first public acknowledgement that Britain possessed a parachute capability, and was a useful fillip for 11 SAS Battalion, which was experiencing difficulty attracting new volunteers and retaining those it already had. Italian reporting of the raid was widely quoted by the British press,[227] and interest in it was heightened by the execution of one of X Troop's interpreters after his captors identified him as an Italian national.[228] There was also at least one unwelcome result. Bruce Williams accompanied the raiders as a despatcher,[229] and ended up facing a court martial charged with 'unlawful disclosure of classified information' after speaking to a reporter on his return to the UK.[230] His removal may have been due to internal CLE politics, a possibility to which we shall return. Be that as it may, by the beginning of 1941 the CLE was functioning properly as a co-ordinating centre, its in-house research and development unit was providing solutions to problems as they occurred, and its parachuting and gliding wings were established and functioning in their own dedicated locations. That, arguably, was as much as could be expected without additional guidance and support from above. This was not immediately forthcoming, because of a growing divergence between the Air Ministry and the War Office over the role, size and composition of the new airborne arm, and no further progress was possible until this was reconciled.

6

Divergence at the Top

The War Office, the Air Ministry and the First Stage of the Development of the British Airborne Force

The trials and tribulations at Ringway in the first months of its existence have effectively overshadowed what was happening above that level. As we have seen, the Air Ministry's preference was for sabotage or small-scale operations to assist conventional forces, which also conveniently required minimal RAF resources. The War Office acquiescence to the Air Ministry's unilateral downgrading of the parachute force from 5,000 to 500 and the integration of the parachute requirement into its Commando raiding effort suggested it concurred with the RAF position. This was not the case, however, for the War Office had its own view on the role, shape, and size of the new parachute force.

Initially, however, the War Office kept this to itself. The Army representatives toed the Air Ministry line at the joint conference at 5 September 1940, although they may have had little choice as only three of the twelve attendees were not serving RAF officers, and one of those was representing Combined Operations.[1] In any case, the conference saw the parachute requirement reduced to 300 in practical terms. These were to act as pathfinders for a projected 3,000-strong glider force, which was to be operational by spring 1941 and employed primarily for raiding. The possibility of secondary employment for spearhead operations was acknowledged but not formally agreed, as was the prospect of deploying the force to the Middle East, and it was recommended that the remaining 200 parachutists be employed as saboteurs rather than being returned to their units.[2]

The War Office may not have objected to this, but its quiescence was purely pragmatic. The Army was having difficulty in recruiting sufficient volunteers to fill the existing parachute requirement and the War Office was still digesting the implications of the Air Ministry's new-found enthusiasm for gliders. This was a poor basis for argument and is presumably why the conference conclusions were not distributed within the War Office until 18 September 1940.[3] Nonetheless, War Office thinking was clearly expansionist in the geographic sense. Middle Eastern Command requested information on setting up a parachute training facility on 16 September 1940,[4] and a similar request was received from India in early October.[5] The former was authorised to establish a PTS on 11 October 1940, with the caveat that no aircraft should be expected from the UK.[6] This prompted requests for parachute instructors and special equipment with a view to starting training in January 1941.[7] In the event, the Middle East initiative appears to have been dropped after HQ RAF Middle East declined to provide any aircraft in December 1940,[8] and the War Office advised Indian Command to postpone its developments until the home situation was clarified at the end of January 1941.[9]

The War Office set out its ideas for the size and scope of the airborne force internally on 4 October 1940 in preparation for a further joint conference announced by the Air Ministry two days earlier.[10] The Air Ministry proposal for a 3,000-strong force by the spring of 1941 was retained, but as an interim step toward a larger force equipped with light tanks, artillery and other heavy equipment. It was also agreed that this should be communicated to the Air Ministry in unambiguous terms, although precisely when was not stated.[11] Nothing was said at the joint conference held on 6 October 1940, apart from a passing comment that the airborne agreement might require modification in the future.[12] This was probably because the War Office was still gathering information to support its position. On 10 November 1940, Major Rock was asked to assess the suitability of a variety of equipment for glider transport, including tanks, Universal Carriers, trucks, motorcycle combinations and Bofors light anti-aircraft guns.[13] The 3.7-inch light howitzer was added to the list twelve days later, along with a list of unit locations, presumably so that the equipment could be examined,[14] and discussion on the carriage of vehicles continued until the beginning of December 1940.[15]

The War Office informed the Air Ministry that it intended to revise its airborne requirement on 11 November 1940.[16] The latter may have been expecting the shift due to a CLE report which had recommended airborne spearhead operations and suggested the airborne force could be expanded to 5,000 with light artillery and motorised transport at relatively short notice; this appeared on 31 October 1940.[17] This would certainly explain the exceedingly swift response from the Director of Military Co-operation, Group Captain Goddard, who issued a draft response for comment the day the War Office letter arrived.[18] The finished minute, incorporating feedback received by 16 November, appeared on 23 November 1940. It began by declaring that the airborne framework agreed on 5 September 1940 was not attainable, and analysed virtually every facet of airborne activity to date.[19] Tentative Army proposals were discussed, the wisdom of training soldiers to fly gliders was questioned, and the absolute necessity of RAF control over the air side of airborne operations was stressed. The need for a binding policy for airborne development and employment with a firm deadline for operational deployment was also pointed out, and it was suggested that the Chiefs of Staff appraise Churchill of the situation.[20]

This did not go down well with the bomber lobby. On 30 November 1940 Deputy Chief of Air Staff Arthur Harris complained that the airborne idea was snowballing out of control, accused the War Office of circumventing the Chiefs of Staff, and demanded clarification of the purpose and strategic justification for the airborne force.[21] Goddard's minute formed the framework for another joint conference, the agenda for which appeared on 9 December 1940 and specifically limited business to determining 'basic principles only for immediate action by the Air Ministry'. The latter agreed that invasion spearhead and battlefield support operations should be added to raiding and sabotage in the airborne repertoire, but there was no shift in the restriction of parachute troops to the latter or securing glider landing zones. In fact the Air Ministry went further, by explicitly ruling out the mass use of parachute troops and demanding that the 500 ceiling be formally recognised. The matter of which service was to provide glider pilots was raised, and it was suggested that the immediate requirement for parachute and glider training be agreed, along with a timetable. A progress report from the CLE and a suggested organisation for an Aerodrome Capture Group were attached to the agenda.[22]

The conference was held on 11 December 1940. The Commander Home Forces challenged the 500-parachute-troop limit and requested that as many British paratroops be trained over that limit as possible, along with a further 500 Polish and Free French troops. Surprisingly, the Air Ministry accepted this, with the caveat that it was achieved without expanding the training organisation and did not assume additional aircraft would be made available for the enlarged force. The fact that the complete group of Whitleys pledged in June 1940 had yet to arrive at Ringway was conveniently overlooked. The RAF representatives were more interested in discussing gliders, and specifically reversing their previous insistence that the Army should provide pilot manpower. The conference chairman claimed 'glider' was a misnomer because the projected twenty-five-seater was the same size as the Short Stirling heavy bomber and at least as demanding to land in restricted spaces without engine power. This view was supported by DCAS Harris, who openly ridiculed the idea of using semi-skilled infantry corporals for such demanding work.

The Army was less concerned with where the pilots were to come from than their actual provision, and pointed out that the War Office had not insisted that the pilots be soldiers in the first place. The Air Ministry justified its new approach with the unsupported assertion that any increase in glider provision would remove 350 bomber pilots from Bomber Command. It was claimed this could be avoided by expanding flying training, and by redirecting war-weary bomber pilots to glider duty, which raises the suspicion that the Air Ministry was looking to use the glider issue to expand its pool of bomber pilots.[23] Whether or not, the 11 December conference thus failed to establish clear principles, and actually threw up more differences than it resolved. It did, however, prompt Air Ministry and War Office into openly clarifying their respective positions.

The Air Ministry's position was set out in a paper entitled 'Provision of Airborne Forces – Air Ministry Aspect', which appeared on 23 December 1940 and was passed to the War Office by 1 January 1941.[24] After pointing out the need for a clear airborne plan and reiterating the contents of the 11 December agenda, this justified freezing the parachute force and its training infrastructure at its current size because there was no strategic plan for its employment. It was claimed that establishing similar provision in India would be more convenient for airborne deployment to the Middle East, and imitating the German practice of air-landing troops was rejected because the bombers employed on airborne work were too valuable to risk. Parachute insertion was to be restricted to minor missions or the initial stage of larger operations, as that method was an inefficient and costly employment of personnel and aircraft. Gliders were the preferred alternative, and while it was recommended that stocks of the machines be established as and when possible, it was stressed that equipping and manning them was not to impinge on the resources of operational RAF Commands until live operations were in the offing. It was recommended that existing plans and programmes be abandoned and new ones drawn up in consultation with the Ministry of Aircraft Production, the War Office and the Director of Combined Operations, and the establishment of a dedicated airborne service was rejected as impractical. The paper by holding out the possibility of obsolete aircraft being assigned to airborne work in 1942, and suggesting that the situation might change if the supply of pilots were to outstrip that of aircraft.

Little of this was new. Air Ministry dissatisfaction with the parachute and the desire to see it replaced by the glider went back to August 1940, and faith in the latter was based on little more than wishful thinking. The marginally useful Hotspur gliders only began to leave the production line in April 1941 and the prototype of the more capable Horsa did not make its first flight until that September. Much of the rest was slanted at best and misleading at worst. The implicit assumption that existing aircraft provision at Ringway was sufficient was simply incorrect, as the Air Ministry well knew, and the reference to setting up a separate airborne service appears to have been a straw man. The idea of setting up an airborne infrastructure in India looks suspiciously like a ploy to hamstring the airborne project by diffusing the CLE's scant resources and moving it away from the centre of events where it could be more easily sidelined. The possible future offer of obsolete aircraft also appears to be little more than window-dressing, given the failure to divert the already obsolete Bristol Bombay and Handley Page Harrow for airborne use and the non-appearance of all the promised Whitleys.

The 23 December paper thus merely restated the Air Ministry's existing position in a clearer and blunter form. The airborne force was still considered an unwarranted diversion of resources, for which the Air Ministry was willing to provide the absolute bare minimum of equipment and effort, which some considered still too much. DCAS Harris' reaction to the paper was to restate his opinion that the idea of soldiers flying gliders was hopeless, and to point out there was no prospect of having even 100 gliders in service by spring 1941. He also insisted that no amount of wishful thinking would alter these facts and suggested the War Office and Churchill should be apprised of them forthwith.[25] Other Air Ministry opinion was less combative but equally firm, as illustrated by a letter from Goddard to the Vice Chief of Air Staff on 31 December to confirm despatch of his paper to the War Office.[26] A post-dated postscript recommended that the Army request for a brigade-size airborne force be rejected, but suggested that his proposals be submitted to Churchill for endorsement.[27]

The War Office finally placed its cards on the table on 10 January 1941. The Army was looking for two parachute

'Aerodrome Capture Groups', also configured to seize small tactical features or similarly sized bridgeheads. These were to be 500-strong, and capable of operating in all terrain for a maximum of thirty-six hours within 500 miles of their launch point. These were also to act as a spearhead for two fully air-portable 'Invasion Corps', consisting of four infantry battalions, a light tank squadron, a 3.7-inch howitzer battery, two light anti-aircraft batteries, an anti-tank battery and medical and supply elements (see Fig. 2). Lifting the whole Corps at once was not envisaged, but sufficient aircraft were required to deliver a small HQ, two infantry battalions, the light tank squadron, the howitzer and both light anti-aircraft batteries and some support elements in a single lift, in all around 1,700 men. The Corps were to be capable of operating unsupported for three days within a 500-mile combat radius, and were authorised to undertake smaller operations. No dates were cited, but the units were to be formed as quickly as resources allowed.[28]

The War Office was thus looking to double the existing airborne establishment. Including the Aerodrome Capture Groups, the two Invasion Corps totalled in the region of 5,000 men and thus met Churchill's original directive, albeit with glider troops rather than just paratroops.[29] The War Office proposals prompted two responses. The first came from the Air Ministry on 14 January 1941. It reiterated the latter's view that parachute troops should be a minority in whatever scheme was finally approved because they required more RAF resources, and recommended that the matter be passed to the Chiefs of Staff Committee for adjudication as the two services' positions were at such variance. It also suggested that the War Office formulate a home airborne establishment for tactical development and anti-invasion training with Home Forces, distinct from any operational organisation for offensive operations.[30]

The second reaction, which appeared on 15 January, emanated from the CLE and was divided into two parts.[31] The first referred directly to the War Office proposals, and among other measures suggested augmenting the Invasion Corps with engineer units and the single lift detachment with anti-tank elements, and expanding the proposed list of missions in a manner reminiscent of Major J.T. Godfrey's 1935 paper 'Winged Armies'.[32] The second was a list of answers to specific questions, which clearly show the War Office had little idea of the airborne force's requirements or the paucity of RAF resources assigned to Ringway. The CLE thus had to explain that there would be insufficient Whitleys to carry a single Aerodrome Capture Group even if all the promised machines were provided, that increments of 250 did not conform to 11 SAS Battalion's existing organisation and that speculation on glider numbers was pointless because the machines had yet to be built. Despite this, a provisional estimate that the War Office proposals would require 163 twenty-five-seaters, sixteen tank carriers and 334 pilots was provided. The anti-aircraft requirement was also problematic because existing glider designs were unable to accommodate Bofors guns, although a modified airborne version was considered feasible. Adopting an unspecified four-ton prime mover also held out the possibility of equipping airborne artillery with larger pieces than the 3.7-inch howitzer. Concentrating resources on the twenty-five-seat glider design was recommended over the larger tank-carrying machine, however, due to the former's higher estimated flying speed and superior landing requirements.

All this points to a degree of mutual misunderstanding over and above mere inter-service rivalry. Even allowing for Air Ministry obstructionism, the War Office proposals were rather optimistic in the prevailing circumstances, while the Air Ministry's position suggests it did not appreciate that the Army viewed 11 SAS Battalion as an operational cadre rather than a research and development tool. The root of this fundamental difference in view lay in the two services' attitudes and operating procedures. The Army had a long history of operating on a shoestring, at short notice and in a variety of far-flung locations. The formation of an airborne force was thus the latest in a long line of improvisations, like the formation of Light Infantry units in the eighteenth century, or of the Machine Corps and Royal Tank Regiment during the First World War. Technology played an important role in these and other battlefield innovations, but as an adjunct rather than a *raison d'être*. However, for the RAF, technology, in the shape of its aircraft, *was* the reason for being. Consequently, virtually everything the RAF did was focused primarily upon the servicing, maintenance, piloting and preservation of its aircraft.

This clarifies much about the two services' divergent approach to the airborne force, over and above internal politicking and inter-service rivalries. For the Army, parachutes and gliders were merely the latest, albeit unusual, methods of delivering soldiers to the battlefield, after which they would revert to type. Effecting that delivery, however, involved placing the RAF's aircraft directly in harm's way; hence the initial prejudice against unarmed aircraft,[33] and the preference for carrying out airborne operations at night.[34] It also explains the Air Ministry's rigid insistence that the RAF exercise total control over the flying side of airborne operations. Perhaps the most extreme example of this was the delivery of the 1st Airborne Division to landing areas many miles from their objectives at Arnhem in September 1944 despite objections from the soldiers, and with disastrous results.[35] These differing perceptions were exacerbated further by mutual incomprehension, if not wilful ignorance, between the two services regarding their respective resources, capabilities and intentions generally. The root of this lay in British government policy through most of the inter-war period, which deliberately fostered inter-service rivalry as a divide-and-rule measure and thus encouraged rigid compartmentalisation and limited intercourse between the Army and RAF at the Whitehall level.[36]

The scale of this mutual incomprehension and the institutional mindsets that underlay it were clearly apparent in the correspondence between Group Captain Goddard and Lieutenant-General Nye in January and February 1941, as the two services sought to clarify matters for presentation to the Chiefs of Staff. Nye passed a draft memo as a suggested basis for a joint paper to Goddard on 19 January 1941. This reiterated the position set out on 10 January, mooted the idea of expanding glider pilot training and production to India and posting some pilots to Ringway on a permanent basis, and closed with a list of suggestions for future policy. These included establishing two Invasion Corps as quickly as possible, posting one to the Middle East, ordering sufficient gliders immediately and storing them until needed, and a request that the Air Ministry form and maintain a pool of bomber pilots for glider duty at short notice. The latter were assumed capable of making the necessary transition in two days, and it was suggested those for service in the Middle East be drawn from the RAF in India.[37] Much of this played directly into the hands of the obstructionists within the Air Ministry. Credibility was undermined by the lack of a realistic timetable or suggested organisation, and it was clearly unreasonable to expect the RAF to allocate resources on the off-chance that the Army might wish to use them. The assumption that bomber pilots could convert to gliders in two days also illustrates War Office ignorance of the realities of training pilots of any description.

It took over two weeks for Goddard to respond, prompting internal Army complaints that the Air Ministry was being 'very sticky',[38] but the hiatus was in fact caused by detailed discussion of Nye's memo. The Director of Plans complained that the trials on which the Army proposals were based relied excessively on the German example,[39] accused the CLE staff of unfairly influencing high-ranking observers, and dismissed Nye's because they took no account of other RAF commitments.[40] Goddard cited these comments verbatim in his reply, which appeared on 5 February 1941 and flatly rejected Nye's proposals. The Air Ministry was willing to continue airborne development for future expansion when the precise need had been clarified, and the CAS was anxious to discuss the future of airborne forces with the CIGS, but progress was unlikely until both parties were able to agree basic principles. Goddard closed by pointing out that the Air Ministry was reluctant to commit itself to the 'provision of specific forces... [for]... unspecified operations', and suggested further discussions.[41]

This was blunt, but Nye's response was blunter still. He felt there was little point in further meetings because the Army and RAF views were so far apart, and gave his personal reaction as being:

> To Hell with principles – give me the problem
> We want to decide either that our Airborne forces are required or that they are not required.
> If they are required we want to decide on what scale, so that orders for the necessary material may be placed at once with no further delay... We are faced with a practical problem which demands practical steps to be taken to meet it and a discussion on abstract principles seems to me will not get us anywhere.[42]

Goddard was not overawed, however, and replied in equally forthright terms the same day. He pointed out that the airborne problem could not be resolved '...by a few snap decisions and a wave of the hand', and blamed the War Office for the impasse because it refused to address the specific points contained in the Air Ministry paper of 23 December 1940. Until this was done principles for further development could not be framed, and Goddard went on to query the necessity for an airborne infrastructure in the Middle East and the need for airborne brigade groups.[43]

Bluntness aside, this was merely a restatement of Air Ministry opinion with the added twist of placing responsibility for the airborne impasse on the War Office. The exchange thus highlighted the fundamental differences between the Air Ministry and War Office approaches. The Air Ministry felt it was being dragooned into an ill-thought-out, potentially costly and open-ended venture, while the War Office considered the latter's attitude to be needlessly negative and obstructive. This was neatly summed up in a letter to Rock on 7 February: 'The whole trouble with the Air Ministry is that they love to discuss a policy on a basis of its limitations and restrictions instead of on the basis of what is needed [and] seeing later if it is practicable'.[44] Ironically, Goddard appears to have been sympathetic to the airborne idea, and his more contentious comments reflected the views of others rather than his own. He also defended the CLE against criticism from the Vice-Chief of Air Staff over low flying time for January 1941, detailing the paucity of CLE staff and extenuating circumstances including bad weather, special operations training and participation in joint exercises. The latter were not logged as CLE flying time.[45] Goddard thus acted in a professional manner, which placed him squarely in the firing line between his own Ministry and the War Office.

The airborne problem was examined in another joint conference at the Air Ministry on 19 February 1941, convened to clarify general Army-RAF co-operation. This acknowledged that changes would have to be made to existing arrangements to accommodate the expanded War Office requirement, and recommended that a provisional order for gliders be placed with the Ministry of Aircraft Production, although the number was as yet undetermined. Both parties also agreed to hold formal discussions to frame the joint paper for the Chiefs of Staff.[46]

Goddard informed a variety of Air Ministry departments of the conference and its outcome on 26 February 1941,[47] and attached a summary of the current situation. Originally intended for No.22 Group, this examined the suitability of new bombers for airborne work, factory modifications to new Whitleys and proposals to expand the glider training programme.[48] Copies were also passed to No.70 Group, HQ Bomber Command, the War Office and the Director of Combined Operations.[49]

Incidentally, the conference also appears to have cleared the air between Goddard and Nye. The latter contacted Goddard in a much more civil letter on 7 March 1941, requesting clarification on where the agreed paper on the airborne force was to originate to avoid duplication of effort.[50] Goddard's response was prompt and equally conciliatory, including an apology for the delay and promising answers as soon as possible. It also included an update on the glider situation and informed Nye that RAF Army Co-operation Command had agreed to an expansion of the parachute-training programme. It closed with assurances that matters were moving as swiftly as possible.[51]

The Chiefs of Staff paper was eventually compiled at the Air Ministry, and a draft was passed to the War Office on 17 March 1940.[52] This, with minor alterations,[53] formed the core of the finished article, which appeared on 24 March 1941.[54] Entitled 'Paper on Airborne Policy', it consisted of a brief background summary and three sections, two of which dealt with the Army and RAF sides of the matter. The third listed specific issues for the Chiefs of Staff Committee to address. These included confirming that an airborne force of the size envisaged by the Army was contemplated, whether more gliders would be required for use in India, and whether a CLE was to be set up in the Middle East and/or India. The paper appeared on 24 March, but it then spent several weeks being circulated for comment prior to transmission to the Chiefs of Staff. The Assistant Chief of Air Staff did not receive a copy until 6 April 1941,[55] and it was not forwarded to the War Office until 12 April.[56] The proposals therein also generated additional problems, notably the Treasury balking at the £8 million quote for glider production from the Ministry of Aircraft Production. This prompted the ironic if not amusing spectacle of the General Staff and Air Staff co-operating to justify their requirement to their financial masters.[57]

Thus, after ten months the Air Ministry and War Office had finally clarified what should have been dealt with at the outset, and appeared to be at least moving toward an airborne consensus. Matters were far from settled, however, and the Air Ministry remained far from convinced about the need for an airborne force as envisaged by the Army, as the former's contribution to the Chiefs of Staff Committee paper clearly showed. There was thus more than sufficient scope for further disagreement and backsliding, had the Air Ministry and War Office been left to their own devices. It was at this point that Churchill took a hand, following a visit to a windy Ringway on Saturday of 26 April 1941 with Ismay and Air Marshal Sir Arthur Barratt, head of RAF Army Co-operation Command.

The CLE was well aware that the impasse between the Air Ministry and War Office might well end with the airborne project being abandoned, and thus pulled out all the stops and indulged in some shameless stage-managing. Around 400 paratroops were drawn up for inspection, demonstrations of ground training and special airborne equipment were arranged in the CLE's two hangars, and six camouflaged Kirby Kite sport gliders and the first production eight-seat Hotspur were trucked in from the GTS. The crowning effort was to be a mock assault on Ringway's control tower, involving a drop by forty-four Free French trainees and their instructors using all five of the CLE's serviceable Whitleys. Wing Commander Norman was to give a running commentary, via a specially rigged public address system that had also been linked to the radio in one of the Whitleys. Strange concealed a further 100 troops on the parachute drop zone on his own initiative, with orders to make the attackers appear more numerous. As the wind was gusting to thirty-five miles per hour, Strange also made a private arrangement with Flight Lieutenant Fielden, the senior CLE pilot, to perform an instructor-only drop if the wind speed remained above the official safety limit. This was done covertly to prevent higher authority countermanding the arrangement.[58]

Predictably, some of these measures almost backfired. The Kite gliders landed on target, but the Hotspur's assault landing turned into an extremely long glide, due to a combination of pilot inexperience and the machine's sailplane-based design.[59] Even worse, the parachute aircraft had their take-off delayed because of the high wind, which obliged the paratroops to spend a considerable period in dark, cramped and uncomfortable positions. Thus when Norman tannoyed the lead aircraft, the pilot replied 'No, I'm not ready to take off – five of my blighters have fainted!' The drop nonetheless went smoothly, although one source claims there were six refusals.[60]

Churchill was impressed with the enthusiasm and effort he found at Ringway. An over-enthusiastic unarmed combat display led to one participant being injured,[61] and Churchill was spotted ferociously attacking an imaginary enemy with a Fairburn-Sykes fighting knife in an unguarded moment.[62] He was also subjected to a good deal of the sales talk. Harvey, Norman, Strange and Rock were seen expounding their views at various times to their distinguished guest,[63] to the extent that the pro-airborne Air Marshal Barratt became concerned over the amount of 'line shooting' going on.[64] Similar sentiments were relayed to the Air Ministry prompting the Director of Plans, who had complained about similar activity in February, to lament that the Prime Minister had received only the possibly one-sided views of 'local enthusiasts'.[65]

Churchill was less impressed with progress and the higher echelons responsible for it. He had gone to Ringway expecting to see, after almost a year of development, something like a fully functioning airborne force. He was presented with a partly trained parachute force that numbered less than a tenth of his original requirement, a glider force consisting of six civilian sport machines and a single purpose-designed one capable of carrying six men, backed up by a willing but poorly equipped research and training establishment. Within two days of his visit to Ringway he passed this demand to Ismay:

> Let me have this day the minute which I wrote in the summer of last year directing that 5,000 Parachute Troops were to be prepared, together with all the minutes of the departments concerned which led to my afterwards agreeing to reduce the number to 500. I shall expect to receive the office files by midnight. Let me have all the present proposals for increasing the Parachute and Glider force together with a timetable of expected results.[66]

Ismay duly supplied a synopsis of developments since June 1940, including justification for reducing the 5,000 figure and Air Ministry reservations on committing resources to a project without firm outlines. He also attached a draft paper from Goddard justifying the RAF's actions and position, and a folder of graphs and charts for estimated glider production.[67]

It took Churchill four weeks to digest this. To his credit, he acknowledged that the blame for the lack of airborne progress rested ultimately, if unfairly, upon him, as his eventual response to Ismay, on 27 May 1941, made clear:

> This is a sad story, and I feel myself greatly to blame for allowing myself to be overborne by the resistance which was offered. One can see how wrongly based these resistances were when we read

> paragraph 6 of the Air Staff paper in light of what is happening in Crete, and may be soon happening in Cyprus and in Syria.[68]
>
> See also my minute on gliders.[69] This is exactly what has happened. The gliders have been produced on the smallest possible scale, and so we have practically now neither parachutists nor the gliders except these 500.
>
> Thus we are always behind-hand the enemy. We ought to have 5,000 parachutists and an Air-borne division on the German model, with any improvements which might suggest themselves from experience. We ought also to have a number of carrier aircraft. These will all be necessary in the Mediterranean fighting of 1942, or earlier if possible. We shall have to try to retake these islands which are being so easily occupied by the enemy. We may be forced to fight in the wide countries of the East, in Persia or Northern Iraq. A whole year has been lost, and I now invite the Chiefs of Staff, so far as is possible, to repair the misfortune.
>
> The whole file is to be brought before the Chiefs of Staff this evening.[70]

The airborne ball was thus placed firmly with the Chiefs of Staff, where it should have been from the outset. Churchill's original error had been to attempt to oversee matters personally, which, given the heavy responsibilities of his office, was impractical. He presumably assumed that the Air Ministry and War Office could be trusted to address the matter in the way he intended, and that petty rivalries could be put aside for the greater good. If so, he was sorely mistaken. Thus, although Churchill blamed himself, real responsibility for the lost year rested with the Air Ministry and War Office, irrespective of degree, for his initial requirement was sufficiently clear to allow a good deal more progress than was actually achieved. This time, however, there could be no excuse for mistaking Churchill's airborne requirement, or any doubt of his resolve to see it realised.

7

To the Verge of Adequate Provision

The British Airborne Infrastructure, April 1941–January 1942

The shift toward an Army-RAF airborne consensus and Churchill's renewed intervention were welcome developments, if somewhat delayed. They brought little practical benefit to the airborne training and development infrastructure, however, at least in the immediate term. When Churchill visited Ringway on 26 April 1941, after ten months of existence the Central Landing Establishment (CLE) remained dependent on a literal handful of unsuitable and increasingly decrepit aircraft, half a dozen civilian sailplanes and a single military glider, and was short of parachutes and qualified instructors. After the better part of a year Ringway thus remained incapable of coping with anything more than relatively small numbers of trainees, and of providing only a basic standard of instruction. Credit for improving this state of affairs is routinely attributed to Churchill, especially in Ringway-oriented accounts. However, while slow and halting, progress was nonetheless being made before this. The Army and RAF had been thrashing out their respective requirements for four months when Churchill visited Ringway. In addition, the speed with which the Air Ministry responded to his subsequent demands for information suggests that it was on top of its side of the matter, and there was growing support for the airborne project within the Ministry and wider RAF. It would therefore be more accurate to say that, as with his original involvement in June 1940, Churchill's intervention focused and hastened a process that was already underway.

Poor to non-existent support from higher in the chain of command exacerbated the CLE's problems for the first six months of its existence. This did not stem from the very top, for RAF Army Co-operation Command, headed by Air Marshal Barratt, and Group Captain Goddard at the Air Ministry Department of Military Co-operation, were broadly supportive of the project.[1] The weak link was Ringway's immediate superior, No.22 Group, which was lukewarm about its responsibility. This changed when the CLE was transferred to No.70 Group, commanded by Air-Commodore Cole-Hamilton, in January 1941.[2] No.70 Group shouldered its new responsibility with enthusiasm. It began lobbying the Air Ministry for additional personnel on behalf of the CLE on 3 March 1941,[3] and weighed in to assist the GTS eleven days later.[4] Ringway was also encouraged to inspect a variety of aircraft to assess their suitability for airborne work.[5] The results were passed to RAF Army Co-operation Command on 9 April 1941, with a candid précis of airborne progress to date. This directly challenged the Air Ministry decree that parachute dropping had to be an alternative and ancillary role for bombers, and criticised No.22 Group for slavishly following this line. It was suggested that the policy be reassessed, and the German use of dedicated transport aircraft in their airborne operations was cited as justification.[6]

This heresy struck a favourable chord with at least some within the Air Ministry. A high-level internal memo in June 1941 bluntly stated that the airborne project was not feasible without dedicated transport aircraft, condemned Army Co-operation Command for not pursuing the matter more diligently, and dismissed claims that there was insufficient production capacity to build transport aircraft. The Blackburn Botha, which continued in production for a full year after its unsuitability had been acknowledged, was cited as evidence and it was claimed that effort was also being squandered producing too many different types of bomber. The memo closed by recommending that the option of acquiring transport aircraft from the US be re-investigated, and pointing out that even allowing for relative priorities '...the importance of transport aircraft to the Army was too obvious to need arguing'.[7]

It is unclear whether this memo reached No.70 Group, but Cole-Hamilton continued to fight Ringway's corner in person, in any case. At a conference to discuss RAF provision and training for the airborne force on 22 August 1941, he sidestepped the agenda to raise serious shortfalls in glider development and production, and questioned the viability of the official production timetable. He also pointed out that the modification of bombers for airborne use was seriously behind schedule, that the viability of the parachute force and projected expansion at home and in India was threatened by under-resourcing, and that the CLE was being denied information necessary to carry out its appointed tasks.[8] Cole-Hamilton's intervention here was courageous and self-effacing, for his unscheduled intervention was not mentioned in the conference minutes or covering letter passed to Ringway at the end of August.[9] It is intriguing to speculate on how matters might have developed had Louis Strange received similar support from No.22 Group a year previously.

Aircraft were thus the most pressing problem facing the CLE. The Air Ministry failure to provide the twenty-one additional Whitleys promised in June 1940 left Ringway dependent on six aircraft whose serviceability was increasingly problematic. A CLE paper in June 1941 pointed out that only three were usually operational, it was rare for more than five to be available at any one time, and that mid-air engine failures were not unknown.[10] Much of the problem was due to the fact the CLE's Whitleys used Armstrong Siddeley Tiger engines rather than the more powerful and reliable Rolls-Royce Merlin units used on subsequent marks. Obtaining spare parts for the Tiger engines became increasingly difficult over time.[11]

The situation was exacerbated by the need to withdraw aircraft from flying duties for modification, such as fitting tail-wheel spats or improving static-line attachment points,[12] and their employment on research and development tasks. Items like supply containers or modified parachutes had to be drop-tested, and Ringway's Whitleys were the only aircraft available.[13] In addition, Ringway was tasked with a number of ancillary tasks and responsibilities. These included parachute training for SOE operatives from August 1940,[14] and an increasing number of foreign military personnel. Contingents of Poles arrived in October 1940 and the following March,[15] and Free French trainees were present in February 1941 and were inspected there by De Gaulle the following month.[16] There was also the matter of providing advanced parachute training for the British parachute cadre and the proliferating involvement of the latter in demonstrations and exercises with the Army and Home Guard.

Combined pressure from No.70 Group and Army Co-operation Command began to secure limited concessions from the Air Ministry in March 1941. Whitleys with factory-fitted parachute modifications began to come off the production line that month, although the benefit was somewhat reduced because the new machines were then issued to Bomber Command squadrons rather than Ringway. The latter was also allotted a single Vickers Wellington for tests, to establish its suitability as an alternative parachute transport, and Bomber Command was instructed to assess the suitability of all its new bombers for parachuting and empowered to allow the CLE to inspect them at its own discretion. No firm guarantees of access were given, however, and the Director of Military Co-operation stressed that RAF operational requirements took precedence over the needs of the CLE.[17]

It was thus perhaps just as well that Ringway had already taken matters into its own hands. Wing Commander Norman examined a Stirling at the Short works on 1 January 1941, and the Avro Manchester, prototype Avro Lancaster and the Handley Page Halifax were also examined at their factories, on 27 and 31 March 1941. The Stirling, Manchester and Lancaster were improperly balanced for carrying passengers, and their stalling speeds were too high for dropping parachutists.[18] This was not a problem with the Halifax, which Norman considered the most promising prospect even though it would require extensive modification. The machine also featured six large wing cells ideal for carrying containers and the manufacturer obligingly offered to supply a mock-up fuselage for troop trials.[19] Norman thus recommended that an example be obtained for tests.[20]

CLE personnel also gained access to the sole surviving example of the De Havilland Hertfordshire, the military version of the Flamingo airliner, on 5 April 1941. The Air Ministry had rejected this aircraft as unsuitable in August 1940, but the

CLE examination directly contradicted this verdict and judged the Hertfordshire to be the most suitable machine of all those examined to date. The allegedly small door was considered easily modified, and the machine had a low stalling speed and ample room for sixteen passengers or an equivalent load of freight.[21] This raises questions about the Air Ministry rejection, and the suspicion that it was not based on any objective criteria but was a measure to avoid the diversion of resources from bomber construction to transport aircraft production. The fact that the Hertfordshire formwork, which was vital for additional production, was being broken up as surplus to requirements at Hatfield when they inspected the aircraft reinforces this conclusion. The sixth new aircraft examined by Ringway was the Vickers Wellington, a detailed report on which was compiled on 12 May 1941 for transmission to No.70 Group. The machine was judged suitable for parachuting with modifications and the roomier fuselage, which was illuminated with Perspex panels, was considered much better for troop morale even if the machine's higher speed was likely to lead to increased stick dispersion on landing.[22]

Ringway's possible options were thus narrowed down to the marginally suitable Whitley or the Vickers Wellington, and therein lay the problem. Bomber Command was shouldering the burden of carrying the war to the Germans virtually single-handed, and Air Ministry concern for its bombing resources was therefore understandable and legitimate. The unfortunate reality for Ringway was that the Whitley and Wellington were the mainstay of Bomber Command's operations in 1940 and 1941. In December 1940, for example, these two types comprised ninety-six of the 134 bombers despatched against the industrial city of Mannheim,[23] and they made up 143 of a total force of 169 machines that raided Berlin in November 1941.[24] Given this, it is scarcely surprising that no Wellingtons were assigned to airborne duty or that the RAF bomber lobby was willing to be economical with the truth to keep its Whitleys. That said, supplying the CLE with a handful of aircraft was unlikely to fatally compromise the strategic bombing effort, and the Air Ministry was probably more concerned with setting a precedent that might tell against them in the future.

The situation was made all the more frustrating by blatant RAF institutional inertia and indifference. On 12 June 1941, for example, Army Co-operation Command asked if the CLE still had any use for two parachute-modified Whitleys that had been in storage for some unexplained reason since February 1941.[25] This arrived the same day the CLE issued its paper highlighting the decrepitude of its existing aircraft, and the dire need for more.[26] Even more galling was the arrival of a Whitley K8991 eleven days previously. The machine was supposed to be broken down so the fuselage could be used for ground training, but its good condition prompted enquiries to the previous owners who happily confirmed the aircraft had indeed been despatched for disposal in an airworthy condition. Ringway therefore sought permission to exchange it for one of its existing aircraft that had been recently written off, but this proved more easily said than done.[27]

It took thirteen days for Army Co-operation Command to respond to the request, and it did so by asking another unit to verify Ringway's verdict on the condition of Whitley K8991.[28] No.75 Maintenance Unit inspected the machine and confirmed this was the case on 10 July 1941.[29] This verdict was duly relayed to Ringway via No.70 Group with the rider that any repairs to the written-off machine were to cease forthwith. The letter also informed the CLE that Whitley K8991 had been discarded in an airworthy condition by an Operational Training Unit simply because '...they had no further use for a Whitley Mark III aircraft'.[30] Resource-strapped Ringway's reaction to this revelation can be well imagined. Final permission to effect the exchange and for the CLE to retain both airframes arrived on 17 July

1941.[31] It had thus taken six weeks to exchange a serviceable aircraft for an unserviceable one at the same location.

Neither was Whitley K8991 the only surplus machine located by the CLE. Flight Lieutenant Williams of the DU discovered another Whitley at RAF Kemble. This machine had been left standing in the open for approximately nine months, so long that the weather had damaged its fabric surfaces. Its owners considered it surplus to requirements as they lacked the engine parts to repair it, and told Williams that they would be happy to part with it. An official request was therefore made for the machine on 15 July 1941,[32] and while the matter was resolved within a week it was not in the way the CLE would have preferred. On 17 July RAF Kemble informed the CLE that the Whitley was officially assigned to a gunnery school in South Wales, and provided its maintenance records as proof.[33] Despite the fact the machine had been standing idle for the better part of a year the request was refused the following day,[34] and a further attempt to secure the machine by No.70 Group met with no more success.[35]

That the CLE had stumbled on two redundant but sound Whitleys within days suggests that there may have been more waiting to be discovered, although there was no guarantee that Ringway would benefit. It would be convenient to ascribe this to deliberate Air Ministry obstructionism, but it is clear that the aircraft had merely fallen through cracks in the RAF administrative machinery. The episode does suggest that the Air Ministry's efforts to locate additional Whitleys for the CLE was not particularly thorough or high priority. Both Whitleys appear not to have been assigned to Bomber Command because they were Tiger-powered Mark IIIs, for which spares were in short supply. If Operational Training Units and Gunnery Schools were willing to scrap such machines or leave them to rot in the weather, it would have cost the Air Ministry nothing to assign all Whitley Mark IIIs to Ringway.

As it turned out, the Air Ministry was ultimately obliged to provide Ringway with the most modern Whitleys to the detriment of Bomber Command. On 4 June 1941, Army Co-operation Command informed No.70 Group that high-level discussions over a significant expansion to the airborne force were underway,[36] and Ringway was requested to prepare to implement the outcome forthwith.[37] The response was swift and blunt. Harvey pointed out that the PTS had trained 600 Army parachutists and 250 foreign and SOE personnel to date, that it would take until January 1943 to achieve the original 5,000 target parachutists, and that this would only be possible with a cessation of CLE participation in joint exercises and demonstrations and the provision of a full Whitley Group.[38]

Harvey was pitching things high, but his forthright response had the desired effect and No.70 Group asked him to draw up a paper proposal.[39] This appeared on 12 June 1941, and listed the implications of expanding the PTS output to 100 parachutists per week in terms of drops per month and flying hours. It also moderated the demand for additional aircraft to an absolute minimum of twelve Mark II or nine Mark V Whitleys, the differential arising from the latter's longer fuselage and more powerful Rolls-Royce Merlin engines.[40] Three pilot-to-trainee ratios were listed, and while these made no provision for aircrew training, modifications or operational exercises, a limited allowance for experimentation and SOE training was included.[41] A training programme based on these projections was produced on 23 June 1941 with a list of additional accommodation and synthetic training requirements,[42] and a number of queries from No.70 Group were answered four days later.[43]

The catalyst for all this was the Army decision to enlarge its parachute force by another 1,800 men, which will be examined in detail later. Detailed proposals prepared for CIGS approval were inadvertently passed to the Air Ministry on

4 July 1941, in response to an enquiry asking why the Army was not making use of Ringway's expanded parachute-training capacity.[44] It is unclear what prompted this, as Ringway had not even compiled a definitive list of additional resources necessary for the 100-per-week output, let alone implemented it. In any event, the Army decision provoked an intensive, month-long argument within the Air Ministry, which was reflected in the rather schizophrenic nature of the resulting discussion paper. This began by objecting to any enlargement of the airborne force or its training infrastructure in principle, citing a variety of supporting evidence, and opined that anything larger than a small raiding force was a '…luxury that this country, and particularly Bomber Command, cannot afford'.[45]

The paper then went on to list a number of positive proposals. It recommended passing all responsibility for the airborne force to the Army, providing sufficient Whitleys for a full battalion lift, and training all pilots from the Whitley- and Halifax-equipped No.4 and No.6 Groups in glider towing. The requirement for 500 glider pilots was also agreed, along with a proposal to utilise low medical category RAF pilots if the Army was unable to find the requisite personnel. Finally, it was recommended that RAF Transport Command should investigate all possible sources of aircraft for parachute dropping and glider towing.[46] This was significant progress indeed, and the Air Ministry actually came up with the goods; Ringway's complement of Whitleys was increased to twelve Mark V machines by 11 October 1941.[47] Most of these recommendations were confirmed by an Air Ministry conference on 22 August 1941. The offer to supply glider-pilots was withdrawn, but was offset by allotting the CLE a new airfield for the Glider Training School at Shobden.[48] The commitment to train RAF aircrew in the necessary specialist techniques was upheld, and the conference concluded that, dependent upon Bomber Command opinion, it would be possible to withdraw bomber crews for a one-week refresher course at Ringway prior to any large-scale airborne operation.[49]

Bomber Command opinion, when it appeared on 30 August 1941, was lukewarm but accepted the proposals with some specific caveats over the training of aircrew in airborne techniques.[50] This was noteworthy because it tacitly acknowledged the Army's proposal to have a parachute brigade formed and parachute-trained by the end of January 1942.[51] That Bomber Command was fully aware of the Army intentions is clear from the fact that copies of the various War Office documents were attached to its letter of 30 August. That this was processed in just two days and passed on to Army Co-operation Command virtually without demur suggests that the Air Ministry was becoming reconciled to the inevitability of a large-scale airborne force.[52]

Ringway began to address increasing its parachute-training output with a change of title and organisation. The CLE became the Airborne Forces Establishment (AFE) on 1 September 1941; all glider pilot training was concentrated in a dedicated organisation under RAF Flying Training Command (see Fig. 3), and recommendations for implementing the output increase was passed to No.70 Group three days later.[53] The latter, however, questioned the wisdom of implementing systemic changes to train just 2,500 additional paratroops, and the ability of the PTS to maintain the output increase through the notoriously poor winter weather at Ringway. The latter was also felt likely to require an expansion of synthetic training facilities for use during inclement weather. These queries, while perfectly valid, are interesting because they show that Ringway's immediate superior was by no means unquestioning in its support of the airborne project. No.70 Group's reservations were shared by Army Co-operation Command, which also questioned the need for an airborne force on the German model on 8 August 1941. A smaller, raiding-oriented option was recommended once again, on the grounds that it was unlikely that Bomber Command would ever be in a position to divert sufficient aircraft from operations to lift anything larger.[54]

These reservations prompted yet another joint conference at the Air Ministry on 9 September 1941,[55] chaired by the head of Army Co-operation Command, Air Marshal Sir Arthur Barratt. Other attendees included Harvey and Rock from the AFE, officers from Barratt's Command, Cole-Hamilton from No.70 Group, representatives from a variety of Air Ministry and War Office departments, and Brigadier Richard Gale MC, the officer selected to command what was to become the 1st Parachute Brigade.[56] Matters discussed included additional personnel, accommodation and facilities for the AFE at Ringway, the poor serviceability of the latter's aircraft and, most importantly, defining the role of PTS. Henceforth this was to deal solely with the provision of parachute training, with physical assessment and preparation of trainees being carried out by a dedicated Army Training Centre (ATC). Selected Army officers and NCOs were to be trained to act as instructors at the ATC, and trainees were initially to commute to the AFE because accommodation at Ringway was limited. The PTS course was to consist of two balloon jumps and four from an aircraft, two individually and two as part of a stick, ideally with one of the latter taking place at night. It was planned to cycle 200 trainees through the PTS every fourteen days, using twelve Whitleys and a single Avro Anson for air experience flights. This schedule included replacement training for five individuals per month, and provision for trained paratroopers to make at least one aircraft jump every two months to maintain their skills.[57]

These recommendations began to be implemented on 8 October 1941 when No.41 Group was ordered to supply the AFE with five Whitley Mark Vs and an Avro Anson immediately, and to exchange the other Whitleys as replacements became available.[58] Army Co-operation Command authorised the issue of the additional aircraft three days later to bring the total to the requested twelve and No.41 Group reported compliance on 12 October 1941.[59] Ringway subsequently discovered that some machines from No.102 Squadron were unmodified for parachuting and that the factory-fitted modifications had been removed on others. This required eight hours' remedial work per machine,[60] prompting No.70 Group to request further information in order to avoid similar problems in the future.[61] No.70 Group began chasing Army Co-operation Command for Ringway's replacement aircraft on 15 October 1941, pointing out that they should be issued within five days if training the parachute brigade was to begin on 1 November as scheduled.[62] Two Whitleys were en route, having been allotted on 14 October, and the Air Ministry was willing to release three more direct from the manufacturer if the AFE would accept them without parachute modifications. The latter were unlikely to be delivered by 20 October, however.[63]

The PTS also required a host of ancillary items. On 21 September 1941, 750 parachutes were requested to augment existing stocks,[64] and within three weeks 394 had been located at a variety of RAF Maintenance Units. The remainder were ordered from Irvin and the GQ Parachute Co., to be delivered at a rate of fifty per week,[65] and an additional 150 protective helmets were ordered, at a cost of six shillings and sixpence each.[66] A request for additional ground training equipment was submitted on 5 October 1941, which included swings, jumping stands, trapezes, Whitley fuselages and mock bomb-cells for container-loading practice.[67] A detailed cost breakdown, including everything from screws and nails by the ounce to ropes and man-hours, was attached, to the total of £326 9s 9d.[68] By 8 October 1941 the AFE reported that progress toward the 1 November 1941 deadline was well in hand,[69] despite unexpected deficiencies. On 21 October, for example, Ringway urgently requested three buses, two vans and a prime mover.[70] In the event, these and the errant Whitleys were obtained, the 1 November 1941 deadline was achieved, and the first parachute course at the increased output was successfully completed on schedule fourteen days later.[71]

This was a notable and praiseworthy achievement, the more so because it was accomplished against a background of discord within the CLE and successor AFE. The accepted line is of unity at Ringway in the face of external difficulties, and only one secondary account refers explicitly to internal politics at Ringway. However, cross-referencing secondary accounts with primary material presents a rather different picture of empire-building, patronage, and shabby treatment of dedicated and courageous men who did not conform to fit the approved profile of the new Ringway hierarchy.

The issue appears to have arisen with Group Captain Harvey's assumption of command on 18 September 1940.[72] Harvey did not approve of Strange's unorthodox methods or the barnstorming mavericks he had recruited, and set about reforming his command in a way more to his liking. The first to fall foul of the new regime was Bruce Williams, following his involvement in the Tragino affair as a despatcher.[73] After speaking to a reporter on his return he was charged with 'unlawful disclosure of classified information', court-martialled, and dismissed from the CLE.[74] This seems somewhat harsh, given that details of the raid were published in newspapers all over Britain.[75] Next to go was Strange himself, posted to the Merchant Shipping Fighter Unit on 12 May 1941.[76] His biography suggests that he was expecting something of the sort: 'He [Wing Commander Nigel Norman, deputy commander at the CLE] used to say to me "You'd better look out Louis… you will go at it bald headed. It attracts too much attention, and you'll find someone taking a pot at you one of these fine days"'.[77]

This implies that Strange's removal originated outside Ringway, but as second-in-command it is unlikely that Norman was unaware of Harvey's opinion of Strange, given Harvey's scathing assessment of Strange and the Ringway staff. On 15 July 1941 he opined to No.70 Group that all Ringway's pilots should be replaced because they had been adversely affected by exposure to Strange. Five were thought salvageable with retraining but Earl Fielden, the former Cobham's Flying Circus pilot, was considered incompatible with the expected pressure involved in increasing the output of the PTS.[78] The tone of this, and the fact it did not emerge until two months after Strange's departure, suggests that Harvey had failed to bend the existing PTS staff to his will. He then embarked upon a wholesale purge to remove all vestiges of Strange's reign at the PTS.

Strange had been succeeded by Ringway's Chief Parachute Instructor, Squadron Leader Jack Benham, with effect from 5 June 1941.[79] Benham had been at the PTS virtually from the beginning,[80] but was superseded by Squadron Leader Maurice Newnham, formerly Ringway's administration officer, on 11 July 1941.[81] Newnham had no obvious qualifications for the job. His sole involvement with airborne forces had been connected to repelling German airborne attack upon the UK at the Air Ministry,[82] and he made his first parachute descent after taking command of the PTS.[83] No official reason was given for Benham's removal, which is not mentioned in the operational records. Newnham's account refers to Benham obtaining a transfer to help set up a parachute school at Chaklala in India, and while offering no explanation as to why Benham left, refers to him losing the posting after failing a medical.[84]

The dearth of detail is suspicious, and suggests Benham was forced out by Harvey, or at his behest. This is reinforced by his advice that any decision on Fielding should be postponed until the 'Newnham-Benham fight' had been resolved in the 15 July letter to No.70 Group.[85] It also fits with Ward's account, which blames Newnham for Fielden's subsequent removal along with Flight Lieutenant Romanov and Pilot Officer MacMonnies, who had also been at Ringway from the beginning.[86] It is therefore difficult to avoid concluding that Newnham was a placeman charged with carrying through Harvey's purge. Such actions by incoming commanders are by no means unusual, and Harvey was of course quite at liberty to reconfigure his command as he saw fit. The problem in this instance is that his dissatisfaction appears to have been based largely on dislike of Strange and his unorthodox methods, rather than any specific operational inadequacy.

This raises the distinct possibility that Harvey was empire-building, for many of those ousted from Ringway for alleged unsuitability were subsequently employed elsewhere in airborne work. For example, being found unfit for his Indian posting did not prevent Benham from continuing to train SOE specials, and indeed from dying with them; he was posted missing while acting as despatcher for an SOE drop somewhere over Europe.[87] Bruce Williams went on to serve as a Lysander pilot in Special Operations,[88] and Strange himself returned to the airborne fold as Wing Commander Operations for No.46 Group in December 1943. The latter unit was one of two transport groups dedicated for airborne service. Fielden and MacMonnies served with the other, No.38 Group.[89] The PTS purge did not end with the removal of Benham and the pilots. Ward and Hire became marked men after they disagreed with Newnham over the length of the PTS basic parachuting course for the 100-per-week output expansion. Ward was slated to go to Iraq when Newnham imported a replacement,[90] but wangled a posting as Air Liaison Officer to HQ 1st Airborne Division at Netheravon. He was joined there by Hire, who had been similarly ousted.[91]

In fairness, Harvey's dissatisfaction may not have been totally unjustified, and the fact that the PTS met the expanded output deadline suggests his remodelling did not interfere with Ringway's operational capabilities. Similarly, Newnham's stated intent was to remove the macho mystique surrounding parachuting by employing a more straightforward technical approach to training, and he was firmly behind restricting RAF involvement to that end and leaving everything else to the Army.[92] His success can be measured by the fact that this template has framed British military parachute training ever since.

Nonetheless, it is arguable whether this justifies the shabby treatment of the original PTS staff, not least because such self-serving behaviour contrasts poorly with that of Strange. It was he who provided Harvey and Newnham with a sound foundation on which to build their empires, as Harry Ward pointed out:

> He [Strange] deserves more credit than he ever got for leading that small band of RAF and Army pioneers… It would be easy for some of those who came later to smile at the naivety and some of the inadequacies of the earliest days of airborne training in Britain. They should remember that Louis Strange had nothing to build on: they built on Louis Strange.[93]

The same could justifiably be applied to Williams, Benham, Fielden, Romanov, MacMonnies, Hire, Ward and a host of others whose contribution has been similarly overshadowed because what early British airborne history there is was been written largely by Ringway's winners rather than the losers.

Be that as it may, the remodelling of Ringway into Harvey's preferred image was part of a wider process that regulated the airborne infrastructure and formally assimilated it into the RAF proper. While Ringway's original orphan-like status caused problems with resources, it also permitted a great deal of autonomy in research, development and equipment modifications, which were carried out in-house. It also engendered the free-spirited, barnstorming attitude that attached itself to the original staff and Commando volunteers alike, which Harvey took such pains to eradicate and which, as we shall see, attracted the ire of Rock and the Army hierarchy too.

This autonomy was gradually whittled away as Ringway acquired a higher profile and became of interest to larger bureaucracies. On 8 May 1941 the Ministry of Aircraft Production (MAP) suggested establishing a MAP technical section within the CLE.[94] Initial discussions at Ringway prompted the Director of Military Co-operation to recommend a higher-level meeting on 13 May 1941.[95] The CLE, which was already in regular contact with the MAP, reacted positively, largely because it assumed a direct conduit would avoid the inertia and delay generated by passing communications through several different departments.[96] No.70 Group, however, saw the idea as a thinly veiled attempt by MAP to take over Ringway's research and development function and judged it a 'most unsatisfactory idea'.[97] No.70 Group may have been simply concerned with maintaining Ringway's freedom of action, or it may have been piqued by MAP approaching Ringway directly rather than through the appropriate channels. Whichever, the proposal prompted a series of joint discussions beginning with a conference on 22 July 1941,[98] and another in early August.[99] While the MAP proposal was not adopted, its involvement in airborne development did increase, particularly after formation of the Airborne Forces Experimental Establishment (AFEE) in February 1942.[100]

The appearance of No.70 Group on the scene also undermined the CLE's autonomy by taking far more interest in the doings of its subordinate. Hitherto, accidents and equipment failures had been investigated by the CLE, and any remedial action or equipment modifications carried out in-house, usually in a matter of days.[101] The DU, for example, designed, tested and released a locking pin for the snap-hook linking the static-line strop to the parachute pack for general use within a week of a failure causing a fatality in November 1940.[102] This convenient practice ceased with the death of a Polish officer trainee on 19 June 1941.[103] Lieutenant Twardawa was killed by a failure of the connection between the strongpoint in the aircraft and the parachute.[104] This time No.70 Group held its own inquiry, using information supplied by the CLE. The verdict took a month to appear and cleared the despatcher but criticised PTS instructional procedures and requested recommendations for amending them.[105]

These were forwarded on 19 June 1941, and suggested limiting the number of trainees to eight per sortie, assigning two RAF instructors to every stick of trainees for fore and aft coverage, and an additional Polish instructor to Polish sticks as a translator. RAF instructors were charged with personally attaching trainee's static-lines and locking the safety pins. This was to be double-checked by each trainee, and completion of the drill was then to be relayed to the pilot before clearance to take-off would be issued.[106] These were reasonable precautions, but on 24 July, No.70 Group ordered a revision of operating procedures and the inclusion of written instructions in the trainee's native language to avoid potentially fatal misunderstandings. Ringway was also instructed to investigate the current method of attaching the static-line to the aircraft strongpoint, with a view to making the snap-hook locking mechanism simpler and foolproof. It was also suggested that a method be devised to allow the trainees to hook up their own static-lines, thereby making them responsible for their own safety.[107]

Such external interference was unheard of, and it appears to have struck a nerve. Ringway pointed out that the snap-hooks used until Lieutenant Twardawa's death were approved by the Air Ministry and that the locking safety pin was an additional CLE refinement. It also pointed out that the DU had developed a special connector socket to replace the strop-hook in January 1941, and that the Air Ministry had approved the design but the connectors had not yet arrived from the manufacturer. It was intended to fit to all the CLE's aircraft with the assistance of No.30 MU.[108] Ringway clearly considered this sufficient, but No.70 Group requested clarification that the new connector would allow trainees to fasten their own static-lines to fixed strops, and assurance as to whether the connector had been fully tested.[109] The CLE demurred by pointing out that the connector had been tested prior to production and that trainee involvement would require longer strops and would increase the chances of entanglement within the aircraft. This was a very relevant point, given the cramped dimensions of the Whitley fuselage.[110] This still failed to mollify No.70 Group, however, which remained unconvinced that procedures did not need improvement and reiterated its desire for trainees to do their own hooking up. The DU was to devise a system for the latter, and demanded details of the connector for examination and approval before it was used.[111]

The CLE's exasperated response was to stress that the first design of the new connector had already been modified once to enhance safety at the CLE instigation, and that a host of non-CLE departments and personnel had been involved in the design and testing. It also pointed out that the CLE's Chief Technical Officer, who would also be responsible for carrying them out, had drawn up an extensive programme of full-scale dummy tests. Copies of all test reports and photographs were to follow.[112] A further report detailing modifications and successful live testing of the secure panel in what were by then the AFE's Whitleys, which allowed them to return to carrying ten rather than eight trainees, followed on 20 September 1941.[113]

This was far from the end of the matter, however. On 13 October 1941 the AFE pointed out that it was not possible for trainees in Wellingtons to connect their parachutes to strops on entering the aircraft. This was because centre of gravity limitations obliged passengers to occupy different positions for take-off and jumping,[114] although a new procedure for the Wellington was designed and tested.[115] Nonetheless, No.70 Group continued to demand clarifications until at least the beginning of November 1941,[116] and its scepticism appears to have been justified. On 5 November the AFE reported that the entire second batch of connectors had failed under test, and all deliveries to date were being returned to the manufacturer for investigation. It also reported that no satisfactory system for making trainees responsible for their own hooking up had yet been devised.[117]

The root of the problem here was the unsuitability of the aircraft rather than the parachutes or personnel, the cramped dimensions of the Whitley fuselage being the clearest case in point. The dilemma was eventually overcome with the introduction of the Armstrong-Whitworth Albemarle and the US-built Douglas C47, christened Dakota by the RAF.[118] These were roomy enough for parachutists to attach their own parachute strops to rails or cables running along the length of the fuselage, and Dakota passengers were able to stand upright.[119] This removed the need for secure panels in the aircraft, and meant the strops could be permanently attached to the parachute, being secured to a shoulder of the harness for convenience. It also made things easier for instructors, who had merely to check that the clips were properly secured to the cable.

Aircraft suitability aside, all this shows that by July 1941 Ringway was starting to lose the autonomy it had enjoyed hitherto, and this applied to administrative as well as operational and safety matters. At the end of August 1941 and at the CLE's suggestion, Ringway's line of communication was to run upward to No.70 Group, then to Army Co-operation Command and wherever thereafter.[120] On 17 September 1941 the PTS forwarded details of parachute training to date to Army Co-operation Command via the CLE HQ.[121] The information had been requested by Army Co-operation Command, but No.70 Group criticised its presentation and provided an approved format for future use.[122] The PTS was obliged to resubmit the information in the new format on 24 September 1941.[123]

Bureaucratic nit-picking was not totally unprecedented at Ringway. In September 1940, for example, Churchill had returned a conference agenda to the Air Ministry with a scrawled complaint about lack of clarity and a demand for the culprit's name;[124] this turned out to be Group Captain Goddard, then Deputy Director of Plans.[125] No.70 Group's sustained campaign was of a different temper, however, and succeeded in making Ringway toe the RAF procedural line. This was certainly necessary, for the airborne project began to overlap with other RAF activities as it expanded. When Ringway wanted to provide night parachute training, for example, it had to liaise with Fighter Command in order to avoid interfering with night-fighter operations by No.9 Group.[126] The Air Ministry may not have been able to limit the size of the airborne force, but it did succeed in establishing firm RAF control over virtually all aspects of the airborne infrastructure, a useful position from which to influence future allocation of resources.

The expansion of the parachute force may have boosted the fortunes of the PTS, but the impressively renamed No.1 Glider Training School (GTS) remained hamstrung by a lack of gliders. Machines were on the way, but the inevitable lag between design and delivery was exacerbated by wider production priorities. The MAP raised the matter with the Air Ministry in early January 1941,[127] prompting discussions on the ramifications of equipping the War Office's projected 'Invasion Corps'.[128] An order for 800 machines was placed on 3 March

1941,[129] with the caveat that quantity production was unlikely before late spring 1942,[130] and a pre-production meeting was held at the MAP on 6 March 1941.[131] The machine involved was the General Aircraft Hotspur, the first British purpose-designed military glider. Test-flown by the CLE on 21 January 1941,[132] the Hotspur was demonstrated before Churchill at Ringway in April 1941 but proved poorly configured for British requirements. The sailplane-based design was influenced by the German DFS 240, and consequently had a high landing and stalling speed. This precluded short, steep landing runs, and the carrying capacity of seven passengers was also considered insufficient.[133]

Consequently, in March 1941 it was recommended that Hotspur production should be restricted to 400, and that they should be employed solely for training purposes.[134] Inspections and tests were conducted on pre-production Hotspurs through March and into April 1941, to determine matters such as the optimum tow-cable length.[135] The tests also led to reductions in wing span, and changes to the cockpit canopy and passenger exit; this was originally via a hinge-top fuselage, which was replaced with two more conventional side-doors.[136] The machines were still unsatisfactory, and following further tests in September 1941 the AFE concluded the Hotspur was unsuitable for operational deployment or large-scale production.[137] Army Co-operation Command nonetheless ordered the continuation of trials,[138] although these created more problems than they resolved,[139] and it was still proposed to use the Hotspur operationally in lieu of more suitable machines.[140] In the event, this did not happen and the Hotspur served as a basic glider trainer until 1945, with over 1,000 being produced.[141]

This illustrates the pitfalls of ordering equipment without properly ascertaining its purpose, although in fairness the Hotspur was a stopgap measure from the outset. The 3 March 1941 order for 800 gliders, which was endorsed by the War

Office on 17 March 1941,[142] actually specified the twenty-five-seat-glider designed to meet Spec. 26/40, later christened the Horsa. The Horsa was to become the mainstay of the British glider force, with 3,655 being built,[143] but as it was still on the drawing board in March 1941 the Hotspur was ordered instead. CLE staff accepted the design at the end of January 1941 after discussions and examining a mock-up,[144] and detailed drawings and a delivery schedule were forwarded to the Air Ministry in April 1941;[145] this information was passed to Churchill the following month.[146] The Horsa made its maiden flight at Heathrow on 3 September 1941,[147] but attaining mass production remained problematic. As the Joint Chiefs of Staff pointed out as early as March 1941, the glider was competing directly for production space and raw material with other wooden aircraft, including the Miles Magister and Avro Anson trainers, and Armstrong Whitworth Albemarle and De Havilland Mosquito bombers.[148]

There was also the matter of cost. The Treasury raised objections over the cost of projected glider production, which it estimated to be in excess of £8 million, in April 1941.[149] This figure may have included the giant tank-carrying glider produced to meet Air Ministry Spec. 27/40, later christened the Hamilcar. A mock-up was inspected by the CLE on 28 May 1941,[150] and it made its maiden flight in March 1942.[151] Treasury concerns were doubtless exacerbated by the fact that adopting the Horsa looked like leading to the resources invested in the Hotspur being written off, and against a machine that might prove to be equally unsuitable. Theoretical calculations in April 1941 suggested that towing the Horsa might be problematic,[152] and the Director of Military Co-operation cautioned against ordering large numbers of Horsas because too little was known about the machine in October 1941.[153] These reservations led to the compromise solution of confining the Hotspur to training, originally mooted in March 1941,[154] pending further investigation of the Horsa.[155] This meant the resources put into the Hotspur were not totally wasted, and allowed the operational glider force to be standardised on the Horsa and Hamilcar when they entered full-scale production.[156]

The second major obstacle facing the No.1 GTS was obtaining sufficient trainee pilots. The issue had been something of an Air Ministry-War Office football ever since August 1940,[157] with the Air Ministry initially insisting that the Army provide pilots and then insisting that only fully trained bomber pilots were equal to the task in December 1940.[158] Nonetheless, the first cohort of pilots consisted of twelve soldiers who, along with sixteen RAF volunteers, had soloed on the available sport gliders by 5 April 1941,[159] and five of the newly qualified Army volunteers flew the gliders demonstrated at Ringway for Churchill at the end of that month.[160] The Air Ministry reversed its position again in August 1941, apparently because the Army was looking to the RAF to provide the promised 800 pilots for its two projected glider brigades.[161] On 22 August 1941 the Air Ministry announced that it could only provide this number of glider pilots by stripping crews from Bomber Command, which it was predictably, and arguably reasonably, unwilling to do. It therefore recommended that henceforth glider pilots should be Army officers and NCOs, fully trained for ground combat, who would be temporarily seconded to the RAF for flying training.[162]

This was accepted by the War Office, which also agreed that candidates should conform to RAF flight-crew medical standards.[163] The Army subsequently developed the idea into the 'total soldier' concept, which required all glider pilots to be fully trained in tactics and on all weapons deployed by airborne forces before undertaking flying training. This led to the establishment of the Glider Pilot Regiment in February 1942, commanded by airborne pioneer John Rock under the aegis of the Army Air Corps, formed the previous December.

By August 1942 the regiment had grown to two battalions, commanded by Lieutenant-Colonel George Chatterton; Chatterton had succeeded John Rock following the latter's death in a gliding accident in October 1942.[164] Glider pilot training thus paralleled its parachute counterpart, with the RAF providing flight training and the Army assuming responsibility for everything else.

While all this was going on, No.1 GTS and the DU were fully occupied at RAF Thame with glider development work in tandem with the soldiers who would ultimately become the Airlanding Brigades of the British 1st and 6th Airborne Divisions. The first joint glider exercise, with troops from the Oxfordshire and Buckinghamshire Light Infantry, took place at Thame on 20 February 1941,[165] with another being held the following month.[166] This began a partnership that climaxed just after midnight on 6 June 1944, at Benouville in Normandy.[167] Gliders also participated in a joint demonstration with the PTS before the King at Windsor on 25 May 1941. As with the PTS, involvement in demonstrations and exercises expanded rapidly, prompting the formation of a dedicated Glider Exercise Flight, later Unit (GXU) at Ringway on 9 July 1941, equipped with ten Hotspurs and the same number of single-engine tug aircraft.[168] The GXU's first duty involved glider experience flights for the Royal Welch Fusiliers on 11 October 1941,[169] following the War Office's decision to transform 31 Independent Brigade Group into an Airlanding Brigade Group.[170] Troops from the Ox & Bucks were lifted to participate in exercise COTTON on 26 October, and were inspected by GOC Western Command after landing. A further demonstration was held for the recently appointed 'Commander Para-Troops and Airborne Troops', Acting Major-General F.A.M. Browning, on 12 November 1941.[171]

Glider development work continued at Thame and other locations in parallel with flying and tactical training. Wing

Commander Norman and Flying Officer Kronfeld attended a conference at the MAP to discuss the Hotspur on 6 March 1941, for example, and an unsuccessful test of a winch for reeling in glider towlines took place at the end of that month. Representatives from tow-rope manufacturer R. Malcolm Ltd visited Thame on 21 March 1941; tests were held to ascertain the type and length of towline required for the Hotspur on 10 April, and DU personnel inspected a mock-up of the Hamilcar on 28 May 1941.[172] GXU gliders also participated in tests to assess the German glider threat at the Air Fighting Development Unit (AFDU) at RAF Duxford in Cambridgeshire between mid-November and December 1941.[173] The GXU also carried out stowage and stability trials with the Hotspur on 19 December 1941, following a fatality and injuries caused by unsecured weapons and equipment during landing.[174]

Thus, by the end of 1941, the PTS was finally in a position to embark upon its original task of training a large-scale parachute force, and the GTS was similarly poised, awaiting only the arrival of sufficient suitable gliders. It now remains to examine how the War Office formulated a role, and provided the men, for the establishment of operational parachute and air-landing brigades.

8

From Maverick Raiders to a Conventional Force

The Transformation of 11 SAS Battalion into the 1st Parachute Brigade

By the end of February 1941 the Army possessed a semi-operational parachute force configured for small-scale raiding, which had carried out a single sabotage operation in southern Italy. Recruiting problems had kept 11 Special Air Service Battalion under-strength, and the raiding focus was obliged more by wider Army manpower shortages and Air Ministry reluctance to provide more than a handful of aircraft than choice. The War Office harboured grander ambitions, however, and within a year this band of raiders had been transformed into a three-battalion parachute brigade, with another battalion in the pipeline. This process was not as seamless or straightforward as many accounts suggest, however, and it began with a widening awareness and interest in the parachute force.

The new arm became an object of public interest due to widespread reporting of the Tragino raid in February 1941,[1] and Army Co-operation Command instructed Ringway to prepare a paper for public consumption five months later.[2] The piece, imaginatively entitled 'British Parachute Troops', was intended to play down some of the more lurid popular perceptions about them. This suggests that the powers-that-be were aware of the maverick image cultivated by the rank and file of 11 SAS Battalion, which was later vigorously suppressed. Nonetheless the piece closed on a rousing note:

> They are some of our finest stormtroopers who are imbued with the one ambition of getting to grips with the enemy in whatever role... We know they will give a good account of themselves in whatever circumstances they may find themselves. Good luck to them.[3]

The written piece was followed by an official press visit to Ringway in October 1941, which included involved a film crew. The resulting Movietone News film included footage of parachute drops and an in-depth interview with Group Captain Harvey.[4]

The new arm was also attracting attention beyond the Home Front. In June 1941 the Army staff at the CLE prepared a paper on parachuting kit and for transmission to the Turkish government, following a request from the latter to the War Office.[5] More significantly, India and Middle Eastern Commands, which had expressed interest in forming airborne forces of their own in the autumn of 1940,[6] had continued to monitor developments.[7] In the event, the Middle Eastern effort was stymied by equipment and lapsed for a time,[8] but that in

India enjoyed the support of Sir Robert Cassels, Commander-in-Chief India. Cassels ordered the formation of three parachute battalions for a future Indian parachute brigade on 2 December 1940, and formed an Airborne Troop Committee in April 1941 despite War Office advice to hold back until the Home airborne situation had been clarified.[9] The committee, headed by Air Commodore Claude-Wright, the senior RAF staff officer in India, was briefed to investigate setting up an Indian parachute-training infrastructure and parachute brigade. Cassels authorised the latter on 15 May 1941, and the 50th Indian Parachute Brigade was officially established the following October.[10]

The Indian airborne effort thus paralleled that in Britain, and was in front in establishing a parachute brigade, a development not settled in the UK until the end of August 1941.[11] This rapid progress was attributable to remoteness from Whitehall and long-standing Army-RAF co-operation for Imperial policing, which had resulted in air transportation being a routine occurrence. Forming a parachute force was therefore merely a variation on a theme rather than a major shift in operational thinking, as had been the case in the UK. In the event, Indian progress was severely hampered by equipment problems, most seriously a lack of parachutes and aircraft, although the Indian airborne force was expanded to divisional size by April 1945.[12]

Initial developments in India provided Churchill with a useful prompt for home use and a pro-airborne political ally, in the shape of the Secretary of State for India L.S. Amery. Amery urged Churchill to establish a multi-division airborne force in India for strategic deployment across the Empire in October 1941, and cited Wavell as a supporter of the project.[13] Churchill passed this to the Chiefs of Staff for comment,[14] who responded with a detailed and fairly accurate appraisal of the airborne situation. The crux of this was that there was no realistic prospect of implementing Amery's proposal without a significant shift in aircraft production priorities. Churchill passed this straight on to Amery with a pencilled footnote asking for further comment.[15] The response, which appeared on 6 November 1941, must have been music to Churchill's ears. Amery questioned the Chiefs of Staff's commitment to the airborne idea and their assumption that glider production had to be governed by the availability of tug aircraft. He also recommended further investigation into obtaining transport aircraft from the US, and suggested that gliders be built in India, Canada and the US to speed production.[16] This list of measures was augmented five days later with the suggestion that cheap and unsophisticated transport aircraft be produced in parallel with bombers and on the same production line.[17]

Amery was rehashing ideas floated a year previously, albeit in a more forthright manner, and the response when Churchill duly relayed them to the Chief of Air Staff on 13 November 1941 was equally familiar.[18] The idea of producing transport aircraft was dismissed out of hand, on the grounds that even large numbers of aircraft could not cope with the demands of large-scale troop transport and logistical support.[19] This verdict not only proved wildly inaccurate, but also conveniently ignored the wealth of contradictory evidence from Imperial policing operations in the inter-war period, and it is therefore difficult to avoid concluding that the Air Ministry was deliberately ignoring facts that did not support current air policy. As the 1st Parachute Brigade had training at Ringway for almost three weeks when the Air Ministry's verdict appeared, it is likely that the latter was looking to avoid diverting even more RAF for an expansion of the airborne effort overseas.

Be that as it may, overseas commands continued to agitate for their own airborne forces. Wavell's successor as senior commander in the Middle East, Sir Claude Auchinleck, vigorously reopened the matter in a telegram addressed to every senior official in the War Office including the Secretary of State for War on 20 January 1942. This demanded the immediate establishment of a parachute battalion, and claimed that Rommel could have been destroyed in Libya if an airborne force had been available.[20] Auchinleck's enthusiasm may have been prompted by his participation in the attempts to relieve the besieged garrison of Kut in 1916, which included air-dropping of a variety of stores and foodstuffs.[21] He also served in Kurdistan and India throughout the inter-war period, latterly as member of the Expert Committee on the Defence of India, which means he would have been well aware of the scale and importance of air transportation in the Empire through the 1920s and '30s.

All this doubtless explains his accurate appreciation of the potential advantages of airborne operations. It also probably also explains why he authorised the formation of David Stirling's Special Air Service raiders,[22] and eventually he got his way with regard to more conventional airborne forces too. No.4 Middle East [parachute] Training School and the 4th Parachute Brigade were established in the Suez Canal Zone in May and November 1942 respectively, and both units moved to more suitable accommodation at Ramat David in Northern Palestine in February 1943.[23] The 1st Parachute Brigade was also deployed to North Africa from the UK in November 1942, for operations in Algeria and Tunisia.[24] However, they came too late to participate in the destruction of Rommel, or indeed to aid Auchinleck, who was replaced as Commander-in-Chief Middle East by Alexander in August 1942.[25]

Be that as it may, the pressure from the Middle East and India appears to have been orchestrated to a degree. Amery wrote to Churchill the same day Auchinleck despatched his telegram to the War Office reiterating the latter's arguments, re-emphasising the advantages an airborne force would bring to the Middle and Far East, and urging Churchill not to be put off by Air Ministry obstruction. At the end of March 1942 Auchinleck berated the Indian War Office for its lack of airborne progress,[26] and Amery kept up the pressure by passing the details to the Indian government on 5 April 1942.[27] Amery's letter to Churchill is particularly noteworthy because it shrewdly identified the root of the problems facing the airborne effort:

> I still believe that the only way to get the [airborne] thing on an adequate scale is to insist on having it, on whatever scale you decide on, entirely separate from the Air Force. Order large quantities of powerful engines, have your transport planes and gliders built, all as a show of its own. Otherwise the Air Staff will always point out how few are the bombers or pilots that can be spared for the task.[28]

These were prophetic words indeed, and it is fascinating to speculate how the airborne effort might have turned out had Churchill placed it in the hands of Amery or an equally capable individual at the outset, rather than relying upon the goodwill of the Whitehall bureaucracies involved.

Back in the UK, the War Office spent the period July to September 1941 refining its airborne requirement. As we have seen, the Army had decided to aim for a brigade-size force in early October 1940, and a consensus of sorts was reached with the Air Ministry by April 1941 after some acrimony and a series of conferences. Little attention was paid to practical matters such as the purpose, composition and training of the new force, however, or indeed to where the necessary personnel were to be drawn from. Thus when the War Office announced that it intended to expand the airborne force by a further 1,800 men on 4 July 1941, the idea was by no means universally accepted within the Army.[29] This is clear from the reaction of Lieutenant-General Haining, Assistant Chief of the Imperial General Staff (ACIGS), on 4 July 1941. Haining pointed out that the Army was short of manpower, and recommended that the expansion should either be postponed until reorganisations scheduled for November 1941 were complete, or that it should be temporarily restricted to a single parachute battalion for the time being.[30]

However, CIGS Sir John Dill was a firm airborne supporter and he ordered the two additional parachute battalions to be formed immediately, irrespective of any adverse effects this might have.[31] Interestingly, at least one senior officer was as shocked as Churchill had been in April at the comparatively puny size of the British parachute force. Lieutenant-General Sir Ronald Adam wrote to the C-in-C Home Forces on 18 August 1941, seeking authorisation to draw parachute recruits from Home Forces infantry units, and closed with the following comment: 'I know you will realise the necessity for doing this and doing it quickly. I am horrified to find how few trained parachutists we have at present in the British Army. We ought at least to have had 5,000 by now.'[32]

The underlying problem of how to raise the additional parachute battalions with as little disruption as possible was addressed by Lieutenant-Colonel Rock two days after Dill's order, on 7 July 1941.[33] Rock acknowledged that there was no easy solution and laid out five possible options. The existing system of drawing volunteers from across the Army was considered too slow for the rapid expansion envisaged, and wasteful of technically trained manpower. Restricting voluntary recruiting to infantry battalions and Infantry Training Centres was rejected because it would merely transfer the existing problems to a smaller pool of potential volunteers. Option three was to raise a battalion cadre of volunteer officers and NCOs via options one or two and flesh the unit out with high-quality recruits selected at their initial call-up. This would ensure a steady flow of suitable recruits, but, while an excellent method for peacetime, it was considered too slow for the current situation. Option four was to draw suitable recruits from a single infantry regiment and its attendant ITC while drafting in non-parachuting personnel from elsewhere. This would ease administration, but suffered from the same drawbacks inherent in recruiting from a limited manpower pool.

The fifth option was the most radical. It advocated scrapping the voluntary principle altogether and converting existing infantry battalions to the parachute role in their entirety, with only the medically unfit being exempt. This would allow the expansion to proceed quickly, while retaining the existing unit's *esprit de corps* and minimising administration. The risks were acknowledged, as was the fact that the conversion would have to be ruthlessly imposed; Rock nonetheless considered it to be the only practical way of expanding the parachute force with the required speed. He therefore recommended that the first new parachute be raised via the existing voluntary system or battalion conversion, that the third parachute battalion be raised by the latter, and that thereafter individual reinforcement/replacements should be volunteers selected at call-up. The desirability of a dedicated parachute brigade headquarters to oversee administration and training was also stressed. Rock closed by considering the likely effects of the airborne expansion on 11 SAS Battalion, the future of which was dependent upon which recruiting method was selected and a revision of the Commando terms under which its personnel were serving.

Rock's proposals were discussed at a War Office conference on 23 July 1941, chaired by Brigadier Nye.[34] The upshot was a series of recommendations for approval by CIGS Dill. Three new parachute battalions were to be raised by 1 March 1942, along with their first increment of reinforcements under the existing volunteer system but without the Commando cash subsistence and option to Return To Unit (RTU). This was to be offset by a new parachute pay allowance, which was also intended to act as a recruiting inducement. 11 SAS Battalion was to have its Commando privileges withdrawn as soon as the first new battalion was trained. A dedicated brigade HQ was to be formed, a parachute War Establishment was to be drawn up on the standard infantry battalion template, and a cadre of volunteer officers and NCOs was to be raised and trained in small batches before the rank and file. The new battalions were to be housed at Hardwick Hall in Derbyshire, with parachute training being carried out at Ringway with the assistance of instructors drawn from 11 SAS Battalion. Finally, the Royal Engineers were to provide an 'Air Troop' for airborne service.[35]

The War Office informed the Air Ministry of its decision to raise two additional parachute battalions at the end of August 1941, and requested that the CLE be ready to begin training them by 1 November 1941.[36] A War Office conference to review progress and address problems was held on 26 August 1941. Attendees included Lieutenant-Colonel E.E. Down, commander of 11 SAS Battalion since June 1941, and the officer selected to command the new parachute brigade, Brigadier Richard Gale MC. A variety of matters were discussed including standardising parachute pay for all ranks, modifying airborne recruiting criteria, the need for a unit shake-down period prior to parachute training at Ringway, and increasing the ratio of trained reinforcements. The conference concluded with another list of recommendations. An administrative section was to be set up at Hardwick Hall; the camp was to be ready to accept the first batch of trainees by 15 September 1941; and the parachute War Establishment was to be finalised as soon as possible. The names of putative battalion commanders were to be forwarded to Gale, and volunteers for airborne service were to be sought from the Royal Engineers and Royal Army Medical Corps.[37]

Recruitment began on 28 August 1941 with a circular to all Field Force, infantry, rifle and machine-gun battalions in the UK from the Assistant Adjutant General on 28 August 1941. Physical fitness was stressed; soldiers with spectacles were ineligible; and volunteers were to be aged between twenty and thirty-two, with exemptions as to age for officers and NCOs who met all the physical standards. All were to be A1 fit with 6/12 vision in both eyes and acuity to at least Army Hearing Standard Two, with a minimum of eight sound teeth including two molars in the upper jaw, and to weigh a maximum of 196lb naked. Signal and mortar officers were especially required, and captains were to be company command-qualified. No special terms of service were offered apart from parachute pay, at a rate of four shillings per week for officers and half that for other ranks, payable on completion of three parachute jumps. Only ten other rank volunteers per unit were permitted, to avoid depleting existing units, and nominal rolls were to be returned to AG17 by 13 September 1941.[38]

The Air Ministry initially rejected the War Office proposals on the grounds that a parachute brigade was a luxury that the country and Bomber Command could not afford, not least because there was no prospect of it being employed operationally before 1943.[39] However, this line softened following internal discussions about aircrew provision toward the end of August 1941,[40] leading to a joint conference at Army Co-operation Command headquarters on 9 September 1941.[41] Attended by the heads and key members of all the units and commands connected to the airborne project, the meeting finalised responsibilities between them. Ground training was to be carried out by parachute brigade staff at Hardwick Hall according to CLE guidelines, while Ringway provided live parachute training. The latter was also to train the Army ground-training instructors and provide a RAF liaison officer, a parachute instructor, a balloon and a five-strong parachute packing party. All Army instructors were to be withdrawn from Ringway by 1 November 1941.

A permanent Army camp was to be constructed for parachute trainees near Ringway, and Nissen accommodation for

250 trainees was to be constructed at Ringway as an interim measure. In the meantime, trainees would commute to the PTS from Hardwick Hall, where they would be cycled through the two-week qualification course of two balloon and four aircraft jumps in batches of 200. It was also decided to expand the CLE's Exercise Unit with the means to provide refresher training from December 1941.[42] Finally, trainees were to be subject to RAF administrative and disciplinary control while at the PTS, following a request from Ringway on 15 September 1941.[43] This was endorsed at the end of the month, at the same time Gale was confirmed CO 1st Parachute Brigade,[44] and the Air Ministry was informed at the beginning of October 1941.[45]

The 1st Parachute Brigade's War Establishment was also settled by the beginning of October 1941. It was made up of a brigade headquarters and three parachute battalions, each of three rifle companies, along with a sixty-four-strong RE Air Troop and a small signal staff. The basic building block of the parachute was the ten-man section, commanded by a sergeant rather than a corporal; expanding the ratio of senior NCOs was intended to counteract dispersal on landing.[46] The War Office also pushed ahead with preparations for the establishment of a glider force. On 10 October 1941, all Army Home Commands were officially notified that 31 Independent Brigade Group, currently undergoing mountain training in North Wales, was to become an Airlanding Brigade Group. The memo laid out the new unit's projected roles and WE, and included a report from the AFE on preliminary trials with the Horsa glider, with details of possible load combinations.[47]

Thus between July and October 1941 a workable relationship was finally achieved between the War Office and Air Ministry, with an agreed formation and training timetable for a full parachute brigade, and the groundwork for a glider equivalent. This was spectacular progress compared with what had gone before and credit appears solely due to the War Office, but there was a little more to it. Air Ministry resistance had been considerably reduced by RAF converts to the airborne cause and the War Office had paid little attention to airborne matters before July 1941, which suggests there was an element of convenience to its new-found enthusiasm. Neither was Army support for the airborne force unanimous, and it is interesting to speculate how events might have developed had Dill and Alanbrooke not been staunch airborne supporters. It is therefore perhaps more accurate to say that War Office design was augmented by favourable circumstances and a modicum of luck. Be that as it may, while the expansion and training of the airborne force were well in hand, little thought had been given to the doctrinal or operational details of how the enlarged force was to be employed. This oversight was resolved with another dose of good fortune.

On 9 June 1941 a Colonel Marecki from the Polish General Staff requested Brigadier Gubbins at the War Office to arrange a visit to Ringway.[48] The request included a nine-page paper addressed to Colonel 'de Rock' at the CLE, and took eleven days to negotiate the system.[49] Gubbins passed the paper straight to Rock for comment,[50] and the latter's reaction was swift and candid:

> Colonel Marecki's paper is most interesting and I hesitate to comment on it, since we have never produced any detailed, connected instructions of the same sort ourselves. The reason is that, in the present phase of parachuting, anything one can say is a little academic. We have, however, produced one paper on the use of parachute troops, for the benefit of Home Forces, but I don't think it has got beyond [War Office department] MT 1. If Colonel Marecki would like a copy, I will send him one, but he must understand that it is unofficial. I enclose a copy of my comments on his paper, offered rather tentatively.[51]

Rock's response shows he was well aware of British deficiencies, and it illustrates the pitfalls of placing total responsibility for the Army side of airborne training, research and development on the shoulders of a single, relatively junior officer. On the other hand, this rings a little hollow considering that the Poles had produced their paper under at least equally trying circumstances.

Hitherto, War Office thinking on the matter was based on Rock's July/August 1940 paper requesting the airborne force be used as an invasion spearhead.[52] This was augmented in October by another paper suggesting six functions including the latter,[53] which was fleshed out slightly in January 1941 with a list of specific missions. These were cutting off enemy units from reinforcement, attacking the enemy rear in conjunction with land forces, capturing airfields and carrying out unspecified 'other enterprises'.[54] While valid, this nonetheless consisted of little more than a series of broad-brush concepts with little if any detail. The Polish General Staff paper took the opposite tack by examining every facet of parachute operations. This included prerequisites, air and ground force command responsibilities, landing drills for opposed and unopposed landings, actions on the objective and recommendations for parachute units supporting air landing, armoured or amphibious operations. More mundane matters, including internal communications and the treatment of POWs, were also covered, although the rather terse treatment of the latter creates the inference they were to be dealt with out of hand.[55]

Rock's initial assessment of the Polish paper was thus fully justified, and he restricted his comments to the sections dealing with daylight drops with air cover and reorganisation on landing.[56] Rock felt drops within 500 yards of an occupied objective would be suicidal, and considered that drops at dawn, dusk or even after dark offered the best prospect of success, even allowing for the attendant assembly problems.

He recommended distinguishing between small operations of up to company strength and larger ones employing a battalion or more, not least because the latter needed longer to reorganise on landing. Rock also felt that large-scale parachute operations would be 'very rare' because of the difficulties inherent in establishing and maintaining air superiority.[57] This provides an interesting window into British airborne thinking, and suggests it was blinkered by equipment shortcomings and largely negative British war experience despite the large-scale German examples in the Low Countries and Crete.

For example, Rock's concern over post-drop reorganisation must have been prompted by the Whitley's awkward exit. This lengthened the time it took for a stick of parachutists to clear the aircraft, expanded the distance between members on landing and thus exacerbated problems with re-assembly. His opinion that large operations would be rare occurrences was likely shaped by the dearth of aircraft at Ringway, and the automatic assumption of German air parity if not outright superiority was clearly the result of events in France in 1940 and more recently in the Mediterranean. On the other hand, Rock questioned whether battalion-size operations as advocated by the Poles were viable, and suggested brigade or even division operations would be a more suitable step up from company-level raiding. He also challenged the Polish idea of controlling airborne operations from aircraft orbiting the battlefield, pointing out that aircraft radios were relatively low-powered and suggesting more powerful ground sets capable of reaching friendly ground stations would be a better option. Both these criticisms were eminently sensible, because the Polish proposals were somewhat over-enthusiastic. Relying on aerial communications and command and control not only assumed air superiority but also entailed risk from ground fire or mechanical failure.[58]

That Rock only felt qualified to comment upon two points from such a large and detailed document also highlights the

British failure to think much beyond their immediate circumstances. This is reinforced by the content of the British parachute paper Rock passed back to Marecki via Gubbins.[59] Intended primarily as a familiarisation aid for non-airborne units, it was high on administrative detail but low on practical information. Less than half was devoted to operational matters such as equipment, weaponry, jump procedures and drills and likely tasks. The larger remainder was headed 'Staff Duties in Connection with British Paratroops' and dealt with administrative matters including lead times for warning orders, transport and messing arrangements, and the establishment of lines of communication between air and ground commanders during operations. It closed with small sections on defence against paratroops and the use of paratroops in joint training exercises.[60]

Circumstances had obliged the British concentration on infrastructure and procedures, but this was nonetheless very much a case of putting the administrative cart before the operational horse. This may have been due to the Army's having a long history of improvisation, which took the ability to formulate drills, procedures and other organisational details at short notice for granted. In addition, Rock can perhaps be forgiven for failing to find the time to consider the nitty-gritty of airborne employment, but this does not absolve the War Office, especially considering the amount of effort expended formulating hypothetical brigade organisation tables. What the Poles made of Rock's paper is unclear, although Marecki did get his visit to Ringway at the beginning of July 1941, along with some American observers.[61]

For their part, the British appear to have been far more impressed with the Polish paper than their overt reaction suggests. On 21 June 1941 the CLE produced a four-section paper, ostensibly dealing with co-operation between the RAF Army Co-operation Command and parachute troops. The bulk of the document was actually focused on the use of paratroops to influence the immediate battle situation, and the transmission of tactical information from parachute troops to ground formations.[62] This was remarkably similar to the Polish General Staff paper and a totally new line of thought for Ringway and Army Co-operation Command, as well as lying outside the latter's official remit. This was the first of a series of studies emanating from the CLE which also bore more than passing similarity to topics examined by the Poles. They included the seizure of bridgeheads for armoured forces,[63] and a wide-ranging doctrinal paper that suggested five roles for airborne forces based on analysis of German experience. Eben Emael was seen as a parallel for attacking beach defences or seizing bridgeheads, and the Norwegian and Greek operations were characterised as tactical operations in indirect support of ground forces. The use of air-landing for rapid reinforcement in the former example was considered of possible utility in Iraq, a possibly tongue-in-cheek suggestion given that the British had been doing just that since the 1920s. The assault upon Holland was considered a useful template for strategic operations, and Crete was classified as an independent airborne operation against an isolated objective.[64]

Of course, not capitalising on the Polish paper would have been blinkered to the point of stupidity. It complemented existing British thinking, such as it was, and offered a firm base for further investigation, if not a significant developmental shortcut. The problem is not therefore that the British plagiarised it, but that they failed overtly to acknowledge the fact at the time or subsequently. There is no mention of it in the official history of British Airborne Forces, for example, and neither does it figure in secondary works. Had the paper been the sole example of Polish input into the expansion of the British airborne force this could be written off as an unfortunate oversight. However, this was not the case, for the Poles made a number of important practical contributions to British airborne development that have also gone largely unacknowledged. This input encompassed both the training side of matters at Ringway, and the conditioning and preparation of troops to undergo that training, which was to be a key requirement in the expansion of the British parachute force to brigade size.

At least three Polish air force officers served on the staff at Ringway. Lieutenant Bleicher, who had been an instructor at the Polish State Gliding School, gave a lecture on Polish gliding experience in May 1941 and subsequently served at the Development Unit.[65] Lieutenants Jerzy Gorecki and Julian Gebolys had been instructors at the Polish parachute-training centre at Bydgoszcz. The operational records make no direct reference to when they arrived at Ringway, although there is a reference to '…new Polish officers [being] separated for Special Parachute Instruction' at the end of September 1940.[66] This may have referred to the Polish instructors or the first increment of Polish special forces trainees, which underwent training at the beginning of October.

Whenever they arrived, there is ample evidence of their service at Ringway. Colonel Jan Lorys, who participated in one of the first Polish special forces courses and later served with the 1st Polish Independent Parachute Brigade at Arnhem, distinctly remembered Gorecki heading a 'Polish section' at Ringway in the autumn of 1940.[67] In mid-July 1941 Gorecki penned a letter on Ringway notepaper,[68] and Gebolys was the object of discussion between the Polish General Staff and the Airborne Forces Establishment in November 1941 following his request for a transfer to the Indian PTS at Chaklala. The Polish General Staff refused to release him because it considered him vital for the training of Polish personnel at Ringway, and suggested that Gebolys be promoted in recognition of his expertise. Group Captain Harvey asked for the request in writing, and promised Gebolys would then be posted to the AFE with the rank of flight lieutenant.[69]

This suggests that Gebolys was serving as an attached supernumerary rather than part of the permanent cadre, despite his nominal RAF rank. This may also explain his transfer request, for it must also have been somewhat galling to serve under men who had far less parachuting experience. Gebolys' position was thus similar to that of Williams, Ward and Hire following Strange's departure and the elevation of Newnham to command of the PTS, although they lacked the backing of a General Staff, exiled or otherwise. Harvey's reaction also suggests both that he was aware of Gebolys' presence at Ringway, and that he shared the Polish General Staff's high opinion of him. It is therefore highly likely that Gebolys was involved in training the large batches of Polish troops who began to arrive at the PTS from mid-April 1941,[70] and possibly the earlier Polish special forces contingents too. He also appears to have remained at Ringway after his transfer to India was denied; Polish primary documentation shows that Newnham consulted him about including a night jump in the training of Polish paratroopers in June 1942.[71]

This consultation is also interesting because it ties in with another Gebolys contribution to British military parachuting. According to Cholewczynski, Gebolys was responsible for introducing the practice of manipulating the parachute rigging lines to spill air from the canopy, thus allowing the parachutist a degree of directional control. The technique was allegedly christened the 'Polish Method' as a result.[72] There is no mention of this in the official history, but Newnham also credited Gebolys with inventing the method and referred to him as one of the best parachutists in the world.[73] Newnham did not specify a date, but the operational records describe the method without mentioning Gebolys in April 1941, and refer to it becoming standard practice.[74] The technique was also discussed in a CLE memo to No.70 Group in June 1941, after a number of paratroopers suffered injuries during a demonstration at Windsor in late May 1941.[75]

There is therefore no doubt that Polish instructors served at Ringway or that they made a major contribution to British military parachuting. Why this was not officially acknowledged or noted in the operational records is unclear, but there was a parallel failure to acknowledge ideas picked up from the Poles as they formed and trained their own parachute formation. The process was initiated by the Polish General Staff in late June 1940, and began with the raising of a small covert operations force by the Sixth or Special Bureau, the Polish equivalent to the SOE that maintained links with the underground Home Army in Poland.[76] Members of the covert operations force were christened *Cichociemni* ('Silent and Unseen'),[77] and the first contingent of twenty officer volunteers, drawn from the Polish 4th Cadre Rifle Brigade, arrived at the Special Training Centre at Lochailort in Scotland in September 1940.[78]

All *Cichociemni* volunteers were parachute-trained, and some may have been trained by the SOE at its own establishments.[79] However, the operational records clearly refer to Polish personnel arriving for training on 28 October 1940, although Colonel Stanislaw Sosabowski, commander of the 4th Cadre Rifle Brigade, claimed that *Cichociemni* volunteers from his unit did not arrive at Ringway for another four months.[80] Be that as it may, at least two contingents of Polish officers were trained at Ringway by 14 March 1941, and one carried out a demonstration drop for Sosabowski on that date.[81] A further twelve all-officer Polish courses were trained at Ringway by mid-August 1941, totalling fourteen courses in all.[82]

The *Cichociemni* effort was followed by a much larger and more ambitious undertaking, the transformation of Sosabowski's 4th Cadre Rifle Brigade into a parachute unit. Sosabowski escaped from Poland in 1939 to join the reconstituted Polish army in France in 1940, was evacuated to Britain via Dunkirk and ended up in Glasgow with many other evacuated Polish personnel. His efficiency in organising a holding camp at Biggar led to him being given command of the Canadian Officers Cadre Brigade in July 1940.[83] This unit was intended to augment Polish émigré volunteers in Canada but was renamed the 4th Cadre Rifle Brigade and assigned coastal defence duties based in Fife in October 1940.[84] Sosabowski claimed the idea of forming a parachute unit was his,[85] but there is evidence that the Polish General Staff were responsible, albeit 'unofficially'.[86] The latter's claim is supported by the pre-war Polish programme, in which Sosabowski does not appear to have been involved, and he does not appear to have been involved in drawing up the Polish General Staff paper either.

Wherever the idea originated, Sosabowski certainly was responsible for retraining the 4th Cadre Rifle Brigade, and oversaw the establishment of a preliminary parachute-training centre in the grounds of Largo House near Leven in February 1941.[87] The Polish effort was set up without official guidance from the British, but doubtless profited from the presence of Polish instructors there and enjoyed unofficial support within the CLE. Two Polish officers visited Ringway specifically to gather information for the Polish brigade effort on 21 July 1941,[88] for example, and the CLE supplied Whitleys for a Polish parachute demonstration in September 1941. In the latter instance, issuing invitations to high-ranking officers at the War Office and Air Ministry may also have eased matters,[89] especially given that a previous request had been refused.[90] Assistance was of course dependent upon British needs and equipment availability, but overall the British appear to have been favourably disposed toward the Polish effort. In the event, it proved to be a fruitful indulgence, for the British adopted several Polish practical innovations in the same way they plagiarised Polish doctrinal thinking.

The Poles tailored their training to British equipment and procedures, perhaps most notably by fabricating mock Whitley exits using barrels mounted in the loft of a stable block at Largo House. This allowed trainees to practise exit drills by dropping onto PT mats or sand and sawdust spread on the floor below, with drops of five, six and eight feet.[91] They also offset lack of access to aircraft by erecting a parachuting tower at Ludlin Links near Leven, using a £500 grant from the Polish General Staff.[92] Polish engineer officers drew up the design with advice from Gebolys, and the construction was contracted out to a local Scottish firm. Between 60 and 100 feet high, the tower was based on the sport parachuting towers used in Poland in the 1930s, and was surmounted by a platform large enough for ten trainees. The parachute canopy was fitted to a metal hoop, which was suspended in turn from a cable that could be raised and lowered by compressed air. This allowed the instructor to control the process and coach the trainee throughout the descent.[93]

The Ludlin Links tower was ceremonially opened on 20 July 1941,[94] and proved its worth when Polish troops began to pass through Ringway in numbers. PTS staff noted that Polish training-related injuries were conspicuous by their absence,[95] and a similar tower was subsequently erected at Ringway after a detailed examination of the Polish example in July 1941.[96] It is unclear when the Ringway tower was built, but it was in use in mid-1943 when the British 6th Airborne Division was undergoing training.[97] The British may also have been influenced by American observers who visited Ringway in April and July 1941,[98] given that US parachute training had incorporated towers from the outset,[99] and a home-grown proposal had been rejected, apparently due to the projected cost.[100] Nonetheless, it cannot be entirely coincidental that the British adopted a previously rejected training device after inspecting the functioning Polish example at Ludlin Links.

The British also borrowed, if not outright adopted, the Polish idea of putting trainees through a pre-parachute toughening process. The Poles used a large obstacle course built by Polish engineers in the grounds of Largo House. Nicknamed the 'Monkey Grove', the course included fences, climbing ropes, swings, jumps and a trapeze, all of which were designed to physically harden trainees for the rigours of parachute training.[101] This idea was incorporated into the British Airborne Depot at Hardwick Hall, which added a series of tests to measure trainees' physical and mental suitability for parachute training into the toughening process. Polish thinking again appears to be complementary rather than inspirational. Not only was there clearly a need for a British preliminary airborne training establishment of some description, but the decision to set one up had been taken by 17 July 1941 and was authorised by the War Office on 23 July.[102] The CLE submitted a detailed report on Polish training facilities in Scotland on 27 July 1941, the day after the minutes of the latter War Office meeting appeared. This suggests that the information was gathered for the War Office conference, and its late arrival was probably due to the distance between the four Polish establishments visited.[103] British observers also visited Leven at least once before the parachute demonstration at the beginning of September 1941, since an unknown major from the War Office wrote to Sosabowski on 20 August to inform him that he had been favourably impressed with all he had seen the previous week.[104]

The final area where Polish developments appear to have influenced British airborne thinking was personnel selection. As we have seen, Rock presented a series of options to address this problem on 7 July 1941, the most radical of which was a proposal to scrap the voluntary principle and convert infantry battalions in their entirety after separating the medically unfit.[105] This was a total and unheralded departure from prior British practice, but it was the very method employed by Sosabowski in converting the 4th Cadre Rifle Brigade into a parachute unit.[106] Officially this policy was adopted to ensure 'equality of sacrifice',[107] but Sosabowski was likely also influenced by a worsening shortage of suitable recruits. The pool of such was beginning to run short by 1941, prompting diplomatic efforts to secure the repatriation of Polish POWs from the Soviet Union, and there was fierce competition for what was available as a result.[108]

Had he adhered to the voluntary principle, Sosabowski therefore ran the risk of losing men with little chance of finding replacements. It is unclear precisely when Sosabowski scrapped the voluntary principle, but it is logical to assume it coincided with or possibly preceded the transformation of the 4th Cadre Brigade. This can be narrowed down to the period late 1940–early 1941, given that the Polish General Staff sanctioned the Leven parachuting tower in January 1941, and that Largo House was functioning by the following month.[109] It is therefore highly likely that Rock's departure from prior practice was influenced by the Polish example, given the degree of contact between Ringway and the Poles and that Sosabowski visited Ringway in March 1941.[110] It is of course possible that similarities between Polish and British airborne development were coincidental, but rather unlikely given the evidence. This begs the question of why the Polish input has not received the acknowledgement it merits, and the evidence suggests it may have been downplayed deliberately.

From a British perspective, the Poles proved to be less than co-operative allies due to their insistence that their units remained answerable to the Polish General Staff and Polish government in exile. This tendency was not confined to Sosabowski's parachute brigade but also applied to the Sixth Bureau, which was reluctant to integrate its covert operations with the SOE.[111] At least some Poles do not appear to have reacted well to

British-style discipline either. Sosabowski requested clarification of disciplinary problems relating to Polish trainees at Lochailort at the beginning of January 1941,[112] and the following year the STC suggested Polish officers be made aware of British disciplinary requirements and that a Polish liaison officer be attached to the STC staff.[113] There also appears to have been friction over Polish treatment of trained men who refused to jump, which the British considered a serious disciplinary offence. The War Office forwarded a detailed explanation of the relevant Section of the British Army Act to Sosabowski on 25 February 1942, followed by a full translation of the Army Act in February 1941.[114]

Relations between Sosabowski's brigade and the British airborne hierarchy took a turn for the worse with the establishment of the British 1st Airborne Division in November 1941, and the elevation of then Brigadier F.A.M. Browning to command.[115] The latter attended the Polish parachute demonstration in Scotland held in honour of Polish Commander-in-Chief, General Sikorski, on 23 September 1941. Sikorski issued specially commissioned Polish parachute qualification wings at the end of the exercise,[116] and Sosabowski's formation was officially redesignated the 1st Polish Independent Parachute Brigade on 4 October 1941.[117] Browning appears to have decided that a complete and fully trained Polish parachute brigade was too useful an asset to ignore. The British view of the matter is neatly summed up as follows:

> At first, Browning was most enthusiastic about the Polish Brigade, and gave Sosabowski every support in acquiring accommodation, supplies and equipment. However, as time passed he noticed that the Polish Brigadier… was reluctant to show any enthusiasm for, or understanding of, the suggestion that his Brigade be attached to one of the British airborne divisions…He [Sosabowski] just could not understand that private, nationalistic wars were

> unacceptable, not only to Browning but also to the Allied command… Sosabowski continued to complain that he had insufficient time to train his troops – although he had longer than anyone else. He stressed that his Brigade was under strength. So intense was his desire to carry out an operation in his native Poland that he may have exaggerated these handicaps. If his unit was not committed to battle until the final stages of the war, then the chance of its being engaged at full strength in the liberation of Poland would be that much greater.[118]

The Poles saw matters rather differently, and doubtless considered that their input into the British airborne effort offset any perceived requirement for gratitude. In the event they lost the ensuing bureaucratic struggle for independence in June 1944, and the 1st Polish Independent Parachute Brigade was incorporated into the British 1st Airborne Division on 10 August 1944.[119] Sosabowski subsequently exacerbated his unpopularity with the British by raising very pertinent objections to Operations COMET and MARKET GARDEN. He then committed the ultimate sin of not only being proven right, but of pointing out the fact at a British staff meeting at Valburg in the closing stages of the battle for Arnhem. This led directly to Sosabowski and his Brigade being scandalously scapegoated for the failure of others, and the Polish government-in-exile were pressured into relieving him of his command on 9 December 1944.[120]

None of this appears in the official British accounts, however. There is no mention at all of the 1st Polish Independent Parachute Brigade in *By Air To Battle*, the official history of the British airborne divisions. Otway's official airborne history merely mentions the formation of the brigade in passing, with a bare-bones mention of its activities at Arnhem, and lists it in the 1st Airborne Division's order of battle.[121] This is presumably because the scapegoating of Sosabowski and his men was still fresh in mind when these accounts were compiled in the immediate post-war period, when the officers who had orchestrated the episode were among the most senior in the British Army. It would therefore have been impolitic, not to say foolhardy, for the officers involved in compiling the official accounts to challenge received wisdom, even in the unlikely event that they had access to all the facts. Be that as it may, all this provides a compelling explanation for the British failure to acknowledge the full extent of Polish input into the establishment of their own airborne force. The important point here, however, is that there can be no doubt that the Poles provided valuable theoretical and practical assistance to the British, which eased the latter's efforts considerably.

The British, meanwhile, were wrestling with the problem of where 11 SAS Battalion was to fit into the formation of the 1st Parachute Brigade. The favoured War Office option was to disband the unit, retain some personnel as instructors at the CLE and disperse the rest across the brigade. This was prompted by 11 SAS Battalion's maverick reputation, in particular, and wider Army dissatisfaction with the Commando terms of engagement, which were considered inimical to discipline, in general.[122] The battalion staff was thus ordered to categorise its personnel on 15 July 1941, and return details of those considered suitable for future parachute service within three days.[123] Faith in the voluntary principle was undermined further by the poor standard of ITC volunteers intended to maintain the Battalion's strength. Rock referred specifically to this on 7 July 1941, claiming that up to twenty-five per cent of such volunteers were subsequently rejected for refusing to jump or involvement in crime.[124]

However, the War Office view failed to appreciate the efforts of Lieutenant-Colonel E.E. 'Eric' Down, who had taken over 11 SAS Battalion from Lieutenant-Colonel C.J. Jackson in June 1941. The change was not popular among some within the battalion, and Down was greeted with boos, catcalls and foot-stamping at his first parade.[125] He responded by jeering at the perpetrators and informing them that their days of ballet dancing were over. This uncompromising attitude earned him the disparaging nickname 'Dracula' and his malign influence was routinely assumed to be behind any untoward happening. On one occasion, for example, a loaded Whitley forced landed due to mechanical failure at Tatton Park, and the parachutists aboard were rushed back to Ringway for another jump to prevent them losing confidence. When the second jump was carried out without mishap, one of the paratroopers wondered aloud if the first run was a deliberate ploy by Down to see how they would react in an emergency.[126]

While reprehensible from a disciplinary standpoint, the troops' reaction was understandable. Down was charged to oversee the withdrawal of their special Commando privileges, which had been a source of dissatisfaction to the Army virtually from the outset.[127] For the troops his arrival therefore meant a reduction in pay and the re-imposition of some of the more tiresome aspects of military life. The blow was softened to an extent by the promise of special parachute pay, which Down later attempted to have paid at the same rate across the board,[128] and his leadership in persuading the majority of the Battalion to remain under the new regime.[129]

Between June and September 1941 Down set about transforming his command from a loose-knit raiding force into a first-rate conventional infantry battalion that merely utilised an unconventional method to reach the battlefield. The Battalion moved to Bury for a period of intensive weapon training, then back to Knutsford for a mixture of long-distance route marches and night descents from the balloon at Tatton Park.[130] Down was a harsh taskmaster, accepting only the highest standards, but he led by example and repeatedly outperformed men several years his junior in everything from routine tasks to setting the pace in route marches.[131] In this way he lost the Dracula tag and gained the more affectionate label 'Charlie Orange', the phonetic code for commanding officer.[132] Down's hard work paid off. Lieutenant-Colonel Richard Gale inspected 11 SAS Battalion in August 1941. He was so impressed by the changes wrought by Down that he argued successfully against the War Office recommendation for disbandment with the C-in-C Home Forces, General Sir Bernard Paget. The unit was redesignated the 1st Parachute Battalion on 15 September 1941, the same day that formation of the 1st Parachute Brigade was formally authorised;[133] Gale was confirmed as its commander fourteen days later.[134]

Gale's job was greatly assisted by the parallel establishment of HQ 1st Airborne Division. The CIGS General Sir Alan Brooke argued for a divisional title despite opposition from the War Office, which felt this inappropriate for what was ostensibly a training and development HQ. Brooke was clearly thinking ahead, however, and wanted the necessary command arrangements set up in advance for future expansion. This became clear in mid-January 1942, when Brooke informed Home Forces that henceforth HQ 1st Airborne Division was to be considered an operational command, and was to be fully integrated into the Army command structure.[135] Brigadier F.A.M. 'Boy' Browning was appointed to command of the new formation on 29 October 1941, and assumed his duties with the rank of acting Major-General on 3 November 1941.[136] This meant that the British airborne force finally had a high-ranking commander tasked specifically to deal with administration and development rather than operational matters, and with sufficient authority to fight its corner in Whitehall. Gale was thus able to concentrate upon training 1st Parachute Brigade without the distraction of fighting for the necessary resources.

The 2nd and 3rd Parachute Battalions began forming at Hardwick Hall under Lieutenant-Colonels E.C.W. Flavell and G.W. Lathbury respectively from 15 September 1941. An administrative headquarters had been set up there to oversee the process as agreed at the War Office conference of 30 August 1941.[137] Formation was to be completed by 1 October,[138] which would allow a month for sorting and incorporating volunteers, and physically hardening them for the rigours of parachute training, which was scheduled to commence on 1 November 1941. This hiatus was also to allow Ringway to make the necessary preparations for increasing its training output, and to gather the necessary parachutes and other training equipment.[139]

The memo circulated to all Home Forces Commands at the end of August 1941 had been quite explicit about the type of volunteer required,[140] but many of the men reporting to Hardwick were nonetheless far below the required standard, as Captain John Frost, the 2nd Parachute Battalion's Adjutant, noted:

> [I was]… astonished to see the way in which commanding officers of units all over Britain had taken the opportunity of playing the old Army game of shunting off their naughty boys and misfits when the call had gone out for volunteers to parachute. Nearly half those who presented themselves at the gates of the parachute battalions during this period were unsuitable for one reason or another. Some of them had conduct sheets… six pages long. There were few good NCOs because commanding officers often would not let them go.[141]

The body of the Army, it seems, considered one call for volunteers – that for Commandos in June 1940 – to be enough. The variable quality of the volunteers arriving at Hardwick resulted in the respective battalion staffs intercepting batches of volunteers further and further from the camp gates in order to cream off the most promising, until things got out of hand and a more equitable consensus was reached.[142]

Despite these difficulties, however, the two new parachute battalions progressed well in their pre-parachute preparation. Lathbury and three of his company commanders visited Ringway on 15 October 1941,[143] and the AFE issued 1st Parachute Brigade with a set of standing orders for parachuting on 24 October 1941.[144] An advance party from Hardwick Hall arrived at Ringway as scheduled on 1 November 1941, and 255 trainees, consisting of the 2nd Battalion's C Company and A Company from the 3rd Battalion, commenced parachute training the next day.[145] On 15 November Ringway informed Army Co-operation Command that No.1 Parachute Training Course had been successfully completed at 1330 hours.[146] This had involved 519 balloon jumps and 1,254 aircraft jumps, some of them in front of Browning, who visited Ringway on 12 November 1941.[147] Of the 250 who started the course, 249 finished it, a success rate that suggests the physical hardening at Hardwick was doing its job.[148]

It took a further four increments to run all the volunteers from the two new battalions through the PTS basic parachuting course. The second, consisting of 270 trainees, commenced on 18 November and concluded twelve days later.[149] The operational records make no reference to any losses from No.2 Course, but its completion brought the PTS's monthly drop total for November 1941 to 1,443 balloon and 2,887 aircraft descents.[150] Course No.3 began training on 5 December 1941, a five-day delay being necessary for parachute-drying.[151] This course tested a new departure for the PTS, running three training syndicates simultaneously. Two of these consisted of the 3rd Battalion's C Company, and A Company from the 1st Battalion, a total of 246 all ranks.[152] The third syndicate was made up of twenty-four Polish trainees from the 1st Polish Independent Parachute Brigade, who had commenced training on 2 December 1941. Poles were undergoing training at the PTS throughout this period.

Completion of Course No.3 brought the total of descents carried out by the PTS in the six weeks since 1 November 1941 to 5,239, in the process of which thirty-nine trainees had been injured to an extent sufficient to prevent them completing the course. This was a ratio of fifty injuries per 5,000 drops.[153] Some personnel from 1st Parachute Brigade also undertook other activities while at Ringway. Men from the 1st Parachute Battalion made a total of 216 night balloon jumps during December,[154] for example, and a party of fourteen drawn from the 2nd and 3rd Parachute Battalions began a parachute packing and maintenance course on 8 December. Others participated in trials to gather data on the incidence of airsickness among airborne troops, and its effect upon efficiency.[155]

The three-syndicate model was carried over into Course No.4, which commenced on 17 December 1941 with 209 trainees from the 2nd and 3rd Parachute Battalions. It concluded on 25 December 1941 and, along with the rest of the AFE, was rewarded with a day off as a double celebration.[156] The final and much smaller Course No.5 began on 30 December, with twenty-five trainees including two padres. This was another first for Ringway, and was marked dryly in the operational records as the '...first time the Parachute Training Squadron has had the honour to be instrumental in teaching reverend gentlemen to descend from the clouds'.[157] The monthly drop total for December 1941 was 1,523 balloon jumps and 2,606 aircraft jumps.[158] The PTS had thus conducted a total of 2,966 balloon descents and 5,493 aircraft jumps in the two-month period beginning 1 November 1941, the vast majority of them by the 1st Parachute Brigade. With the completion of Course No.5 the brigade became fully parachute-qualified, as all its jumping personnel had completed the basic parachuting course and received their qualification wings.

Two entire battalions thus completed their basic parachute course in a period of eight weeks, and virtually without a hitch.

The minor exception was a brief dispute between Hardwick Hall and Ringway over transportation in mid-December.[161] This was a tribute to the careful planning and preparation carried out by the Ringway and Hardwick Hall staffs, which laid the foundation for truly mass training in the future. 1st Parachute Brigade greeted 1942 by moving straight onto advanced parachute training on 3 January 1942, with every man making two stick descents and a night balloon jump.[159] Night training on such a scale was a new departure, but proceeded largely without mishap.No.1 Advanced Course was completed on 10 January 1942, with only two injuries from a total of 196 balloon descents in total darkness. There were no refusals, and while the experience was described as eerie, Ringway recommended that henceforth such training be included in the standard training syllabus.[160]

The British Army was therefore finally able to field a trained parachute force shaped to its preferred configuration by the middle of January 1941. A similarly sized glider force was in the offing, backed by a fully functioning training and research and development infrastructure. It had therefore taken eighteen months to meet Churchill's 1940 parachute requirement, a time-scale that could have been reduced considerably had the War Office and more especially the Air Ministry applied their energies more diligently to the task. This is clear from the subsequent course of events. Over the next three years this parachute embryo expanded to a force in excess of two full divisions, which spearheaded the largest seaborne invasion in history and participated in the largest airborne operations to date. In the process these descendants of the handful of Commando parachute volunteers forged an enduring military reputation, second to none in the British Army or elsewhere.

Notes

CHAPTER 1: DEVELOPMENTS IN TRANSPORTING TROOPS BY AIR BEFORE 1940

1 See for example Hickey, *Out of the Sky*, p.9

2 Kennett, *The First Air War 1914-1918*, p.46

3 *ibid.*, p.57

4 *Kagohl: Kampfgeschwader der OHL* (Battle Squadrons of the High Command). For details see Morrow, *Great War in the Air,* p.149; and Kilduff, *Germany's First Air Force,* pp.68–70

5 Morrow, pp.116–117; and Kilduff, pp.70–74

6 For the origins of this policy, see Malcolm Cooper, *The Birth of Independent Air Power,* pp.14–15

7 R.D. Layman, *Naval Aviation in the First World War,* pp.67–68

8 Morrow, pp.122–123

9 *Ibid.*, pp.243–244; and Layman, pp.74–75

10 Morrow, p.319; and Cooper, pp.131–132

11 Figures quoted from Morrow, p.322; for a contemporary account of the activities of the Independent Force, see Sir Walter Raleigh and H.A. Jones, *The War in the Air,* Volume V, pp.135–164

12 Morrow, p.320; and Kennett, p.99

13 For the British view, see Roderick Grant and Christopher Cole, *But Not in Anger,* pp.16–17; for the wider view, see for example Kennett, p.36

14 According to one source, the French, Italians and Russians all dropped

reconnaissance and sabotage teams by parachute; see Bruce Quarrie, *Airborne Assault,* p.28

15 Raleigh and Jones, Volume V, pp.278-280; for a more detailed account, complete with contemporary photographs, see Grant and Cole, pp.7-14

16 Christopher Cole (ed.), *Royal Air Force Communiqués 1918,* p.208

17 Grant & Cole, pp.14-16

18 For details of Mitchell's scheme, see for example Hickey, pp.13-14

19 See for example Maurice Tugwell, *Airborne to Battle,* p.18

20 The paper is reproduced in Vernon Blunt, *The Use of Airpower,* pp.163-169, especially pp.168-169

21 Jafna L. Cox, 'A Splendid Training Ground: The Importance to the Royal Air Force of its Role in Iraq, 1919-32', *The Journal of Imperial and Commonwealth History,* Volume 13, No.1 (October 1984), pp.157-184

22 Two squadrons of 0/400s, totalling fifty-one aircraft, were despatched to Egypt, and in the period April to October 1919 fifteen were written off in accidents, while several more were damaged and eight crew members were killed; see Grant and Cole, p.41

23 *Ibid.*, pp.41-44

24 *Ibid.*, pp.91-94

25 Captain R.G. Thorburn, 'The Operations in South Kurdistan, March–May 1923', *The Army Quarterly* Volume 31 (October 1935-January 1936), p.275

26 Grant and Cole, pp.91-99

27 *Ibid.*, p.56

28 *Ibid.*, pp.71-80

29 *Ibid.*, p.54.

30 *Ibid.*, pp.44-45; and Tugwell, p.21; for aircraft details, see Owen Thetford, *Aircraft of the Royal Air Force*

31 AIR 5/1253, Chapters 9 & 12; David Omissi, *Air Power and Colonial Control,* p.72; and Grant and Cole, pp.57-65

32 For contemporary comment see AIR 5/1255, Chapter 35; and Captain J.R. Kennedy MC, RA (Retd) *This, Our Army*, pp.149-150; see also Omissi, p.72, and Grant and Cole, p.66; for aircraft details see Thetford, pp.513-514

33 Grant and Cole, p.80

34 *Ibid.*, pp.80-83

35 See for example Louis Allen, *Burma: The Longest War*, pp.242-244, 318-320, 324-325

36 'Notes of the Week', *The United Services Review,* (14 April 1938), p.4; see also Grant and Cole, p.90

37 Lt-Col. James A. Bassett, 'Past Airborne Employment', *Journal of Military History,* Volume 12, No.4, Winter 1948, pp.206-207

38 F.O. Mischke, *Paratroops*, p.22

39 Details of this operation were kindly supplied via personal communication by the late Professor John Erickson following a written enquiry

40 See A. Borisov, '*Desant* onto the Sand in Aircraft', *Vestnik vozdushnovo flota* (January 1929) pp.11-13; A.N. Lapchinsky 'Airborne Landings', *Voyna i Revolyutsiya* (1930) Book 6, as printed in A.B. Kadishev (ed.) *Voprosy Taktiki v Sovetskikh Voyennykh Trudakh 1917-1940* (Moscow: Voyenizdat, 1970), pp.348-

354: cited in H.F. Scott and W.F. Scott (eds), *The Soviet Art of War*, pp.64-65. I am indebted to Dr James Sterrett for locating and translating the Borisov article

41 For details see Col. N. Ramanichev, 'The Development of the Theory and Practice of the Combat Use of Airlanding Forces in the Inter-War Period', *Military-Historical Journal*, No.10 (October 1982), p.72 (Russian-language publication), which is also cited in David M. Glantz, *The History of Soviet Airborne Forces*, p.4. I am again indebted to Professor Erickson for providing a copy of the Ramanichev article, and to Dr James Sterrett for translating it

42 Glantz, p.4

43 *Ibid.*, pp.4-7

44 *Ibid.*, pp.11-12

45 Scott, p.65

46 See for example John Connell Wavell, *Soldier and Scholar*, pp.182-183; and Lt-Gen. Sir Giffard Martel, *An Outspoken Soldier*, pp.139-140; for Churchill's paper, see CAB 120/10, War Cabinet Paper dated 16/06/1940

47 AIR 2/3897, '1938 - Formation of Parachute Troops in Germany: Report from British Air Attaché, Berlin', dated 30/08/1938; and WO 190/811, '1939, May 19: Note on Parachute Units in German Defence Forces', report from M.I.3b, dated 19/05/1939

48 'Wings of the German Air Force', *The United Services Review*, (13 October, 1938), p.9

49 Brian Bond, *British Military Policy Between the Two World Wars*, p.24

50 'Statement Relating to Defence, 1935', Cmd. 4827: cited in Kennedy, *op cit.*, p.18

51 Bond, pp.24-25, 33

52 49.5 to 52.6 per cent between 1918 and 1935; figures quoted from Kennedy, p.75

53 For details of the Army's expanded commitments and the problems thus generated, see Bond, pp.15-22

54 Lt-Col. Graham Seton Hutchinson, DSO, MC 'The Army of Tomorrow: How to Make it a Corps d'Elite', *The Army Quarterly*, Volume 30, pp.71-85; Capt. R.L. Telfer, 'The Army of Today', *The Army Quarterly*, Volume 31, pp.124-130; and Lt-Col. Seton Hutchinson, 'Recruiting: The Real Problem and its Solution'; Maj.-Gen. J.F.C. Fuller, 'Our Recruiting Problem, and a Solution'; A. Decurion, 'The Recruiting Problems of the British Army'; and I.A.M. Maclennan, 'Recruiting Stagnation: A Younger View', in *The Army Quarterly*, Volume 33, pp.79-90, 222-233, 285-292, 293-302

55 Seton Hutchinson, 'The Army of Tomorrow', *The Army Quarterly*, Volume 30, pp.76, 80

56 'The Army of Today', *The Times*, 25, 26 and 27 November 1935

57 Maj.-Gen. J.F.C. Fuller, *Lectures on F.S.R.* III, p.16; Liddell Hart, *The Future of Infantry*; see also Major-General H. Rowan-Robinson, *The Infantry Experiment*; anon., 'The New Warrior', *The Army Quarterly*, January 1934; LVSB, 'Three Infantries, Not One Infantry', *The Army, Navy and Air Force Gazette*, Volume LXXVII (14 May, 1936), pp.395-396; Lt-Col. W. Wilberforce DSO, MC 'The Infantry of the Future', and Capt. J.R.J. MacNamara MP, 'Army Methods of Training: Approach of the Modern Reorganised Infantry Platoon Toward the Enemy', *The United Services Review*, 22 April, 1937, p.5 and 26 August 1937,

p.5, respectively

58 David Fraser, *Alanbrooke*, pp.80-81

59 David French, *Raising Churchill's Army*, p.205

60 For details of this strife, see for example Bond, pp.127-190; and Charles Messenger, *The Art of Blitzkrieg*, pp.37-48, 67-76, 105-114

61 RAF personnel figures broke down as 27,906 Officers and 263,842 Other Ranks, as quoted in CAB 4/8, Committee for Imperial Defence paper 349-B, n.d., *c.*1918; cited in Omissi, p.8; statistics and squadron totals are from Cooper, pp.154-155

62 See for example Cooper, p.154

63 Omissi, pp.14-17; Smith, p.28; and Philip Towle, *Pilots and Rebels*, p.12

64 Cox, pp.162-165

65 The RAF's first two monoplane twin-engined bombers, the Handley Page Harrow (Air Ministry Spec. 29/35) and Bristol Bombay (Air Ministry Spec. C. 26/31), which entered service in 1937 and 1939 respectively, were officially classified as bomber transports; see Thetford, pp.136-137, 310-311

66 Omissi, p.21

67 For a balanced, in-depth study of Air Control, see Omissi; and Towle, pp.19-34; for a participant account, see Sir John Slessor, *The Central Blue*, pp.45-75. For a predictably pro view, see also D.J. Dean, 'Air Power in Small Wars: The British Air Control Experience', *Air University Review*, Volume 34, No.5 (1983); for a more balanced view see C. Townshend, 'Civilisation and Frightfulness: Air Control in the Middle East Between the Wars', in Chris Wrigley (ed.), *Warfare, Diplomacy and Politics* (London: Hamish Hamilton, 1986), pp.142-162

68 Omissi, pp.60-63; and W. Michael Ryan, 'The Influence of the Imperial Frontier on British Doctrines of Mechanised Warfare', *Albion*, Volume 15, No.2 (1983), p.136

69 Omissi, p.60

70 See for example Captain H.S. Broad, 'If it Happened To-day! War From the Air', *The Army, Navy and Air Force Gazette*, Volume LXXVII (30 July 1936), p.620

71 Uri Bialer, *The Shadow of the Bomber*, pp.155, 20-24; and John Terraine, *The Right of the Line*, p.8-13

72 Smith, especially pp.44-75, 140-197; and Terraine, pp.12, 45-53

73 Smith, pp.45-46

74 Terraine, pp.98-107

75 Ryan, p.136; and Omissi, pp.60-63

76 Bond, p.106; see also Omissi, pp 70-75

77 See for example Norman Dixon, *On The Psychology of Military Incompetence*, especially pp.36-79; Geoffrey Regan, *Someone Had Blundered*, pp.192-208; and *idem*, The Guinness Book of Military Blunders, pp.31-39, 76-78; all three works are widely available in public libraries, an indication of their popularity, and by extension the popularity of the negative portrayal of the British Army. Regan has been especially prolific in this regard, having published around a dozen books around the issue of military incompetence, although it must be acknowledged that the British Army is not his sole target

78 According to one source, a company-sized unit of Rangers was operating in

Nova Scotia from 1744 until the expansion of the unit by the original leader's son into Gorham's Rangers in 1750. The same source also claims this unit was the only American Ranger unit to offer regular commissions; for these and other details see Alan M. and Frieda W. Landau, *Airborne Rangers*, pp.8-12

79 David Gates, *The British Light Infantry Arm*, pp.12-13; and Arthur Bryant, *Jackets of Green*, pp.21, 31-32

80 Moreman, pp.37-43

81 Brian Bond, 'Doctrine and Training in the British Cavalry, 1870-1914', in Michael Howard (Ed.), *The Theory and Practice of War*, pp.96-125, especially pp.104-110; and Edward M. Spiers, 'The British Cavalry, 1902-1914', *Journal of the Society for Army Historical Research*, Volume 57 (1979), pp.71-79

82 For details of PFF artillery, see Moreman, p.41; and Michael Barthorp, 'The Mountain Gun', *Military Illustrated Past and Present (MI)* No.78 (November 1994)

83 David Fletcher, 'Steam Sappers: Steam Engines in the Boer War', *MI* No.47 (July 1994), pp.28-30

84 Quoted from Brian Bond, *Victorian Military Campaigns*, p.309; cited in T.R. Moreman, 'The British and Indian Armies and the North-West Frontier, 1846-1914', *Journal of Imperial and Commonwealth Studies*, Volume 20 No.1 (1992), pp.35-64

85 Tony Geraghty, *Who Dares Wins*, pp.69-79

86 Major J.T. Godfrey, RE, P.S.C., 'Winged Armies', *The RUSI Journal* (August 1935), pp.486-499

87 Otway, *Airborne Forces*, p.3; and Martel, *An Outspoken Soldier*, p.139

88 See for example LVSB, 'Three Infantries, Not One Infantry', *The Army, Navy and Air Force Gazette*, Volume LXXVII (14 May, 1936), pp.395-396; and Major-General H. Rowan Robinson, 'Air Infantry: How Can This Development Assist Great Britain?', *United Services Review*, Volume LXXVII (17 December 1936), pp.5-6

CHAPTER 2: A FEASIBLE METHOD OF TACTICAL DELIVERY

1 For a detailed account of these pioneering jumps, see Gerard M. Devlin, *Paratrooper!*, pp.7-13. A photograph of Berry leaving his aircraft appears on p.12

2 Quarrie, *Airborne Assault*, pp.26-28

3 Grant & Cole, pp.16-17

4 Omissi, p.72

5 Thorburn, p.270

6 Grant & Cole, pp.80-83

7 Morrow, *Great War in the Air*, p.239

8 Quarrie, p.27

9 *The United Services Review*, (16 June 1938), p.3

10 Tugwell, p.24; and Otway, *Airborne Forces*, pp.16-17

11 Glantz, pp.5-7

12 *Ibid.*, p.11

13 *Ibid.*, pp.17-20
14 *Ibid.*, pp.20-22
15 *Ibid.*, p.27
16 Hickey, p.15; and Glantz, p.13
17 Mischke, *Paratroops*, p.17
18 Glantz, p.44, and Figure 13, 'Airborne Corps Dispositions, June 1941', p.45
19 See for example 'Soviet Film of Kiev Manoeuvres', *The Army, Navy and Air Force Gazette* (12 March 1936), p.206
20 Martel, p.139; Connell, pp.182-183; and Otway, p.3
21 Glantz, p.4
22 *Ibid.*, pp.8-9
23 For details see Simpkin, *Deep Battle*, especially Chapters 12-16
24 Glantz, p.32
25 Alvin D. Coox, *Nomonhan*, Chapter 30
26 Glantz, pp.38-39
27 *Ibid.*, pp.39-44
28 *Ibid.*, pp.52, 70-289
29 *The United Services Review* (10 December 1936), p.1; and Rowan Robinson, 'Air Infantry: How Can This Development Assist Great Britain?', *ibid.*, (17 December 1936), pp.5-6
30 Mischke, p.19
31 Cholewczynski, *Poles Apart*, p.47
32 Opinion expressed by Lt-Col. Jan Jozef Lorys (Retd), during an interview at the Polish Institute and Sikorski Museum, Prince's Gate, London, on 16 June 1998. Col. Lorys participated in parachute training as an officer cadet in Poland before 1939, and later served with the 1st Polish Independent Parachute Brigade, including a liaison tour to observe airborne training in the United States. I an indebted to both Col. Lorys and his wife, whose assistance proved invaluable in translating the present author's regional English accent, and also to Mr Andrzej Suchcitz, Keeper of Archives at The Polish Institute and Sikorski Museum, for both making the interview possible, and locating relevant files from his archive
33 Col. J.T. Godfrey was commissioned into the Royal Engineers on 27 October 1915 and held a number of staff appointments in the inter-war period, including Staff Captain at the War Office in 1927, Assistant Military Attaché to Washington in 1929, and Military Attaché to Warsaw, 1935-1938. I am indebted to Dr John Rhodes, Curator of the Royal Engineers Museum, for supplying this information
34 Major J.T. Godfrey, RE, PSC, 'Winged Armies', *The RUSI Journal* (August 1935), pp.486-499
35 Lorys interview, 16/06/98
36 Cholewczynski, p.47
37 *Ibid.*, p.47
38 Quarrie, *Airborne Assault*, p.29
39 For Student's involvement, see Zeidler, *Reichswehr und Rote Armee 1920-1933*, pp.71, 107, 138-140, 161, 174, 272. I am indebted to Professor Hew Strachan for drawing my attention to this work and translating the appropriate sections

40 Macdonald, *The Lost Battle*, p.9
41 Zeidler, p.215
42 Lucas, *Storming Eagles*, pp.16-17; and Hickey, p.18
43 MacDonald, pp.11-12; and Quarrie, *German Airborne Troops*, p.5
44 Lucas, pp.17-18; and Quarrie, *German Airborne Troops*, pp.5-6
45 The date of this unit's establishment is somewhat confused, being cited as 1936 and 1937; see Quarrie, *German Airborne Troops*, p.6; and Lucas, p.18
46 MacDonald, pp.13-14; and Hickey, pp.19-21
47 Lucas, pp.19-20
48 MacDonald, p.13
49 Lucas, p.20
50 Glantz, p.9
51 Jean Gottman, 'Bugeaud, Gallieni, Lyautey: The Development of French Colonial Warfare', in Edward Meade Earle (Ed.), *Makers of Modern Strategy*, p.248
52 MacDonald, pp.14-15
53 *Ibid.*, p.15; for 22nd *Luftlande* Division, see Lucas, pp.19-21
54 For the Commandments in full, see Hickey, pp.21-22
55 'Wings of the German Air Force', *The United Services Review,* (13 October 1938), p.9
56 MacDonald, pp.18, 258-259, 304-306
57 *Ibid.*, pp.9, 16-17
58 Glantz, pp.41-43, especially the organisation details on p.43
59 MacDonald, p.25

CHAPTER 3: CATALYST AND EXAMPLE

1 Ellis, *The War in France and Flanders*, pp.244-246. 305
2 *Militargeschichtliches Forschungsamt* (Research Institute for Military History), *Germany and the Second World War*, Volume II, p.254; for details of the *Brandenburger* unit and operations, see Lucas, *Kommando*, pp.56-67
3 Bekker, *The Luftwaffe War Diaries*, pp.58-59, 97-113
4 MacDonald, *The Lost Battle*, p.17; and Bekker, pp.124-125
5 Bekker, pp.119-120
6 For overall details see *Militargeschichtliches* Volume II, pp.275-276
7 Bekker, p.132
8 Lucas, *Storming Eagles*, p.33; and Bekker, p.118
9 Bekker, pp.120, 126-127
10 See *ibid.*, pp.121-128; and Mrazek, *The Fall of Eben Emael*
11 Bekker, pp.130-139
12 *Militargeschichtliches* Vol. II, p.281
13 German paratroopers jumped carrying only sidearms, other weapons being dropped in special containers for recovery after landing; see Lucas, *Storming Eagles,* pp.367-368
14 Bekker, pp.138-139
15 *Ibid.*, pp.149-150
16 MacDonald, p.37

17 See for example *ibid.*, pp.37-39; and John P.Campbell, 'Facing the German Airborne Threat to the United Kingdom, 1939-1942', *War in History*, Volume 4, No.4 (1997)

18 Otway, *Airborne Forces*, p.6

19 Bekker, p.128. The technique was subsequently used by the Allies in the invasions of Sicily and Normandy; see Otway, pp.119, 124, 177

20 *The Times*, Monday 20 May 1940, p.8; and 21 June 1940, p.8

21 For details and illustrations of this and other copied equipment, see Steven and Amodio, 'British Airborne Forces, 1940-42', *Military Illustrated Past and Present (MI)* No.54 (November 1992), pp.21-23

22 According to Otway, the *coup de main* idea occurred independently to Major-General Gale, commanding the British 6th Airborne Division, and his subordinate Brigadier Hill. Gale admitted to being inspired by the German examples cited; see Otway, pp.173-174; for details of the German operation against the Corinth Canal, see MacDonald, pp.66-67. For the Orne operation, see Ambrose, *Pegasus Bridge*, and Shannon and Wright, *One Night in June*

23 The German Z1 parachute obliged the parachutist to land on all fours, and the door of the Junker 52 was so small that exiting the aircraft was a gymnastic exercise, which precluded the carriage of weapons larger than a pistol; see Lucas, *Storming Eagles*, pp.367-368

24 For details of initial British reliance on containers, see AIR 32/4 Document 7A, dated 19/06/1941; for the sleeves and valises see Otway, pp.98, 410-411, and plates 22-25, between pp.196-197

25 All figures quoted from Ellis, pp.326-327

26 Fraser, *And We Shall Shock Them*, p.28

27 MTP No.33, March 1940 'Training in Fieldcraft and Elementary Tactics'; cited in Harrison Place, pp.74-75

28 Quoted from Lucas and Cooper, *Hitler's Elite*, p.68

29 Fraser, pp.28-29

30 *Ibid.*, pp.27-29

31 See for example Alistair Horne, *The Price of Glory: Verdun 1916*, pp.339-347

32 Fraser, p.30

33 See for example Bond, *Chief of Staff: The Diaries of Lieutenant-General Sir Henry Pownall*, Volume One, pp.280-281, 296

34 Terraine, *Right of the Line*, pp.96-97; for a table of organisation and list of the RAF units involved, see Ellis, p.372

35 Ellis, p.325; for a detailed breakdown of the aircraft loss figure by Command, see Wood and Dempster, *The Narrow Margin*, Appendix 12, p.311

36 Ellis, p.307; and Terraine, pp.123, 133-134, 146-147

37 Air Historical Branch (AHB)/II/117/2(A): 'The Air Defence of Great Britain', pp.100-102; cited in Terraine, p.73

38 For pre-war policies and the provision of fighters for Home Defence, see Smith, *British Air Strategy*, pp.317-319; and Terraine, pp.72-76

39 For fighter component of the AASF, see Terraine, p.122; for organisation and a full list of the RAF units involved, see Ellis, p.372

40 CAB 65/13, War Cabinet minutes 15/05/1940; and Terraine, pp.137-140

41 Bryant, *Turn of the Tide*, pp.89-156

42 Pilot Officer H.A.C. Bird-Wilson, 17 Squadron, RAF; cited in Franks, *The Air Battle of Dunkirk*, p.165

43 Squadron Leader J.M. Thompson, 111 Squadron, RAF; cited in *ibid.*, p.198

44 Pilot Officer H.M. Stephens, 74 Squadron, RAF; cited in *ibid.*, p.190

45 Flight Lieutenant A. Hope, 601 Squadron, RAF; cited in *ibid.*, pp.67-70

46 Attributed to Air Marshal Sir Cyril Newall, CAS in 1937, referring to the close support of ground forces in the Spanish Civil War; cited in Terraine, pp.64, 80

47 For details see Terraine, pp.140-143; and Gilbert, *Finest Hour*, pp.334-335, 342-343

48 The scheme for striking the Ruhr originated in 1938; see Smith, pp.291-296

49 For details see Terraine, pp.71-77, 138-141

50 For the Bomber Command Order of Battle on 15 September 1940, see Wood and Dempster, Appendix 3, pp.303-304

51 Classifications from RAF expansion Scheme 'F' of 1936; see Terraine, p.34

52 For the Stirling's shortcomings, see Terraine, pp.278-279; for technical details see Thetford, *Aircraft of the Royal Air Force*, pp.459-462

53 For a detailed account of these operations see Terraine, pp.95-111

54 Quoted from AHB/II/117/1(B), pp.72-73; for details of the Hörnum raid, see Terraine, pp.112-113

55 CAB 120/414, minute from PM to Ismay, dated 03/06/1940

56 CAB 120/414, minute from PM to Ismay, dated 05/06/1940

57 For a comprehensive list see Ladd, *Commandos and Rangers of World War II*, pp.251-275

58 CAB 120/414, minute from PM to Ismay, dated 05/06/1940

59 CAB 120/262, document 1B, letter from PM to Ismay, dated 22/06/1940; the letter also appears in AIR 2/7338, document 1A, same date

60 See for example the diary of John Colville, entry for 29/05/1940: cited in Gilbert, *The Churchill War Papers*, Volume II, pp.192, 426

61 CAB 69/1, minutes of Defence Committee meeting, dated 19/06/1940

62 Ladd, pp.21-38

63 Figures from Neillands, *By Sea and Land*, pp.49 & 52

64 Blunt, *The Use of Air Power*, Appendix 'C', pp.163-169

65 CAB 120/10, War Cabinet Paper dated 16/06/1940

66 CAB 120/414, minute from PM to Ismay, dated 03/06/1940

67 CAB 120/262, letter from PM to Ismay, dated 22/06/1940; the letter also appears in AIR 2/7338, document 1A, same date

CHAPTER 4: IMMEDIATE REACTIONS

1 MI(R) File 3, paper dated 5 June 1939; cited in M. R.D. Foot, *SOE in France*, p.2

2 *Ibid.*, p.3

3 *Ibid.*, pp.4-5

4 *Ibid.*, p.6

5 Messenger, *The Commandos*, pp.19-25

6 Massam, *British Maritime Strategy and Amphibious Capability*, Chaps. 1 & 2

7 *Ibid.*, pp.124–135
8 *Ibid.*, pp.140–147
9 *Ibid.*, pp.150–151
10 'Notes of the Week', *The United Services Review*, Vol. LXXVII (10 December 1936), p.1
11 See for example AIR 2/3897, '1938 - Formation of Parachute Troops in Germany: Report from British Air Attaché, Berlin', dated 30/08/1938; and WO 190/811, '1939, May 19: Notes on Parachute Units in German Defence Forces', report from M.I.3b, dated 19/05/1939
12 See for example WO 193/697, minute from Balfour Davey to MI 3, dated 26/09/1939; and WO 190/879, appendix 'A', minute from MI 3, dated 01/11/1939
13 'Parachute Troops Technique: How the Germans are Trained', *The Times*, Wednesday 15 May 1940, p.6
14 *The Times*, Saturday 8 June 1940, p.3; the four-view originals, printed on high-quality card, are filed in WO 32/4723
15 The 1,600 figure is cited in MacDonald, *The Lost Battle*, p.37; see also the photograph of German POWs in *The Times*, Monday 20 May 1940, p.8. The prisoners all appear to be wearing *Heer* uniform, and were presumably from 22 *Luftlande* Division. Another photograph of *fallschirmjäger* with distinctive airborne items was published in a later edition; see *The Times*, Friday 21 June 1940, p.8
16 See AIR 2/7239, doc. 3A, 'Parachute Troops' from AM Director of Intelligence, dated 10/06/1940
17 'Fighting in Rotterdam' and 'Parachutists In British Uniforms', *The Times*, Saturday 11 May 1940, p.6
18 Editorial 'Parachutists', *The Times*, Saturday 11 May 1940, p.7
19 'Parachute Attacks Mastered', *The Times*, Tuesday 14 May 1940, p.6
20 'The Parachute Invasion: German Techniques Described - Lessons from Holland', *The Times*, Tuesday 21 May 1940, p.5
21 Miksche, *Paratroops*, p.25
22 'Local Defence Volunteers - Guarding Against Parachutists: Mr Eden's Appeal', *The Times*, Wednesday 15 May 1940, p.3; see also S.P. Mackenzie, *The Home Guard*, pp.33–34
23 Parl. Deb. 5th Series, CCCLXI, p.750, 4 June 1940
24 WO 193/27, doc. 1A, minute with appended Commons Notice 1939/40 - 1439, Question for Tuesday 4/6/40 by Mr Cocks, 'Organisation of Corps of Parachutists and Gliders', n.d., c.03/06/1940; and doc. 2A, minute with appended reply in full, n.d., c.03/06/1940
25 *Ibid.*, doc. 2B, 'Creation of a Parachute Corps', from General Staff MO1 to MO7, dated 04/06/1940
26 See for example Otway, *Airborne Forces*, p.21
27 Messenger refers to the 6 June meeting, and Ladd to approval being granted on 8 June. Messenger implies that Clarke's note was not considered until 10 June 1940, when Dill replaced Ironside as CIGS, and that the 9 June call for Volunteers for Special Service originated independently. However, Clarke's note suggested the name Commando, and that term appears twice in the

9 June letter, which would suggest that the latter was drafted with knowledge of the former. Ladd's account would therefore appear to be the more accurate: see Ladd, *Commandos and Rangers*, p.17; and Messenger, *The Commandos*, p.26

28 WO 32/4723, doc. 1B

29 *Ibid.*, doc. 11A, memo from WO DMO&P to WO DRO, dated 12/06/1940

30 *Ibid.*, doc. 18A, memo from WO DMO&P, dated 13/06/1940; the memo also appears in PRO WO 193/384, doc. 3A, same date

31 *Ibid.*, doc. 18A; the memo is reproduced in full in Messenger, *The Commandos*, pp.28-29

32 WO 193/384, doc. 1A, signal from WO DMO&P, dated 20/06/1940

33 WO 32/4723, doc. 14A, copy of letter from WO DRO to All Home Commands, dated 17/06/1940, and doc. 15A, telegram from WO DRO to All Home Commands, also dated 17/06/1940; for copies of individually addressed telegrams see docs. 1 - 10 & 13

34 *Ibid.*, doc. 11A, addendum dated 17/06/1940; 3rd Division, commanded by future Field Marshal Montgomery, had performed well on the continent and having been evacuated in relatively good order was earmarked for invasion defence

35 *Ibid.*, doc. 7A, 'Record of Meeting Held at 12.00, 20 June 1940 to Consider Organisation of Irregular Forces', dated 21/06/1940

36 *Ibid.*, doc. 19C, 'Formation of Irregular Commandos' from WO DSD to All Home Commands, n.d., c.20/06/1940

37 *Ibid.*, doc. 19B, telegram from GOC Southern Command to Forcedly Seventeen, dated 23/06/1940

38 Being RTU'd, became the ultimate disciplinary sanction in Commando and Airborne units

39 WO 32/4723, doc. 19A, memo from WO DRO to All Home Commands, dated 26/06/1940

40 From 15 October 1940 the rate was reduced to ten shillings per day for officers and four shillings per day for other ranks for the first seven days of leave or illness, after which the special allowance ceased until the individual returned to duty; WO 32/4723, doc. 91A, memo to All Home Commands and Pay Offices, dated 15/10/1940

41 *Ibid.*, doc. 1A, telegram from Commandeth Chester to WO SD1, dated 29/06/1940; and doc. 2A, telegram from WO SD1 to Commandeth Chester, dated 02/07/1940

42 *Ibid.*, doc. 29A, letter from WO DRO to All Home Commands, dated 03/07/1940

43 *Ibid.*, docs. 38 - 44, various dates

44 *Ibid.*, doc. 19A, memo from WO DRO to All Home Commands, dated 26/06/1940

45 *Ibid.*, docs. 4 , 5, 6, & 7, letters from Ministry of Food to WO, dated 01, 02, & 05/04/1941 respectively, and doc. 109A, memo from WO DMO&P to Commander Special Service Brigade, dated 15/04/1941

46 The exceptions were No.10 Commando, which was temporarily shelved when Northern Command were unable to locate sufficient suitable volunteers, and No.12 Commando, raised in Northern Ireland, where only 250 suitable

volunteers were found; see Messenger, *The Commandos*, p.30

47 For details and brief participant accounts see *ibid.*, pp.30-31

48 CAB 120/262, letter from Lt-Col. Jacob RA to Lt-Col. Hornby MC, dated 14/08/1940

49 See for example Richard Gale, *Call To Arms*, p.117. Gale is referring specifically to the later Army reaction to the expansion of airborne forces, but the point made is equally valid for the earlier Commando establishment

50 WO 32/4723., doc. 96A, telegram from WO AG 17 to Eastern Command, dated 22/10/1940

51 *Ibid.*, doc. 49A, letter from GOC Northern Command to the WO, dated 28/07/1940

52 CAB 120/262, doc. 7, 'Meeting of the War Cabinet Chiefs of Staff Committee, 6 August 1940', dated 06/08/1940

53 WO 32/4723, doc. 84, signal from GOC Southern Command to WO AG 17, n.d., c.3/10/1940

54 *Ibid.*, doc. 87A, telegram from HQ Western Command to WO AG 17, dated 06/10/1940

55 *Ibid.*, doc. 64A, letter from WO SD4 to All Home Commands, dated 22/08/1940.

56 *Ibid.*, docs. 73 - 76, various dates between 16/09/1940 and 01/10/1940

57 *Ibid.*, doc. 76A, note from WO DOR to WO AG 17, dated 01/10/1940

58 *Ibid.*, doc. 76B, teleprint from WO AG 17 to HoFor, All Commands, dated 01/10/1940

59 *Ibid.*, doc. 81A, signal from HoFor to All Home Commands, n.d. c.01/10/1940

60 *Ibid.*, doc. 82, signal from WO AG 17 to HoFor, dated 04/10/1940; doc. 84, signal from Southern Command to WO AG 17, n.d. c.03/10/1940; doc. 85, message form from WO AG 17 to Southern Command, dated 05/10/1940; and doc. 86A, teleprint from HoFor to WO AG 17, n.d. c.05/10/1940

61 WO 193/27, doc. 3A, minute from War Office MO1 to War Office SD1, dated 10/06/1940. Given the timing, 'division' is probably meant in its literal sense rather than as a formal military unit

62 WO 32/4723, doc. 11A, memo from WO DMO&P to WO DRO, dated 12/06/1940

63 *Ibid.*, doc. 15A, telegram from WO DRO to All Home Commands, dated 17/06/1940

64 *Ibid.*, doc. 7A, 'Record of Meeting Held 20 June 1940 to Consider Organisation of Irregular Forces', dated 21/06/1940

65 *Ibid.*, doc. 19C, 'Formation of Irregular Commandos', from WO DSD to All Home Commands, n.d. c.20/06/1940

66 *Ibid.*, doc. 20A, telegram from Southern Command to WO AG 17, dated 26/06/1940

67 *Ibid.*, doc. 27A, memo 'Formation of Commando and Irregular Troops', from Southern Command to various units under command, dated 28/06/1940

68 AIR 2/4586, doc. 1A, Secret Organisation Memo, 'Formation of a Parachute Training Centre', n.d. c.20/06/1940

69 Otway, p.31

70 Peter Hearn, *Flying Rebel*, p.114
71 AIR 29/512, entry for 09/07/1940
72 WO 32/4723, doc. 37, telegram from WO MO 9 to GOC Belfast, dated 14/07/1940
73 *Ibid.*, doc. 72A, telegram from Scottish Command to WO AG 17, dated 16/09/1940
74 *Ibid.*, doc. 46A, letter from DA & QMG NI to WO and various subordinate units, dated 26/07/1940
75 *Ibid.*, doc. 26A, telegram 'Volunteers for Special Service' from WO DRO to All Home Commands, dated 30/06/1940
76 AIR 2/4586, doc. 6A, letter from AM Deputy Director of Operations, dated 20/06/1940
77 Otway, p.32
78 WO 32/4723, doc. 99A, teleprint message from WO AG 17 to All Home Commands, dated 21/10/1940
79 *Ibid.*, doc. 103A, telegram from WO AG 17 to Northern Ireland Command, dated 10/11/1940
80 AIR 2/7239, doc. 1B, 'Development of Parachute Troops' from AM Department of Plans to various AM departments, dated 08/06/1940
81 *Ibid.*, doc. 2A, minutes of conference held at the Air Ministry, dated 10/06/1940
82 *Ibid.*, doc. 4A, 'Development of Para Troops - Air Requirements: Conclusions of Conference held at the Air Ministry June 10, 1940', dated 10/06/1940
83 *Ibid.*, doc. 6A, 'Parachute Training Centre' from AM Department of Plans and Department of Operations, dated 14/06/1940
84 AIR 2/4586, doc. 1, AM Form 1455, request to open New File on 'Formation of Parachute Training Centre', dated 20/06/1940; and doc. 1A, Secret Organisation Memo, 'Formation of a Parachute Training Centre', n.d.
85 *Ibid.*, doc. 4A, 'Table of War Establishment for Parachute Training Centre', n.d., c.14-20/06/1940
86 AIR 2/7239, doc. 4A, 'Development of Para Troops - Air Requirements: Conclusions of Conference held at the Air Ministry June 10, 1940', dated 10/06/1940
87 AIR 2/4586, doc. 5A, signal from Air Ministry to 22 Group, n.d., *c.*21/06/1940
88 There does not appear to be any official notification of this change, but the term CLS appears on all documents referring to the airborne unit at Ringway apart from those ordering its initial establishment, and is used for the title of the unit's operational record book, in which entries commence on 1 July 1940; see AIR 29/512, Operational Record Book, Central Landing Establishment
89 Lawrence Wright, *The Wooden Sword*, p.12; and Saunders, *The Red Beret*, p.33. Wright was a RAFVR officer closely involved in British combat glider development from October 1940
90 For Shore's accident see Hearn, *Flying Rebel*, p.114; and AIR 29/512, Introduction
91 According to the official Royal Engineers account, Captain Rock arrived at Ringway on 24 June, but Hearn claims that the pilots arrived on that date

and that Rock arrived on 27 June. Rock's service record merely states he was assigned to Ringway on 24 June 1940; see *The History of the Corps of Royal Engineers* (Chatham: The Institution of Royal Engineers, 1951), Volume VIII, p.191; and Hearn, *Flying Rebel*, p.114. I am indebted to Dr John Rhodes, Curator of the Royal Engineers Museum, for supplying the relevant details from the Royal Engineer account

92 For details of Strange's trip to the Air Ministry, see Hearn, *Flying Rebel*, p.114; for official confirmation, see AIR 29/512, entry for 01/07/1940

93 Hearn, *Flying Rebel*, pp.115-116

94 AIR 2/4586, doc. 6A, letter from AM Deputy Director of Operations, dated 20/06/1940

95 *Ibid.*, doc. 5A, signal from Air Ministry to 22 Group, n.d., c. 21/06/1940

96 AIR 29/512, entries for 01/07/1940 and 02/07/1940

97 *Ibid.*, entry for 04/07/1940

98 For a list of appointments and the names of the personnel involved, see *ibid.*, introduction

99 The precise date of Rock's promotion is unclear, and his service record merely states that he was referred to as Major in documentation after 24/06/1940. I am again indebted to Dr John Rhodes for providing a summary of the late Lt-Col. Rock's service record, prepared by Major J.R. Cross of the Museum of Army Flying, Middle Wallop, *c.*August 1988

100 AIR 29/512, entry for 05/07/1940

101 Hearn, *Flying Rebel*, p.114

102 For a picture of this method in action from the wing of a Vickers Victoria 'Empire Day Thrills', *The United Services Review* (10 June 1937), p.18

103 AIR 29/512, entry for 09/07/1940

104 AIR 2/7338, doc. 11A, 'Development of Parachute Troops', from Air Ministry to Chiefs of Staff, n.d., c.01/08/1940

105 Jozef Garlinski, *Poland, SOE and the Allies*, pp.47-48

106 Newnham, *Prelude To Glory*, p.5. Newnham served in an administrative capacity from October 1940, and was promoted to command what was by then entitled the Parachute Training School in July 1941

107 AIR 29/512, entry for 06/07/1940

108 AIR 2/4586, doc. 7A, request from CLS to AM for aerial photography of Tatton Hall Park, n.d., *c.*July 1940

109 Interestingly, Strange had known Lord Egerton's son, a pioneer aviator killed at an air meeting in 1910; Hearn, *Flying Rebel*, pp.116-117

110 AIR 29/512, entry for 07/07/1940; and AIR 2/4586, doc. 10A, Action Copy Signal from CLS to DDCO (AIR), dated 07/07/1940

111 AIR 29/512, entry for 08/07/1940; and AIR 2/4586, doc. 11A, Postagram from AM to CLS Ringway, and doc. 15A, Message Form from AM to CLS Ringway and 22 Group, both dated 08/07/1940

112 AIR 2/4586, doc. 14A, Message Form from AM to Commander, Chester Area, dated 08/07/1940

113 *Ibid.*, doc. 28C, letter from Ringway to HQ 22 Group, dated 20/07/1940; and doc. 28B, Postagram from 22 Group to HQ Works Area No.4, request for survey of Tatton Park to assess suitability as a powered aircraft landing zone,

dated 13/08/1940. It is unclear whether the CLS produced the proposal on its own initiative, or as the result of prompting from above

114 *Ibid.*, doc. 21A, letter from Lord Egerton to Vice Secretary of State for Air, dated 24/07/1940

115 The documentation generated by this affair is too extensive to be listed in full. For highlights, see *ibid.*, doc. 28D, dated 11/08/1940; doc. 31A, letter from GHQ Home Forces to AM, dated 18/08/1940; doc. 32A, letter from AM DO to 22 Group, dated 23/08/1940; doc. 34A, dated September 1940; docs. 36A & B, dated 28/09/1940 and 03/09/1940 respectively; and doc. 53C, letter from Cheshire War Agriculture Executive Committee, dated 24/03/1941

116 AIR 29/512, entry for 11/07/1940

117 For a sample verse, see Victor Dover, *The Sky Generals*, p.25

118 Newnham, pp.78-82

119 AIR 29/512, entries for 15/07/1940 and 16/07/1940; and Newnham, pp.54, 56

120 Otway, p.31

121 Nine dummy drops, using sandbags for aircrew training and to test parachute and aircraft modifications were carried out at Ringway on the day the Commando pupils arrived, and these flights were subsequently used to give the trainees air experience; see AIR 29/512, entries for 09 & 14/07/1940

122 According to operational records, flying was suspended for two out of three days in the period 10-12 July 1940, due to high winds and rain; *ibid.*, entries for 10 & 12/07/1940

123 Hearn, *Flying Rebel*, p.117

124 AIR 29/512, entry for 13/07/1940; for Strange's involvement, see Hearn, *Flying Rebel*, p.117. Curiously, the operational records specifically refer to the use of X-type parachutes, but this was not developed until August 1940, following a fatal parachute accident on 25 July 1940. Entries in the CLS Operational Record Book appear by date, and the error presumably arises from the entry being written in after the X-type was in general use

125 AIR 29/512, entries for 14 & 15/07/1940

126 *Ibid.*, entry for 16/07/1940. Curiously, this precisely replicated German experience, for the same mishap occurred at the demonstration to sell the parachute idea to the Luftwaffe's Hermann Göring Regiment on 1 October 1935; see MacDonald, pp.11-12

127 Hearn, *Flying Rebel*, p.114

128 See for example WO 32/4723, doc. 76B, teleprint from WO AG 17 to HoFor, All Commands, dated 01/10/1940; doc. 82A, signal from WO AG 17 to HoFor, dated 04/10/1940; and doc. 96A, telegram from WO AG 17 to Eastern Command, dated 22/10/1940

CHAPTER 5: LAYING THE GROUNDWORK

1 AIR 29/512, CLE Operational Record Book, entry for 13/07/1940

2 *Ibid.*, entries for 14, 15 & 16/07/1940

3 *Ibid.*, entry for 22/07/1940

4 *Ibid.*, entry for 23/07/1940

5 *Ibid.*, entry for 25/05/1940

6 For specific mention of the strap being tape rather than canvas webbing, see Otway, *Airborne Forces*, p.29

7 For details see *ibid.*, Appendix C, pp.403-404; and Peter Hearn, *Sky High Irvin*, p.156

8 Newnham, *Prelude to Glory*, pp.119-120

9 See for example L. Minov, 'Obuchenie Parashiutnim Prizhkam' (loosely 'Training in Parachute Jumps'), *Vestnik Vozdushnovo Flota*, No.2, 1931, pp.19-23. I am indebted to Dr James Sterrett for drawing my attention to and translating this article

10 Devlin, *Paratrooper!*, pp.45-46

11 Max Arthur, *Men of the Red Beret*, pp.320-321

12 AIR 29/512, CLE ORB, entry for 26/07/1940

13 *Ibid.*, entry for 29/07/1940

14 *Ibid.*, entry for 26 & 27/07/1940

15 Hearn, *Sky High Irvin*, p.156

16 Quoted from Otway, p.403; see also Hearn, *Sky High Irvin*, p.156

17 AIR 29/512, CLE ORB, entry for 30/07/1940; and Hearn, *Sky High Irvin*, p.156

18 *Ibid.*, entry for 30/07/1940

19 Hearn, *Sky High Irvin*, pp.156-157

20 *Ibid.*, p.157

21 AIR 29/512, CLE ORB, entry for 31/07/1940

22 *Ibid.*, entry for 07/08/1940

23 *Ibid.*, entry for 23/07/1940

24 Hearn, *Sky High Irvin*, p.156

25 AIR 29/512, CLE ORB, entry for 27/08/1940

26 Otway, p.29

27 AIR 2/7239, doc. 4A, 'Development of Para Troops [*sic*] - Air Requirements: Conclusions of Conference Held at the Air Ministry June 10, 1940', dated 10/06/1940

28 CAB 120/262, doc. 3, letter from Keyes to PM, dated 27/07/1940

29 Strange arranged for a demonstration drop from a KLM DC 3 at Ringway for Keyes, through the chief KLM pilot who was a personal friend; Hearn, *Flying Rebel*, p.119

30 CAB 120/262, doc. 4, letter from Sir Arthur Street (AM) to Ismay, dated 02/08/1940

31 *Ibid.*, doc. 5, note from Street to Ismay, dated 03/08/1940

32 *Ibid.*, doc. 6, letter to Ismay, dated 05/08/1940

33 Frobisher was the individual name given to the first De Havilland D.H. 91 Albatross four-engine airliner produced for Imperial Airways in the late 1930s. Only seven were built; four were destroyed in crashes, Frobisher was destroyed by enemy action, and the remaining two were scrapped; see A.S. Jackson, *De Havilland Aircraft*, pp.380-384; I am indebted to Mr Simon Moody, Department of Research at the Royal Air Force Museum, Hendon, for providing this information

34 CAB 120/262, doc. 8, letter from Ismay to van Kleffens, dated 09/08/1940

35 *Ibid.*, doc. 11, letter from van Kleffens to Ismay, dated 12/08/1940
36 AIR 2/7338, doc. 01C, 'Present Situation in Respect of the Development of Parachute Training', dated 12/08/1940
37 CAB 120/262, doc. 9, letter from PM to Ismay, dated 10/08/1940
38 *Ibid.*, doc. 10, memo from Ismay to PM, dated 10/08/1940
39 AIR 2/7338, doc. 11A, paper 'Development of Parachute Troops', n.d., c.08/1940;
40 Quoted from the Colville Papers, diary entry for 27 June 1940; cited in Gilbert, *The Churchill War Papers* Vol. II, p.426
41 Thetford, *Aircraft of the Royal Air Force*, p.28
42 Newnham, pp.21-22
43 Ward, *The Yorkshire Birdman*, p.146
44 Cholewczynski, *Poles Apart*, p.55
45 AIR 29/512, CLE ORB, entry for 31/07/1940; and Newnham, p.18
46 Newnham, pp.18-19. The incident is not recorded in the operational records, but the arrival of an RAF officer at Ringway to investigate it is; see AIR 29/512, CLE ORB, entry for 05/08/1940; for results of the investigation, see *ibid.*, entry for 06/08/1940
47 AIR 29/512, CLE ORB, entry for 27/09/1940
48 *Ibid.*, entry for 07/08/1940
49 Newnham, p.19
50 AIR 29/512, CLE ORB, entry for 08/08/1940
51 AIR 2/7338, doc. 01C, 'Present Situation in Respect of the Development of Parachute Training', dated 12/08/1940
52 Newnham, pp.19-21
53 AIR 29/512, CLE ORB, entry for 15/08/1940
54 The Flamingo was a limited production-run airliner; see Thetford, p.584
55 And these were apparently earmarked for despatch to the Middle East; see Francis K. Mason, *The British Bomber Since 1914*, p.301
56 Otway, p.22
57 Newnham, pp.19-20
58 Thetford, pp.459-462
59 AIR 2/4586, doc. 57B, letter/report from Air Marshal Barratt, OC ACC to Air Ministry, dated 28/04/1941. The Stirling examination is dated 01/01/1941; other aircraft examined were the Avro Manchester and Lancaster, and Handley Page Halifax; and AIR 32/3, doc. 2B, report 'Note on Unofficial Visit by AOC and McPherson to Hatfield to Inspect The Hertfordshire', dated 05/04/1940
60 For line drawing, see Jackson, p.384
61 Other RAF machines using the Pegasus included the Handley Page Harrow and Hampden, and Vickers Wellesley and Wellington; see Thetford, manufacturer-specific entries
62 Bombays serving in the Middle East from September 1939 were used as night bombers and retained their armament. Only fifty Bombays were produced, so if the Air Ministry figure of twenty-one in the UK is accurate, only half were deployed overseas; see Thetford, pp.136-137
63 AIR 29/512, CLE ORB, entry for 06/08/1940
64 Interview with Sergeant Lawley, No.2 Commando; cited in Thompson, *Ready*

for Anything, pp.9–10

65 AIR 29/512, CLE ORB, entry for 12/08/1940

66 *Ibid.*, entries for 13/08/1940 & 14/08/1940

67 *Ibid.*, entry for 09/08/1940

68 I am again indebted to Mr Simon Moody, Department of Research and Information Services at the RAF Museum, Hendon, for providing information on the Harrow

69 C. H. Barnes, *Handley Page Aircraft Since 1907*, pp.372–375

70 *Ibid.*, p.378; and Mason, pp.301–302

71 This figure is reached by subtracting the Harrow's empty weight of 13,600lb from its gross loaded weight of 23,000lb; figures quoted in Thetford, p.311; for a clear illustration of the door see *ibid.*, lower plate, p.312

72 The Harrow was equipped with gun turrets for its bombing role, and while some transports had these removed and faired over this was not universal and some retained the turret cupolas; see Barnes, p.378

73 *Ibid.*, p.378

74 Mason, p.302; and Thetford, p.312

75 Barnes, p.379

76 AIR 2/7338, doc. 01C, conference conclusions 'Present Situation in Respect of the Development of Parachute Training', dated 12/08/1940

77 *Ibid.*, doc. 2A, 'Note on the Employment of Parachute Troops', dated 31/08/1940

78 AIR 29/512, CLE ORB, entry for 02/08/1940

79 See Wright, *The Wooden Sword*, p.16

80 AIR 29/512, CLE ORB entry for 07/08/1940

81 Hearn, *Flying Rebel*, pp.118–119; and AIR 29/512, CLE ORB, entry for 03/08/1940

82 *Ibid.*, p.119

83 AIR 29/512, CLE ORB, entry for 09/08/1940

84 *Ibid.*, entry for 11/08/1940

85 *Ibid.*, entry for 13/08/1940

86 *Ibid.*, entry for 23/08/1940

87 AIR 2/7206, 'Counter-measures Against Possible Enemy Parachute Attack', dated 1940; AIR 20/296, Chiefs of Staff Report (40)432 (JIC), dated 06/06/1940; and AIR 40/1637, Combined Intelligence Chiefs Report No.18, dated 17/06/1940; the latter two are cited in John P. Campbell, 'Facing the German Airborne Threat to the United Kingdom, 1939–1942', *War In History*, Volume 4, No.4 (1997)

88 Otway, Appendix A, p.390; and Thetford, p.621

89 In its original format, 1st Airborne Division fielded three parachute brigades and one air-landing brigade, each of three infantry battalions. This was later reduced to two parachute and one air-landing brigade, the organisation used by 6th Airborne Division in Normandy in 1944 and at the Rhine Crossings in 1945, and by 1st Airborne Division at Arnhem; see Otway, Appendix O, pp.438–445

90 Thetford, pp.620, 622–623; and Otway, Appendix A, pp.390–397

91 Wright, p.45; for details of the Vermork raid, see Otway, pp.70–73; and Richard

Wiggan, *Operation Freshman: The Rjukan Heavy Water Raid 1942*

92 AIR 29/512, CLE ORB, entry for 07/08/1940

93 Wright, p.16

94 Operational records merely record when these aircraft arrived at Ringway and not their intended purpose; see AIR 29/512, CLE ORB, entries for 09/08/1940 & 10/08/1940

95 Wright, p.12

96 AIR 29/512, CLE ORB, entry for 30/11/1940

97 Wright, p.13; according to the operational records, there was a Wellesley airframe at Ringway in October 1940, although it is unclear if it was used as a glider; see AIR 29/512, CLE ORB, Appendix A, following entry for 31/10/1940

98 Wright, p.15

99 AIR 2/7338, doc. 01C, 'Present Situation in Respect of the Development of Parachute Training', closing paragraph, dated 12/08/1940

100 *ibid.*, doc. 01B, extract from Chiefs of Staff Meeting on 6 August 1940, dated 06/08/1940; for the minutes in full, see CAB 120/262, doc. 7, 'Conference Minutes: Meeting of War Cabinet Chiefs of Staff Committee on 6 August 1940 at 10.30 a.m. Re: Raiding Policy', dated 06/08/1940

101 CAB 120/262, letter from PM to Ismay, dated 10/08/1940

102 *ibid.*, letter from DCO Keyes to PM, dated 24/08/1940

103 AIR 2/7338, minute from Ismay to PM, dated 31/08/1940

104 CAB 120/262, doc. 19, letter from PM to Ismay, dated 01/09/1940

105 AIR 2/7338, doc. 4B, letter from Ismay to CAS, dated 02/09/1940

106 *ibid.*, doc. 4A, letter from VCAS to AM Dept. Plans, dated 03/09/1940

107 CAB 120/262, doc. 21, letter from VCAS to Ismay, dated 05/09/1940

108 AIR 29/512, CLE ORB, various entries between 22/08/1940 and 31/08/1940; the total may have been higher because it was not policy at that time to record the number of parachute descents on a daily or weekly basis

109 *ibid.*, 'Appendix A – Progress up to 1/9/40', and 'Appendix B – Training Schedule', inserted between entries for 31/08/1940 and 01/09/1940

110 *ibid.*, entry for 11/08/1940

111 *ibid.*, entry for 12/08/1940

112 *ibid.*, entry for 13/08/1940

113 *ibid.*, entry for 26/08/1940

114 For Rock's injury, see *ibid.*, entry for 22/08/1940. According to Harry Ward, the Irvin parachute canopy oscillated during descent, meaning any '...trainees landing on a down-swing... was heading for a bad knock'. Rock was concussed in these circumstances; see Ward, p.152; for reference to the Ringway conference and No.22 Group assuming total administrative control of the CLS, see AIR 29/512, entry for 31/08/1940

115 AIR 2/7338, doc. 3B, 'Proposed Agenda for Future Conference to [delineate] Policy Governing Airlandings', dated 31/08/1941

116 AIR 29/512, CLE ORB, entry for 03/09/1940

117 AIR 2/7338, doc. 6A, letter from AM to WO rescheduling conference, dated 03/09/1940; and doc. 6B, 'Revised Agenda for Conference 5 September 1940', dated 03/09/1940; and doc. 9A, 'Minutes of Joint Conference, 5 September

1940', dated 07/09/1940

118 AIR 29/512, CLE ORB, entry for 06/09/1940

119 AIR 2/7338, docs. 15A, 16A, 18A & 19A, drafts and final instructions to No.22 Group from AM, various dates between 20/09/1940 & 02/10/1940

120 AIR 29/512, CLE ORB, entry for 01/10/1940; the former entry still refers to the PTS as the CLS, which may have been a genuine error, or a deliberate one to conceal the extent of the change over prior to official sanction

121 AIR 2/7338, doc. 23A, report from 22 Group to AM, dated 06/10/1940

122 *ibid.*, doc. 25A, letter from AM to 22 Group calling conference on 18/10/1940, dated 14/10/1940; doc. 27A, agenda for conference, dated 14/10/1940; doc. 32B, minutes of conference 18/10/1940, dated 23/10/1940; and doc. 35B, 'Note of Continuation of AM Meeting Begun 18 October 1940', dated 19/10/1940

123 *ibid.*, doc. 36B, report 'CLE: Report by 22 Group on [airborne] Results and Experience to Date – Including Graphs for Projected Glider Production', dated 03/11/1940; and doc. 37A, report 'Organisation for Training Air Borne (*sic*) Troops' from AM Dept. Plans, dated 04/11/1940

124 AIR 29/512, CLE ORB, Introduction

125 *ibid.*, entry for 18/09/1940

126 *ibid.*, entry for 19/09/1940

127 *ibid.*, entries for 21/09/1940, 03/10/1940 & 04/10/1940

128 *ibid.*, entry for 23/09/1940

129 *ibid.*, entry for 07/10/1940

130 *ibid.*, entry for 11/09/1940

131 The Boulton Paul Defiant was a single-engine, two-seat fighter armed with a power turret mounting quadruple machine-guns to the rear of the cockpit. It was briefly successful but became something of a liability when the Luftwaffe became aware that it had no forward firing armament; it was then used for a time as a night-fighter before being retired from operational service

132 Ward, pp.142-143; DCO Keyes also referred to an 'RAF machine-gunner who had been a pre-war parachutist'; see CAB 120/262, doc. 3, letter from DCO to PM, dated 27/07/1940

133 See Ward, pp.142-143

134 *ibid.*, p.149; the fan was a drum of cable attached to a standard parachute harness, mounted atop a high platform. The drum was fitted with paddles and the air resistance slowed the drum to the speed of a parachute descent when a trainee stepped off the platform; it therefore took some cold courage to take that step.One trainee who used the apparatus in the 1970s likened the impact to that of 'jumping from a six-foot wall'; see Michael Asher, *Shoot To Kill*, p.81

135 AIR 29/512, CLE ORB, entries for 27/07/1940, 31/10/1940 & 27/11/1940; operational records are not particularly precise on non-flying personnel, or those below a certain level in the Ringway hierarchy

136 *ibid.*, entry for 05/08/1940; and Ward, p.143

137 *ibid.*, entries for 01/08/1940 & 02/08/1940; Newnham, p.49; and Ward, p.149

138 Newnham, p.49; for details of balloon observer's use of parachutes in the First World War, see for example Quarrie, *Airborne Assault*, pp.26-28

139 Poles first feature in the CLE operational records in late October 1940, in a reference to 'New Polish officers [being] separated for Special Parachute Instruction'; it is unclear whether this was as trainees or instructors. It is thus possible that Strange picked up on the idea of using balloons at some earlier, unrecorded meeting; see AIR 29/512, CLE ORB, entry for 28/10/1940; Polish input into the establishment of British Airborne Forces is discussed more fully below

140 Parachute training was included in the training of Polish Army officer cadets from August 1937 as one of several character-building activities that included sport gliding. The parachute course lasted four weeks and included ground training, parachute packing, two or three jumps from a captive balloon with a rip-cord-operated parachute, and three similar descents from an aircraft; notes from interview with Lt-Col. Staff Jan Jozef Lorys (Retd), 16/06/1998. I am indebted to Mr Andrzej Suchcitz, Secretary of the Polish Institute and Sikorsky Museum, for both arranging and providing a location for the interview; and to Col. Lorys and his wife for taking the time to answer my questions

141 AIR 29/512, CLE ORB, entry for 27/11/1940

142 Ward, pp.149-152

143 The balloon was superseded by the Brittan Norman Islander aircraft, on the grounds of economy; see David Reynolds, *Paras: An Illustrated History of Britain's Airborne Forces*, p.11

144 Newnham, p.50

145 Ward, p.152; interestingly, the operational records make no mention of Captain Elliot's involvement, although he is cited by Newnham. On the other hand, neither Newnham nor Ward mentions the involvement of RAF Warrant Officer Brereton who, according to the operational records, accompanied Ward to Cardington for the balloon test: see Newnham, p.50; and AIR 29/512, CLE ORB, entry for 27/11/1941

146 See Ward, p.152; and AIR 29/512, CLE ORB, entry for 08/04/1941

147 *Ibid.*, p.149. A tower was eventually constructed at Ringway, influenced by the Polish example at Leven in Fife in 1941, rather than Williams' suggestion. The Polish tower was 100 feet high and was paid for with a £500 grant from Polish Army HQ and whatever the Poles were able to beg, borrow or steal, including the help of a local Scottish construction firm. It was opened at a public ceremony on 20 July 1940; see Cholewczyski, p.49; for details of the Ringway tower, see Peter Harclerode, *'Go to It': The Illustrated History of the 6th Airborne Division*, pp.27-28, and plates on pp.29, 30

148 AIR 2/4586, doc. 49A, letter from Works Area No.4 to Air Ministry re: permission to establish Balloon Landing Ground at Tatton Park, dated 20/02/1941; doc. 53A, letter from RAF Army Co-operation Command to Air Ministry, dated 02/04/1941; doc. 53C, letter from Lord Egerton's Estate Manager to Air Ministry giving owners permission for establishment of balloon installation at Tatton Park, dated 07/02/1941; doc. 53C, letter from Cheshire War Agriculture Executive Committee to CLE withdrawing ploughing order for Tatton Park, dated 24/03/1941

149 Newnham, p.50

150 AIR 2/4586, doc. 54A, letter from Director of Works to Supervising Engineer No.4 Works Area authorising construction of balloon installation at Tatton Park, dated 12/04/1941; and doc. 56A, letter from Air Ministry Director of Organisation to HQ RAF, Bracknell authorising establishment of Balloon Landing Ground at Tatton Hall Park, dated 16/04/1941

151 AIR 29/512, CLE ORB, entry for 29/09/1940

152 *Ibid.*, entry for 06/10/1940

153 *Ibid.*, entry for 14/10/1940

154 *Ibid.*, entry for 26/10/1940

155 *Ibid.*, entry for 13/12/1940

156 *Ibid.*, entry for 19/11/1940

157 *Ibid.*, DU ORB, entry for 27/11/1940

158 *Ibid.*, entry for 30/11/1940

159 *Ibid.*, entries for 04/12/1940 & 10/12/1940

160 *Ibid.*, entry for 09/12/1940

161 *Ibid.*, entry for 11/12/1940

162 Wright, p.13; and Claude Smith, *The History of the Glider Pilot Regiment,* p.8

163 AIR 29/512, DU ORB, entry for 06/11/1940; and Wright, p.14

164 *Ibid.*, entries for 13/12/1940 & 14/12/1940

165 Wright, p.14; and AIR 29/512, DU ORB, entry for 09/11/1940

166 *Ibid.*, pp.14, 35-36, 44.

167 AIR 32/2, doc. 7A, 'Provisional Training Programme using Sporting Gliders at Ratcliffe and Rearsby or Similar Site', dated 23/10/1940; and doc. 8A, 'Suggested Training Scheme for Coxwains of Troop Carrying Gliders', also dated 23/10/1940; for air photograph interpretation training, see Wright, p.44.

168 Otway, p.31

169 AIR 2/7338, doc. 3A, minutes of meeting at Air Ministry, dated 05/09/1940

170 AIR 29/512, DU ORB, entry for 05/11/1940

171 *Ibid.*, entry for 11/11/1940

172 *Ibid.*, entry for 24/11/1940

173 *Ibid.*, CLE ORB, entries for 14/03/1941 & 18/03/1941

174 AIR 32/2, doc. 4A, memo from Hodges to 22 Group, dated 12/09/1940

175 *Ibid.*, doc. 6A, letter from 22 Group to CLE, dated 19/09/1940

176 AIR 2/7338, doc. 12A, letter from 22 Group to AM, dated 19/09/1940

177 *Ibid.*, doc 14A, letter from AM DTO to ACAS, dated 23/09/1940; and doc. 14B, letter headed 'Subject: Air Landing Troops', from DCO/WO to 22 Group, dated 20/09/1940

178 Otway, Appendix A, pp.391-393

179 Wright, pp.18-19

180 Newnham, pp.54, 56

181 AIR 2/4586, letter from Air-Commodore Hollinghurst, Air Ministry Dept. Organisation to Air Ministry 01, dated 08/10/1940

182 *Ibid.*, doc. 39A, letter from Air Ministry to HQ, Bomber Command, dated 12/10/1940

183 AIR 29/512, CLE ORB, entry for 16/10/1940

184 *Ibid.*, entry for 18/10/1940

185 AIR 2/7338, doc. 33A, letter from AM Dept. Plans to DCAS, dated

23/10/1940

186 *Ibid.*, doc. 36B, report 'CLE: Report by 22 Group on Results and Experience to Date', dated 03/11/1940; and doc. 37A, report from AM DPlans, 'Organisation for Training Airborne Troops', dated 04/11/1940

187 AIR 29/512, CLE ORB, entries for 8/11/1940, 13/11/1940, 14/11/1940 & 15/11/1940; and AIR 2/7338, doc. 49A, letter from Hollinghurst, Dept. Organisation to DDO1, dated 18/11/1940

188 AIR 29/512, CLE ORB, entry for 17/11/1940

189 *Ibid.*, entries for 20/11/1940, 21/11/1940 & 22/11/1940

190 Wright, pp.25-27

191 AIR 29/512, CLE ORB, entries for 24/11/1940 & 06/12/1940

192 *Ibid.*, entry for 05/12/1940

193 *Ibid.*, entries for 12/12/1940 & 17/12/1940

194 AIR 2/7338, doc. 55B, 'Minutes of Air Ministry Meeting', dated 11/12/1940; AIR 2/4586, doc. 46A, letter from Air Ministry DDOPs to OP1, dated 20/12/1940; and Wright, pp.27-28

195 AIR 29/512, CLE ORB, entries for 20/12/1940, 30/12/1940 & 31/12/1940

196 *Ibid.*, entry for 01/01/1941

197 AIR 2/4586, doc. 45A, letter from AM DOrg to RAF ACC, dated 18/12/1940; for a participant account see Wright, pp.28-30

198 *Ibid.*, doc. 44A, Postagram from Supervising Engineer No.11 Works Area to AM, dated 20/12/1940. Bessoneau hangars were wire-braced wood and canvas structures of French design, first used by the RFC in France 1915; for details see Raleigh and Jones, *The War in the Air* Volume 1, pp.186-187; and AIR 29/512, CLE ORB, entry for 02/01/1941

199 AIR 29/512, CLE ORB, entries for 03/01/1940 and 04/01/1941

200 AIR 2/7338, doc. 71C, letter from AM DMC to AM DTO, dated 17/01/1941

201 AIR 29/512, entries for 16/01/1941, 27/01/1941, 03/02/1941& 05/02/1941. The January 1940 trials incorporated tests to ascertain glider detection from the ground at night with and without moonlight, and with searchlights; for a participant account, see Wright, pp.37-42. Similar trials were held at the same location at the end of 1941, using the Hotspur.; see AIR 39/52, doc. 7A, minute from Major Fyffe, detailing the necessary personnel, equipment and aircraft, dated 28/11/1941; doc. 9A, granting approval for the trials, dated 01/12/1941; and AIR 40/298, 'Defence Against Glider Attack by Night: Joint Note by Director Fighter Operations and Deputy Director of Air Tactics', dated December 1941

202 AIR 29/512, CLE ORB, entry for 21/03/1940

203 Sergeant Strathdee was an RAF pilot who resigned his commission to participate in the Spanish Civil War; he was killed in Operation FRESHMAN, the abortive glider raid upon the German heavy water production plant at Vermork in occupied Norway, in November 1942; for details of the March firsts, see Wright, p.45; for Operation Freshman, see Otway, pp.70-73; and Richard Wiggan, *Operation Freshman: The Rjukan Heavy Water Raid 1942*

204 AIR 29/512, CLE ORB, entry for 10/04/1941; and Wright, p.16

205 *Ibid.*, entries for 02/10/1940 & 11/10/1940

206 *Ibid.*, entry for 22/12/1940

207 *Ibid.*, entry for 10/09/1940

208 Hearn, *Flying Rebel*, p.121. Hearn may be mistaken about the date, for while operational records show that PTS personnel successfully participated in an 'Army co-operation exercise' on that date, a later entry specifically refers to King Olaf observing a parachute demonstration in February 1941, although the Norwegian monarch may have attended two demonstrations; see AIR 29/512, CLE ORB, entries for 03/12/1940 & 19/02/1941

209 AIR 29/512, CLE ORB, entries for 26/10/1940 & 13/12/1940

210 *Ibid.*, entries for 02/01/1940, 06/01/1941 & 19/02/1940

211 Otway, p.32

212 WO 32/9778, doc. 24A, letter from Rock to WO SD4, dated 07/07/1941; and doc. 24B, paper 'Formation of Further Parachute Battalions', n.d., *c*.07/07/1941

213 CAB 106/8, 'Account of Operation Colossus, Combined Operations Raid in Italy, 1941 February 10, by Lt A.J. Dean Drummond'; for a detailed and well-illustrated secondary account, see Karel Margry, 'Tragino 1941: Britain's First Paratroop Raid', *After The Battle*, No.81, 1993; and Otway, pp.63-65

214 AIR 29/512, CLE ORB, entry for 01/02/1941

215 Otway, pp.64-65

216 Newnham, p.25; and Margry, p.9

217 AIR 29/512, CLE ORB, 'Colossus Details', entry for 11/01/1941

218 *Ibid.*, entry for 13/01/1941; and Ward, p.155

219 *Ibid.*, entry for 14/01/1941

220 *Ibid.*, entry for 22/01/1941; and Ward, p.156

221 *Ibid.*, entry for 01/02/1941; and Newnham, p.28

222 *Ibid.*, 'Colossus Details', entry for 02/02/1941; the aircraft were from Nos 51 and 78 Squadrons. The Air Ministry originally tried to substitute four Bombays for the operation, and were only dissuaded following protests by the CLE; see Margry, pp.11-12; for the Bombays see AIR 29/512, CLE ORB 'Colossus Details', entry for 11/01/1941; and Newnham, p.27

223 Margry, p.18; and Otway, p.65

224 Margry, p.18; and Raymond Foxall, *The Guinea Pigs*

225 Margry, p.10; and Newnham, p.25

226 Otway, p.65 and plates 27-29, between pp.356-357. Examples of the 'CLE Container' can be seen on display at the Airborne Forces Museum, Aldershot, Hampshire

227 See for example 'Our Paratroops Strike', *The Sheffield Telegraph and Independent*, Saturday 15 February 1941, p.1, reproduced in Margry, p.23

228 Margry, p.24

229 In RAF parlance, a despatcher is an aircrewman tasked to oversee a parachute jump from within the aircraft; his duties include ensuring that parachutist's static-lines are correctly hooked up, ensuring the pilots orders via the red and green jump lights are obeyed, the safe removal of refusals from the stick, and the recovery of static-lines into the aircraft after the jump

230 Hearn, *Flying Rebel*

CHAPTER 6: DIVERGENCE AT THE TOP

1 CAB 120/262, doc. 22, list of attendees appended to 'Air Ministry Conference Held on 5 September 1940', dated 07/09/1940
2 AIR 32/2, doc. 3A, minutes of Air Ministry Conference, 5 September 1940, dated 06/09/1940
3 WO 193/27, doc. 6A, letter from WO DMO&P to WO DSD, dated 18/09/1940
4 *Ibid.*, docs. 4A & 5A, teleprints from C-in-C Middle East to WO, dated 16/09/1940
5 *Ibid.*, doc. 8A, teleprint from C-in-C India to C-in-C Middle East & WO, dated 04/10/1940
6 *Ibid.*, doc. 12A, teleprint from WO to C-in-C Middle East, dated 11/10/1940
7 *Ibid.*, doc. 13A, teleprint from C-in-C Middle East to WO, dated 15/10/1940
8 *Ibid.*, doc 14A, teleprint from C-in-C Middle East to WO, dated 04/12/1940
9 *Ibid.*, doc 17A, teleprint from WO to C-in-C India, dated 29/01/1941
10 AIR 2/7338, doc. 20A, 'Agenda for Meeting on Parachute and Glider Troops', dated 02/10/1940
11 WO 193/27, doc. 10A, note 'Regarding Conference Scheduled for 5 October 1940' to WO DMO&P, dated 04/10/1940
12 AIR 2/7338, doc. 22A, 'Record of Meeting Held 5 October 1940 on Parachute and Glider Troops', dated 06/10/1940; and WO 193/27, doc. 11A, same title and date
13 AIR 32/2, doc. 4, letter from Stephenson WO MO7 to Rock CLS, dated 10/11/1940; and doc. 4A, list of weights and measures, n.d., attached to doc. 4
14 *Ibid.*, doc. 11, letter from Fyffe WO to Rock CLE, dated 22/11/1940. The 3.7-inch howitzer was designed for mountain warfare, and could be broken down into manageable loads. At the time of writing, an example was on display on the upper level of the Land Warfare Hall at the Imperial War Museum, Duxford, Cambs.
15 *Ibid.*, doc. 12, letter from Fyffe WO to Rock CLE, dated 10/12/1940
16 Air 2/7338, doc. 45A, letter from WO MO7 to AM Plans, dated 11/11/1940
17 AIR 32/2, doc. 10A, CLE to AM, 'Brief Appreciation of the Envisaged Functions of an Airborne Force', dated 31/10/1940
18 AIR 2/7338, doc. 43A, covering letter for draft from Goddard AM to Harvey CLE, dated 11/11/1940; doc. 43B, letter with comments to above from Harvey CLE to Goddard AM, dated 14/11/1940; and doc. 44A, commented draft from Capel, AM DTO to Goddard, dated 12/11/1940
19 *Ibid.*, doc. 48B, minute 'Provision of an Airborne Force', dated 16/11/1940
20 *Ibid.*, doc. 48A, covering letter from Goddard AM DMC to AM Plans, dated 23/11/1940; and doc. 48B, 'Provision of an Airborne Force', dated 16/11/1940
21 AIR 2/7470, doc. 8B(1) (attached to doc. 8A), letter from AM Director of Plans

to VCAS, dated 30/11/1940

22 AIR 2/7338, doc. 53A, 'Agenda for Air Ministry Conference 2.45 p.m. 11 December 1940', dated 09/12/1940

23 *Ibid.*, doc. 55B, 'Minutes of Meeting, Air Ministry 11 December 1940', dated 11/12/1940

24 *Ibid.*, doc. 62A, paper from AM DMC Goddard to various AM recipients, 'Provision of Airborne Forces – Air Ministry Aspect', dated 23/12/1940; and doc. 67A, letter from AM DMC Goddard to AM VCAS, dated 31/12/1940; the latter refers to the forwarding of the paper to the War Office

25 *Ibid.*, doc. 61A, letter from DCAS Harris to AM VCAS, dated 24/12/1940

26 The War Office appears to have received Goddard's paper on 30 December 1940, as it is referred to with that date in a later War Office response; see AIR 32/2, doc. 14, 'Airborne Troops – Policy For', from WO SD4 Stephenson to AM DMC Goddard, dated 10/01/1941

27 AIR 2/7338, doc. 67A, letter from Goddard to VCAS, dated 31/12/1940

28 AIR 32/2, doc. 14, 'Airborne Troops – Policy For', from WO SD4 Stephenson to AM DMC Goddard, dated 10/01/1941

29 CAB 120/262, letter from PM to Ismay, dated 22/06/1940

30 AIR 2/7470, doc. 3A, letter from AM DMC Goddard to WO SD4 Stephenson, dated 14/01/1941

31 AIR 32/2, doc. 15, paper from CLE Ringway to WO SD4 Stephenson, dated 15/01/1941

32 See Chapter Two above

33 Otway, *Airborne Forces*, p.22

34 See for example AIR 2/7239, doc. 4A, 'Development of Para Troops [*sic*] – Air Requirements: Conclusions of Conference Held at the Air Ministry June 10, 1940', dated 10/06/1940

35 See for example Martin Middlebrook, *Arnhem 1944*, pp.17–18

36 See Chapter One above

37 AIR 2/7470, doc. 4A, letter from Maj.-Gen. Nye DSD WO to Goddard DMC AM, dated 19/01/1941; and doc. 4B, draft memo, n.d., c.19/01/1941

38 AIR 32/2, doc. 18, letter from Stephenson SD4 WO to Rock CLE, dated 31/01/1941

39 For details of Exercise DRAGON, see AIR 29/512, CLE ORB, entries for 02/01/1941, 04/01/1941, 06/01/1941

40 AIR 2/7470, doc. 8B(3), letter from Medhurst Dir. Plans AM to Goddard DMC AM, dated 04/02/1940

41 AIR 2/7470, doc. 5A, letter from Goddard, DMC AM to Nye, DSD WO, dated 05/02/1941

42 *Ibid.*, doc. 6A, letter from Nye, DSD WO to Goddard, DMC AM, dated 07/02/1941

43 *Ibid.*, doc. 7A, letter from Goddard, DMC AM to Nye, DSD WO, dated 07/02/1941

44 *Ibid.*, doc. 20, letter from Stephenson SD4 WO to Rock CLE, dated 07/02/1941

45 AIR 2/7338, doc. 82A, letter from Goddard DMC AM to VCAS AM, dated 11/02/1941. Goddard's claims are supported by the operational records. The

reference to 'special operations' refers to preparations for the Tragino Raid, which tied up the bulk of Ringway's assets for virtually the whole of January; see AIR 29/512, CLE ORB, entries for 01/01/1941 to 30/01/1941

46 *Ibid.*, doc. 89A, 'Minutes for Meeting at the Air Ministry on 19 February 1941', dated 25/02/1941

47 *Ibid.*, doc. 85A, letter from Goddard DMC AM to Plans, DTO, DoR & DWC AM, dated 26/02/1941

48 *Ibid.*, doc. 85A, letter from Goddard DMC AM to No.22 Group, dated 26/02/1941

49 *Ibid.*, doc. 85B, letter from Goddard DMC AM to ACC, HQ Bomber Cmd., No.70 Group, CLE, WO, DCO, dated 07/03/1941

50 AIR 2/7470, doc. 12A, letter from Nye, DSD WO to Goddard, DMC AM, dated 07/03/1941

51 AIR 2/7470, doc. 13A, letter from Goddard AM to Nye WO, dated 07/03/1941

52 *Ibid.*, doc. 16A, covering letter from Goddard, DMC AM to Stephenson, SD4 WO dated 17/03/1941; and doc. 14A, 'Draft of Chiefs of Staff Paper: Policy for Airborne Forces', n.d., c.17/03/1941

53 *Ibid.*, doc. 17A, letter from SD4 WO to AM, dated 17/03/1941

54 *Ibid.*, doc. 18B, 'Paper on Airborne Policy', dated 24/03/1941

55 *Ibid.*, doc. 19A, covering letter to ACAS(1), dated 06/04/1941

56 *Ibid.*, doc. 21A, covering letter from VCAS AM to VCIGS WO, dated 12/04/1941; and doc. 21B, 'Paper on Airborne Policy', dated 12/04/1941

57 *Ibid.*, doc. 20A, letter from VCIGS WO to VCAS AM, dated 10/04/1941

58 AIR 29/512, CLE ORB, entry for 26/04/1941; Hearn, *Flying Rebel*, pp.122-123; Wright, p.51; and Ward, p.158

59 Wright, p.51; the Hotspur was a sailplane based design optimised for long shallow descents. This was a tactical flaw, and subsequent designs were configured for short, steep approaches. Attempts were made to modify the Hotspur were unsuccessful and the machine was relegated to training duties. It was not employed operationally; see Otway, pp.390-391

60 Newnham, *Prelude to Glory*, p.3

61 Reg Curtis, *Churchill's Volunteer*, p.70

62 Wright, p.51. The Fairburn-Sykes (F-S) fighting knife was designed by two former Shanghai police officers employed as Commando close-combat instructors. The knives were standard issue to Commando and Airborne troops, and the special Airborne-pattern battle dress (BD) trousers incorporated a special snap-fastened pocket for it on the outside of the right leg; see Ladd, *Commandos and Rangers*, Appendix 3, p.240; and Davis, *British Army Uniforms*, p.188, and the plate on p.201.

63 Newnham, p.3; Ward, pp.158-159; and Hearn, *Flying Rebel*, p.123

64 Newnham, p.3

65 AIR 2/7470, File Minute Sheet, Note 25, n.d.

66 CAB 120/262, letter from PM to Ismay, dated 28/04/1941

67 AIR 2/7470, doc. 23D, letter from Ismay to PM, dated 28/04/1941; and doc. 23E, 'Note on the Development of Airborne Forces', dated 29/04/1941

68 This is presumably a reference to Goddard's draft Chiefs of Staff, which

repeated the Air Ministry view that German airborne success stemmed from a combination of novelty and surprise which had dissipated; see AIR 2/7470, doc. 14A, 'Draft CoS Paper: Policy for Airborne Forces'

69 CAB 120/262, letter from PM to Ismay, dated 01/09/1940

70 *Ibid.*, letter from PM to Ismay, dated 27/05/1941

CHAPTER 7: TO THE VERGE OF ADEQUATE PROVISION

1 See for example AIR 32/3, doc. 1A, letter from DMC Goddard AM to OC ACC, dated 07/03/1941

2 AIR 29/512, CLE ORB, entry for 01/01/1941

3 AIR 39/4, doc. 15A, letter from OC 70 Group to HQ ACC, dated 08/03/1941

4 *Ibid.*, doc. 21A, letter from OC 70 Group to HQ ACC, dated 14/03/1941

5 AIR 32/3, doc. 2B, 'Note on Unofficial Visit by AOC and Squadron Leader MacPherson to Hatfield to Inspect "The Hertfordshire"', dated 05/04/1940; for details of the Hertfordshire, see Thetford, *RAF Aircraft Since 1918*, p.584

6 AIR 39/4, doc. 2A, letter from OC 70 Group to ACC & CLE, dated 09/04/1941

7 *Ibid.*, doc. 69A, 'Re: Lack of Transport Aircraft', from Air 1 AM to various AM departments, dated 02/06/1941

8 AIR 32/3, doc. 14B, '70 Group Notes from Air Ministry Conference on 22 August 1941', dated 24/08/1941

9 *Ibid.*, doc. 14A, covering letter from OC 70 Group to CLE, dated 29/08/1941; and doc. 14C, 'Minutes of Meeting at Air Ministry on August 22 1941 to Discuss Provision and Training of Flying Personnel for Airborne Forces', dated 24/08/1941

10 AIR 39/7, doc. 37A, CLE to 70 Group, 'Pilot and Aircraft Requirements for Expanded Output of PTS', dated 12/06/1941

11 *Ibid.*, doc. 66A, letter from CLE to 70 Group, dated 15/07/1941

12 AIR 29/512, CLE ORB, entries for 16/11/1940 & 07/12/1940

13 *Ibid.*, CLE ORB, entries for 10/05/1941 and 04/07/1941

14 Ringway was providing aircraft for SOE by the end of August 1940, and was training SOE personnel from at least the beginning of September 1940; see AIR 29/512, CLE ORB, entries for 23/08/1940 and 01/09/1940. By January 1942 SOE had its own small-scale parachute-training operations utilising Ringway's resources. One was located in a requisitioned merchant's house at Altrincham, according to M.R.D. Foot, who did his parachuting course there. I am indebted to Professor Foot for his opinion and details of the Altrincham installation provided via a private communication dated 30/11/1999

15 AIR 29/512, PTS ORB, entries for 28/10/1940 & 03/03/1941

16 *Ibid.*, CLE ORB, entries for 13/02/1941 & 03/03/1941

17 AIR 32/3, doc. 1A, letter from DMC Goddard AM to OC ACC, dated 07/03/1941

18 Norman's misgivings were well founded. According to Arnhem veteran James Sims, the 1st Parachute Brigade used the Stirling for parachute training in

April 1944, the machine was a '…terrifying aircraft to jump from… the hole in the floor was an enormous looking rectangle about six feet by four feet… [and]… you could see a huge U-shaped bar, which was lowered for the strops of the parachutes to go under so they didn't foul the tailplane. [When a man jumped]… his helmet appeared to shave the lowered U-bar'. Sims claims that at least one of his colleagues broke an arm on this bar, that the fierce slipstream from the aircraft's four engines resembled a rabbit punch, and that the Stirling was discontinued following an extremely high rate of refusals from even seasoned paratroopers; see Sims, *Arnhem Spearhead*, pp.16–19

19 The Halifax was used extensively as a glider-tug, beginning with the ill-fated Operation FRESHMAN in November 1942. It was the only tug capable of towing the Hamilcar, was employed on SOE missions, and served in a modified form as a parachute transport after 1945; see Thetford, pp.299, 302; and Otway, Appendix B, p.399

20 AIR 2/4586, doc. 57B, Appendix A, 'Memo on Visits by Wing-Commander Norman to Messrs. A.V. Roe Ltd., Handley Page and Shorts to Examine Possibility of Adopting Manchester, Halifax or Stirling for Parachute Dropping', n.d., attached to document dated 28/04/1941; the individual reports on the specific aircraft include the inspection dates cited

21 AIR 32/3, doc. 2B, report 'Note on Unofficial Visit by AOC and Squadron Leader MacPherson to Hatfield to Inspect "The Hertfordshire"', dated 05/04/1940; for details of the Hertfordshire, see Thetford, p.584

22 AIR 29/512, CLE ORB, entry for 01/05/1941; and AIR 39/7, report from HQ 70 Group to ACC 'Employment of Heavy Bombers for Parachute Dropping', dated 18/05/1941

23 Terraine, p.269

24 *Ibid.*, p.459

25 AIR 39/7, doc. memo from ACC to No.70 Group, 'Aircraft Establishment – PTS', dated 12/06/1941; see also doc. 29A, dated 18/12/1940; and doc. 30A, memo from ACC to No.70 Group & CLE, 'Modifications of Whitley V's for Parachute Dropping', dated 12/06/1941

26 *Ibid.*, doc. 37A, CLE paper 'Pilot and Aircraft Requirements for Expanded Output of PTS', dated 12/06/1940

27 *Ibid.*, doc. 45A, letter from CLE to No.70 Group 'Allotment of Aircraft Whitley III No.K8991 Allotted for Synthetic Training', dated 26/06/1941. Harvey refers to the aircraft previously belonging to No.41 Group, but subsequent documentation suggests that it may have come from No.43 Group, although the latter unit may have been the parent unit for the MU that re-issued the aircraft to Ringway

28 *Ibid.*, doc. 48A, letter from No.70 Group to ACC, dated 29/06/1941; and doc. 55B(i), note from ACC to No.43 Group, dated 09/07/1941

29 *Ibid.*, doc. 59B, memo from 75 MU to No.43 Group, dated 10/07/1941; and doc. 55B(ii), note from No.43 Group to ACC, dated 10/07/1941

30 *Ibid.*, doc. 55A, letter from ACC to 70 Group, dated 10/07/1941

31 *Ibid.*, doc. 65A, Postagram from ACC to 70 Group, dated 17/07/1941

32 *Ibid.*, doc. 66A, letter from Harvey CLE to Cole-Hamilton 70 Group, dated 15/07/1941

33 *Ibid.*, doc. 68B, covering letter from RAF Kemble to CLE, dated 17/07/1941; and attached doc. 68C, 'Maintenance History of Whitley Mark III K8998', n.d., *c.*17/07/1941

34 *Ibid.*, doc. 68A, memo from CLE to 70 Group 'Additional Aircraft for PTS', dated 18/07/1941; and

35 *Ibid.*, doc. 67A, note from 70 Group to ACC, dated 19/07/1941; and doc. 69A, note from 70 Group to ACC, dated 21/07/1941

36 *Ibid.*, doc. 18A, 'Training of Parachutists', from ACC to 70 Group, dated 04/06/1941

37 *Ibid.*, doc. 19A, letter from 70 Group to CLE, dated 05/06/1941

38 *Ibid.*, doc. 20A, CLE paper 'Brief Aide Memoire for AMT', dated 04/06/1941

39 *Ibid.*, doc. 23A, covering letter from 70 Group to CLE, dated 07/06/1941; and attached doc. 22A, questionnaire 'Training of Parachute Troops at CLE', n.d., c.07/06/1941

40 Thetford, pp.28-29

41 AIR 39/7, doc. 37A, CLE paper to 70 Group 'Pilot and Aircraft Requirements for Expanded Output of PTS', dated 12/06/1941

42 *Ibid.*, doc. 38A, CLE paper to 70 Group, 'Training Capacity of PTS', dated 23/06/1941

43 *Ibid.*, doc. 49A, letter from CLE to 70 Group, dated 27/06/1941

44 AIR 2/7574, doc. 4, letter from Air Chief Marshal Freeman AM to Brigadier Nye WO, dated 02/07/1941; and doc. 5, letter from Nye WO to Freeman AM, dated 04/07/1941

45 AIR 39/4, doc. 102B, paper from AM to various Departments 'British Airborne Force Policy', dated 08/08/1941

46 The reference to 'Transport Command' in this document is curious, for that organisation was not officially established until 25 March 1943; see Humphrey Wynn, *Forged In War*, p.1

47 AIR 2/7574, doc. 20A, telegram from AM to 41 Group, dated 08/10/1941; doc. 21A, telegram from 41 Group to AM, dated 12/10/1941; and AIR 39/7, doc. 158A, Postagram from ACC to 70 Group, dated 11/10/1941

48 Shobden had been considered for the original move from Ringway on New Year's Day 1941, but was rejected because it was unfinished; the fact that it was still unfinished eight months later suggests that it was not considered a high priority; AIR 2/7338, doc. 55B, 'Minutes of Air Ministry Meeting', dated 11/12/1940; AIR 2/4586, doc. 46A, letter from DDOPs AM to OP1, dated 20/12/1940; and Wright, *The Wooden Sword*, pp.27-28

49 AIR 2/7574, doc. 3C, 'Minutes of Air Ministry Conference to Discuss the Provision of Flying Personnel for Airborne Forces', dated 22/08/1941

50 *Ibid.*, doc. 4A, letter from Director Bombing Operations to ACC, dated 30/08/1941

51 *Ibid.*, doc. 1A(2), letter from SD4 WO to DMC AM, dated 27/08/1941; AIR 39/7 doc. 88B Appendix A, SD4 WO to DMC AM, 'Formation of Parachute Brigade', n.d., *c.*27/08/1941; and doc. 88C, chart headed 'Organisation of Parachute Battalion', n.d., *c.*27/08/1941

52 Copies of the War Office communications were attached to the Air Ministry

letter. The latter accepted the fact that an additional 2,500 paratroops were to be trained, asking only for confirmation as to whether the parachute training course could be fitted into the three-month window, and that additional personnel and equipment be provided to the CLE on the minimum scale; AIR 39/7, doc. 88A, covering letter from ACC to 70 Group, dated 31/08/1941

53 AIR 39/7, doc. 83A, letter 'Increased Output of PTS', dated 11/08/1941

54 AIR 39/4, doc. 102A, letter from ACC to 70 Group, dated 07/08/1941

55 AIR 39/7, doc. 96A, letter from 70 Group to CLE [*sic*], dated 06/09/1941; for the agenda see *ibid.*, doc. 106B, n.d., *c.* 05/09/1941

56 For a full list of attendees, see AIR 39/7, doc. 107B. For Gale's selection, see Otway, p.34. According another secondary source, Gale was offered the command on 15 September while a Lt-Col. commanding a battalion of the Leicester Regiment, but the minutes of the 9 September conference clearly list him as 'Brigadier i/c 1 Para Brigade'; see Dover, The Sky Generals, pp.26-27; and AIR 39/7, doc. 10B

57 AIR 39/7, doc. 107A, covering letter from ACC to various, dated 10/09/1941; and doc. 107C, 'Minutes of Meeting at Air Ministry on September 9 1941', dated 09/09/1941

58 AIR 2/7574, doc. 20A, telegram from AM to 41 Group, dated 08/10/1941

59 AIR 39/7, doc. 158A, Postagram from ACC to 70 Group, dated 11/10/1941; and AIR 2/7574, doc. 21A, telegram from 41 Group to AM, dated 12/10/1941

60 AIR 39/7, doc. 154A, memo from AFE to No.70 Group, 'Modifications to Whitley Aircraft for Parachute Dropping', dated 11/10/1941

61 *Ibid.*, doc. 160A, letter from 70 Group to AFE, 'Modifications to Whitleys for Parachute Dropping', dated 14/10/1941; and doc. 160B, suggested draft of letter from CLE [*sic*] to ACC, n.d., *c.*14/10/1941

62 *Ibid.*, doc. 161A, Postagram from 70 Group to ACC, 'Training of Parachute Troops', dated 15/10/1941

63 *Ibid.*, doc. 190A, letter from ACC to 70 Group, dated 18/10/1941

64 *Ibid.*, doc. 130A, letter from CLE [*sic*] to 70 Group, 'Parachutes and Parachute Equipment', dated 21/09/1941; doc. 131A, letter from 70 Group to ACC 'Provision of Training Statichutes', dated 23/09/1941; and doc. 138A, letter from ACC to AM 'Provision of Training Statichutes CLE [*sic*] Ringway', dated 27/09/1941

65 *Ibid.*, doc. 148A, letter from ACC to 70 Group 'Provision of Training Statichutes', dated 08/10/1941

66 *Ibid.*, doc. 135A, letter 'Protective Headgear' from CLE [*sic*] to ACC, dated 23/09/1941. The date of this request suggests these were the final pattern training helmet; photographs show the new battalions of 1st Parachute Brigade wearing them while training. Nicknamed the 'rubber bungee', these were canvas with a ring of sorbo rubber padding at forehead level, and remained in service with RAF Parachute Jump Instructors until at least the late 1950s. Initially, parachute trainees wore leather flying helmets, which were temporarily replaced by a crude sorbo rubber model with a neck guard. The bungee helmet was superseded by the rimless airborne pattern steel helmet; see Davis, *British Army Uniforms*, pp.222-224; for photographs of the various models see James G. Shortt, *Uniforms Illustrated* No.10: The Paras,

plates 4, 6 & 15, on pp.6, 7 & 12

67 AIR 39/7, doc. 144A, memo from AFE to 70 Group 'Increasing Output of Parachute Troop Training', dated 05/10/1941

68 *Ibid.*, doc. 144B, n.d., c.05/10/1941

69 *Ibid.*, doc. 150A, AFE to 70 Group & ACC 'Interim Report on 100 per week Paratroop Training', dated 08/10/1941

70 *Ibid.*, doc. 173A, signal from AFE to 70 Group, dated 21/10/1941

71 *Ibid.*, doc. 197A, signal from AFE to ACC, dated 16/11/1941

72 AIR 29/512, CLE ORB, entry for 18/09/1940

73 In RAF parlance, a despatcher is an aircrewman tasked to oversee a parachute jump from within the aircraft; his duties include ensuring that parachutist's static-lines are correctly 'hooked up', ensuring the pilot's orders via the red and green jumping lights are obeyed, the safe removal of refusals from the stick, and the recovery of static-lines into the aircraft after the jump

74 Hearn, *Flying Rebel*, p.122.

75 Hearn, *Flying Rebel*, p.122; and Ward, p.157. There is no mention of the court-martial in the operational records, although Williams' name does not figure after the date of the raid

76 The War Office released a 'short, guarded report about the raid' on 20 February, 1941; see Margry, *Tragino 1941*, p.29

77 AIR 29/512, CLE ORB, entry for 12/05/1941

78 Hearn, *Flying Rebel*, p.124

79 AIR 39/7, doc. 66A, letter from Harvey to OC 70 Group, dated 15/07/1941

80 AIR 29/512, CLE ORB, entry for 05/06/1941

81 Benham reported to Ringway on 4 July 1940; see *ibid.*, CLE ORB, entry for 04/07/1940

82 *Ibid.*, CLE ORB, entry for 11/07/1941

83 Newnham, *Prelude to Glory*, pp.10–11

84 Newnham completed his first jump from a balloon on 28 July 1941; *ibid.*, pp.46–48

85 *Ibid.*, p.41

86 AIR 39/7, doc. 66A, letter from Harvey CLE to Cole-Hamilton, 70 Group, dated 15/07/1941

87 Ward, p.160; Romanov arrived at Ringway on 3 July 1940, and MacMonnies was present by 8 July; see AIR 29/512, CLE ORB, entry for 03/07/1940; and Introduction, list of CLS staff as of 08/07/1940

88 Ward, p.159; and Newnham, p.41

89 *Ibid.*, p.157

90 Hearn, *Flying Rebel*, p.144

91 Flight Lieutenant John Kilkenny, from the RAF's physical training branch, arrived at the PTS sometime in September 1941, although the event is not recorded in the operational records. He is usually credited with inventing the synthetic apparatus used at the PTS, which was referred to as 'Kilkenny's Circus'. Ward claims that much of the credit for this belonged to Bruce Williams, and that Kilkenny's role was hyped by Newnham; see Ward, pp.161–162

92 *Ibid.*, pp.161, 168

93 Newnham, pp.54–55

94 Ward, p.159

95 AIR 39/4, doc. 65B, letter from MAP to CLE, dated 08/05/1941

96 *Ibid.*, doc. 61B, letter from DMC AM to ACC, dated 13/05/1941

97 *Ibid.*, doc. 65A, letter from CLE to MAP, dated 18/05/1941

98 *Ibid.*, doc. 63A, letter from 70 Group to ACC, dated 19/05/1941

99 *Ibid.*, doc. 86A, letter from ACC to 70 Group, dated 17/07/1941

100 *Ibid.*, doc. 108A, conference minutes, dated 08/08/1941; and doc. 108B, conference conclusions, dated 08/08/1941. The same file contains numerous other documents relating to this matter

101 Otway, p.50

102 This was the case with all three previous fatalities at the PTS. Driver Evans and Corporal Watts were killed by parachute failure in July and August 1940 respectively, and Corporal Carter was killed when the snap-hook linking the parachute strop to the strongpoint in the aircraft snagged on the edge of the aperture on 19 November 1940; see AIR 29/512, CLE ORB, entries for 25/07/1940, 27/08/1940 & 19/11/1940; and Newnham, p.23

103 *Ibid.*, DU ORB, entry for 27/11/1940

104 *Ibid.*, CLE ORB, entry for 19/06/1941

105 There were two parts linking the static-line parachute to the aircraft: a secure panel attached to the aircraft, which was later replaced by a cable running the length of the fuselage, and a reinforced canvas strap called the strop, one end of which was attached to the secure panel or cable with a snap-hook, and the other to the parachute canopy via the pack cover and nylon ties designed to break once the canopy was fully developed. Lt Twardawa was killed when the snap-hook linking the strop to the secure panel came undone, apparently from snagging on another snap-hook. The documents suggest this may have been the result of clipping ten strops to a secure panel designed for eight, and it is also possible that the safety pins designed at the DU after an earlier fatality were only attached to the snap-hooks linking the strop to the parachute

106 AIR 39/7, doc. 111A, letter from 70 Group to CLE 'Flying Accident Ringway on 20 June [*sic*] 1941 Resulting in the Death of 2nd Lieutenant Jan Twardawa', dated 18/07/1941

107 *Ibid.*, doc. 112A, covering letter from OC CLE to 70 Group, dated 19/07/1941; and doc. 112B, 'Parachute Dropping', dated 18/07/1941

108 *Ibid.*, doc. 74A, letter from 70 Group to CLE 'Flying Accident – Whitley K7262, at Tatton Park near Ringway on 19 June 1941 – PTS', dated 24/07/1941

109 *Ibid.*, doc. 115A, letter from CLE to 70 Group, dated 27/07/1941

110 *Ibid.*, doc. 117A, letter from 70 Group to CLE, dated 31/07/1941

111 *Ibid.*, doc. 119A, letter from CLE to 70 Group, dated 15/08/1941

112 *Ibid.*, doc. 122A, letter from 70 Group to CLE, dated 25/08/1941

113 *Ibid.*, doc. 124A, letter from CLE to 70 Group, dated 29/08/1941

114 *Ibid.*, doc. 128A, letter from CLE [*sic*] to 70 Group, dated 20/09/1941

115 *Ibid.*, doc 163A, memo from AFE to 70 Group, dated 13/10/1941

116 *Ibid.*, doc. 188A, letter from AFE to 70 Group & PTS 'Suitability of Wellington Aircraft for Parachute Dropping', dated 05/11/1941; and doc. 188B, 'Pilot's Order Book: Special Orders to Apply when Parachutists Carried in Wellington Aircraft', n.d., *c.*05/11/1941

117 *Ibid.*, doc. 181A, letter from AFE to 70 Group, dated 01/11/1941

118 *Ibid.*, doc. 187A, letter from AFE to 70 Group 'Attachment of Static Line', dated 05/11/1941

119 Otway, Appendix B, pp.398-399

120 Photographs of fully equipped parachutists in these aircraft clearly illustrate their varying degrees of suitability. For the Whitley and Albemarle, see Thompson, *Ready For Anything*, plates between pp.116-117; for the DC3, see Otway, plate 24, between pp.196-197

121 AIR 39/7, doc. 124A, memo from CLE to 70 Group, dated 29/08/1941

122 *Ibid.*, doc. 109A, covering letter from Newnham OC PTS to ACC, dated 17/09/1941; and doc.109B, PTS to CLE 'Training: Parachutists', dated 16/09/1941

123 *Ibid.*, doc. 110A, letter from 70 Group to CLE, dated 18/09/1941

124 *Ibid.*, doc. 136A, covering letter from PTS to 70 Group, dated 24/09/1941; and doc. 136B, two-page breakdown of parachute training statistics from July 1940 to September 1941, n.d., *c*.24/09/1941

125 CAB 120/262, doc. 23, 'Provision of Air Borne Force: Conference at the Air Ministry 5 September 1940', dated 02/09/1940

126 *Ibid.*, doc. 25, letter from Air Ministry to Prime Minister, dated 11/09/1940

127 AIR 39/7, doc. 24A, paper from 70 Group to CLE 'Night Flying from Ringway Aerodrome', dated 09/06/1941; doc. 26A, covering letter from 70 Group to CLE, dated 08/06/1941; doc. 26B, letter from HQ fighter Command to 'relevant authority' regarding curtailing night fighter operations over Ringway, dated 08/06/1941; doc. 27A, letter from 70 Group to Fighter Command, dated 10/06/1941; doc. 32A, letter from 9 Group to 70 Group, dated 11/06/1941; and doc. 33A, letter from CLE to 70 Group, dated 13/06/1941

128 AIR 2/7338, doc. 73A, letter from MAP to DMC AM, dated 04/01/1941

129 *Ibid.*, doc. 86A, letter from AM to MAP, dated 22/02/1941; and doc. 89A, 'Minutes of Air Ministry Meeting 19 February 1941'', dated 25/02/1941

130 *Ibid.*, doc. 91B, signal from ACAS (T) AM to DMO AM, dated 03/03/1941

131 *Ibid.*, doc. 91A, signal from ACAS (T) AM to DMC AM, dated 04/03/1941

132 AIR 29/512, CLE ORB, entry for 06/03/1941

133 *Ibid.*, CLE ORB, entry for 21/01/1941

134 AIR 32/3, doc. 19A, letter from CLE (*sic*) to 70 Group 'Provision of Gliders', dated 11/09/1941

135 AIR 2/7470, doc. 14A, 'Draft Chiefs of Staff Paper: Policy for Airborne Forces', n.d., *c*.17/03/1941

136 AIR 29/512, entries for 25/03/1941, 28/03/1941, 30/03/1941 & 10/04/1941

137 Thetford, p.621; and Otway, p.390

138 AIR 32/3, doc. 19A, letter from CLE (*sic*) to 70 Group 'Provision of Gliders', dated 11/09/1941; and doc. 21A, letter from 70 Group to ACC, dated 15/09/1941

139 *Ibid.*, doc. 24A, letter from 70 Group to CLE (*sic*), dated 21/09/1941

140 AIR 29/512, CLE ORB, entry for 26/09/1941; AIR 32/3, doc. 27A, letter from AFE to 70 Group 'Provision of Gliders', dated 15/10/1941; and doc. 36A, letter from TDS to AFE 'Hotspur II, Full Load Trials', dated 02/11/1941

141 see for example AIR 32/3, doc. 41A, 'Present Proposals for Glider Borne

Forces', dated 28/10/1941; and doc. 45A, agenda and minutes 'Meeting to Consider Army Requirements for Airborne Forces', dated 30/12/12941 and 01/01/1942 respectively

142 Thetford, p.621

143 AIR 2/7470, doc. 17A, letter from WO to AM, dated 17/03/1941

144 Thetford, p.620

145 According to the operational records, Wing Co. Buxton from the DU inspected a mock-up glider at the Airspeed works on 15 January, but another entry six days later refers to other CLE officers discussing production of a mock-up glider, also for Spec. 26/40. Possibly this was related to competing designs for the specification; see AIR 29/512, CLE ORB, entries for 15/01/1941 & 21/01/1941

146 AIR 2/7338, doc. 77A, letter from MAP to ACAS (T) AM '25 Seater Glider to Specification S.26/40', dated 30/01/1941

147 CAB 120/262, doc. 36, 'Note on Horsa Glider', n.d., *c.*05/1941

148 AIR 29/512, CLE ORB, entry for 03/09/1941

149 AIR 7470, doc. 18B, 'Chiefs of Staff Paper: Policy for Airborne Forces', dated 24/03/1941

150 *Ibid.*, doc. 20A, letter from VCIGS WO to VCAS AM, dated 10/04/1941

151 AIR 29/512, CLE ORB, entry for 28/05/1941

152 Thetford, p.622

153 AIR 2/7470, doc. 22A, letter from MAP to AM 'Towing 25 Seat Glider', dated 11/04/1941

154 AIR 32/3, doc. 28B, letter from DMC AM to ACC, dated 17/10/1941

155 AIR 2/7470, doc. 18B, 'Chiefs of Staff Paper: Policy for Airborne Forces', dated 24/03/1941

156 AIR 32/3, doc. 41A, CLE [*sic*] paper 'Present Proposals for Glider Borne Force', dated 28/10/1941

157 *Ibid.*, doc. 40B, Air Ministry paper 'Air Borne Forces – Policy', dated 02/11/1941

158 AIR 2/7338, doc. 01C, Air Ministry paper 'Present Situation in Respect of the Development of Parachute Training', dated 12/08/1940

159 *Ibid.*, doc. 55B, 'Minutes of Meeting, Air Ministry 11 December 1940', dated 11/12/1940

160 AIR 29/512, CLE ORB, entry for 05/04/1941

161 Smith, *Glider Pilot Regiment*, p.17

162 AIR 32/3, doc. 10B, letter from AM to 70 Group, dated 25/07/1941

163 AIR 2/7570, doc. 3C, 'Minutes of Air Ministry Conference to Discuss the Provision of Flying Personnel for Airborne Forces', dated 22/08/1941

164 Otway, p.36

165 *Ibid.*, pp.42, 55–56

166 AIR 29/512, CLE ORB, entry for 20/02/1941

167 *Ibid.*, CLE ORB, entry for 12/03/1941

168 A company of Ox & Bucks under Major John Howard were the first Allied troops to land on D-Day, seizing the vital bridges over the Orne River and Canal in Normandy to link the invasion beaches and the 6th Airborne Division holding the Eastern shoulder of the invasion area; for details see Otway, pp.173–

174, 178; and Shannon, *One Night in June*

169 AIR 2/4586, doc. 58A, telegram from AM to 41 Group, dated 8-9/07/1941

170 AIR 29/512, entry for 11/10/1941

171 AIR 32/3, doc. 30A, letter from C-in-C HoFor to All Army Home Commands, dated 10/10/1941. 31 Brigade Group was a full-strength formation made up from units recalled from India, and was carrying out mountain training in Wales; see Otway, pp.37, 41-42

172 AIR 29/512, CLE ORB, entry for 26/10/1941. Browning was appointed on 29/10/1941; and Otway, p.39

173 AIR 29/512, CLE ORB, entries for 06/03/1941, 21/03/1941 27/03/1941, 10/04/1941 & 28/05/1941

174 AIR 39/52, docs. 1A & 1B, letters from Deputy Director Air Tactics to ACC, both dated 15/11/1941; doc. 3A, Postagram from DDAT to AFE, dated 23/11/1941; doc. 7A, minute from Airlanding Bde. Gp., dated 28/11/1942; doc. 9A, signal approving trials, dated 01/12/1941; doc. 11A & 11B, covering letter and attached AFE questionnaire (dated 25/10/1941) from 70 Group to ACC, dated 25/12/1941; and Doc. 11C, detailed response to questionnaire from GXU to AFE, dated 02/12/1941

175 *Ibid.*, doc. 17A, letter from ACC to GOC Airborne Div., dated 12/01/1942 and attached letter from Principal Medical Officer, ACC (dated 08/01/1942); and doc. 21A, letter from ACC to 70 Group, dated 27/01/1942

CHAPTER 8: FROM MAVERICK RAIDERS TO A CONVENTIONAL FORCE

1 See for example *The Sheffield Telegraph*, 15 February 1941; reproduced in Margry, *op, cit.*

2 AIR 39/4, doc. 71A, letter from CLE to ACC, dated 07/06/1941

3 *Ibid.*, doc. 71B, CLE paper 'British Parachute Troops', dated 07/06/1941

3 AIR 29/512, CLE ORB, entry for 20/10/1941

4 AIR 32/4, doc 4A, enquiry from Turkish govt. to WO, dated 03/06/1941; and doc. 7A, CLE paper, 'Details of Equipment Carried by Parachute Troops', dated 19/06/1941

5 WO 193/27, docs. 4A & 5A, teleprints from C-in-C Middle East to WO, dated 16/09/1940; and doc. 8A, teleprint from C-in-C India to C-in-C Middle East & WO, dated 04/10/1940

6 *Ibid.*, doc. 12A, teleprint from WO to C-in-C Middle East, dated 11/10/1940

7 *Ibid.*, doc 14A, teleprint from C-in-C Middle East to WO, dated 04/12/1940

8 *Ibid.*, doc 17A, teleprint from WO to C-in-C India, dated 29/01/1941

9 Otway, Airborne Forces, pp.331-332

10 AIR 2/7574, doc. 1A(2), letter from WO to AM DMC, dated 27/08/1941

11 For details of the convoluted evolution of this unit, see Otway, pp.341-346

12 CAB 120/262, doc. 37B, letter from Amery to PM, dated 06/10/1941. Wavell had been appointed C-in-C India in mid-1941; see Fraser, *We Shall Shock Them*, pp.160, 204

13 CAB 120/262, doc. 37A, letter from PM to CoS, dated 06/10/1941

14 *Ibid.*, doc. 38, letter from CoS to PM, dated 04/11/1941
15 *Ibid.*, doc. 39, letter from Amery to PM, dated 06/11/1941
16 *Ibid.*, doc. 40, letter from Amery to PM, dated 11/11/1941
17 *Ibid.*, doc. 41, letter from PM to CoS, dated 13/11/1941. Churchill also forwarded Amery's letter of 06/11/1941 on the day it was received, as shown by his pencil footnote
18 *Ibid.*, doc. 42, letter from CAS to PM, dated 19/11/1941
19 *Ibid.*, doc. 43B, cipher telegram from C in C Middle East to WO, dated 20/01/1941
20 Raleigh and Jones, *The War in the Air*, Volume V, pp.278-280; for a more detailed account, complete with contemporary photographs, see Grant and Cole, *But Not In Anger*, pp.7-14
21 See David Warner, 'Auchinleck', in John Keegan (Ed.), *Churchill's Generals*, pp.130-147
22 Kabrit suffered from high winds, frequent sandstorms and extremely high temperatures, which were inappropriate for parachute training; see Otway, pp.107-109
23 Otway, pp.61-62, 74-75
24 Auchinleck followed Wavell to high command in India in June 1943; see Fraser, pp.160, 232, 302
25 CAB 120/262, doc. 47, telegram from C-in-C ME to WO South India, dated 31/03/1942
26 *Ibid.*, doc. 46, telegram from Amery to Indian Government, dated 05/04/1942
27 *Ibid.*, doc. 44, letter from Amery to PM, dated 19/01/1942
28 AIR 2/7574, doc. 5, letter from Nye WO to Freeman AM, dated 04/07/1941
29 WO 32/9778, doc. 25A, memo from VCIGS to CIGS, dated 04/07/1941
30 *Ibid.*, doc. 25A, pencilled addendum from CIGS, dated 05/07/1941
31 *Ibid.*, doc. 33A, letter from Adam WO to CinC HoFor, dated 18/08/1941
32 *Ibid.*, doc. 24A, covering letter from Rock CLE to WO SD4, dated 07/07/1941; and doc. 24B, paper 'Formation of Further Parachute Battalions', n.d., *c.*07/07/1941
33 *Ibid.*, doc. 26A, 'Agenda for WO Meeting on 23 July 1941, to Discuss Raising 2 Parachute Battalions', dated 17/07/1941
34 *Ibid.*, doc. 27A, 'Notes of Meeting at WO on 23 July 1941 to Consider Plan for Raising Additional Parachute Battalions', dated 26/07/1941
35 AIR 2/7574, doc. 1A(2), letter from WO to AM DMC, dated 27/08/1941
36 WO 32/9778, doc. 34A, 'Minutes of Meeting Held at Hobart House on August 26 1941 at 1500 to discuss Formation of Two New Air Battalions', dated 30/08/1941
37 *Ibid.*, doc. 35A, 'Urgent Memo Re; Formation of 2 Additional Airborne Battalions', from WO AAG to all HoFor Commands, dated 28/08/1941
38 AIR 39/4, doc. 102B, paper 'British Airborne Force: Policy', from AM to WO, dated 08/08/1941
39 AIR 2/7574, doc. 3C, 'Minutes of Air Ministry Conference to Discuss the Provision of Flying Personnel for Airborne Forces', dated 22/08/1941
40 AIR 39/7, doc. 106B, 'Agenda for Air Ministry Meeting on 9 September 1941',

n.d., *c.*09/09/1941

41 AIR 2/7574, doc. 10C, 'Minutes of Meeting at Army Co-operation Command to Discuss Measures to Increase CLE Output to 100 Parachutists Per Week', dated 09/09/1941

42 AIR 39/7, doc. 108C, letter 'Expanding Parachute Training Scheme', from CLE to 70 Group & ACC, dated 15/09/1941

43 AIR 2/7574, doc. 19B, letter from WO MT1 to OC, 1 Para Brigade, dated 29/09/1941

44 *Ibid.*, doc. 19A, covering letter for doc. 19B, from ACC to AM DMC, dated 04/10/1941

45 *Ibid.*, doc. 18A, letter from WO SD4 to AM DMC, dated 03/10/1941; and attached doc. 18B, letter from C-in-C HoFor to GOC Northern Command, dated 31/08/941; and doc. 18C, Appendix A, TOE chart for parachute brigade, n.d., *c.*31/08/1941. See also Otway, p.34

46 AIR 32/3, doc. 30A, letter and appendix from C-in-C HoFor to All HoFor Commands, dated 10/10/1941

47 AIR 32/4, doc. 10C, letter from Marecki, Polish GS to Gubbins WO, dated 09/06/1941

48 *Ibid.*, doc. 10B, letter from Gubbins WO to Marecki, Polish GS, dated 20/06/1941

49 *Ibid.*, doc. 10A, letter from Gubbins WO to Rock CLE, dated 20/06/1941

50 *Ibid.*, doc. 11A, letter from Rock CLE to Gubbins WO, dated 03/07/1941

51 AIR 32/2, doc. 1A, 'Training and Organisation of Air-Landing Troops', from Rock CLE, n.d., *c.*08/1940

52 *Ibid.*, doc. 10A, 'Brief Appreciation of the Envisaged Functions of an Airborne Force', dated 31/10/1940

53 AIR 2/7470, doc. 4B, draft memo on airborne employment, from Nye WO to Goddard AM, dated 19/01/1941

54 The paragraph regarding POWs merely drew attention to the possible danger that large numbers of such could pose to a parachute force; see AIR 32/4, doc. 10D, paragraph 32 'Prisoners', in 'Provisional Instructions for Parachute Units', from Polish GS, n.d., *c.*06/1941

55 *Ibid.*, doc. 10D, paragraph 23 'Re-assembly of Landing Parachute Unit'; and paragraph 24, 'Daytime Descents Protected by Fighting Aircraft', in 'Provisional Instructions for Parachute Units', Polish GS, n.d., *c.*06/1941

56 *Ibid.*, doc. 11B, paper 'Comments on Colonel Marecki's Paper', from Rock CLE to Gubbins WO & Polish GS, n.d., *c.*03/07/1941

57 *Ibid.*, doc. 11B, paper 'Comments on Colonel Marecki's Paper', from Rock CLE to Gubbins WO & Polish GS, n.d., *c.*03/07/1941

58 *Ibid.*, doc. 13A, cover slip from Rock CLE to Gubbins WO, dated 10/07/1941; and doc. 13B, 'Notes on the Use of Parachute Troops (Paratroops)' from Rock CLE, n.d., *c.*10/07/1941

59 *Ibid.*, doc. 13B, paper 'Notes on the Use of Parachute Troops (Paratroops)' from Rock CLE, n.d., *c.*10/07/1941

60 AIR 29/512, CLE ORB, entry for 01/07/1941

61 AIR 32/4, doc. 14A, cover slip from CLE, dated 21/06/1941; and doc. 14B, 'Army Co-operation Command and Parachute Troops', n.d., *c.*21/06/1941

62 *Ibid.*, doc. 16A, 'Seizing a Bridgehead for an Armoured Division', from CLE, n.d., *c.*06/1941
63 *Ibid.*, doc. 17A, 'Précis: Airborne Forces Theory', from CLE, n.d., *c.*06/1941
64 AIR 29/512, CLE ORB, entry for 14/05/1941
65 *Ibid.*, CLE ORB, entry for 28/10/1940
66 Personal comment during interview with Colonel Jan Lorys (Retd) 16/06/1998
67 AV 20/3, doc. 105, letter (in Polish) from Gorecki on Ringway headed notepaper, dated 15/07/1941
68 *Ibid.*, doc. 201, covering letter from Harvey AFE to Marecki Polish GS, dated 26/11/1941; and attached report 'Re: Conference with Polish Army HQ Staff on 21 and 22 November 1941', n.d., *c.*23/11/1941
69 AIR 29/512, CLE ORB, entry for 14/04/1941, and numerous entries thereafter
70 AV 20/4, doc. 151, letter from Newnham PTS to Sosabowski OC 1st Polish Independent Parachute Brigade, dated 01/06/1942
71 Cholewczynski, *Poles Apart*, pp.46-48
72 Newnham, p.264
73 AIR 29/512, CLE ORB, entry for 10/04/1941
74 AIR 39/7, doc. 12A, note from AOC to CLE, 'Re: Windsor Demonstration on 25/05/1941', dated 27/05/1941; and doc. 25A, memo from CLE to 70 Group, dated 06/06/1941
75 Garlinski, *Poland, SOE and the Allies*, p.39
76 Cholewczynski, p.50
77 Cholewczynski refers to the 'British Commando School', but primary documentation connected to Polish special training clearly refers to the STC. Commando training was carried out at Achnacarry; see Cholewczynski, p.46; Garlinski, p.60; and Stanislaw Sosabowski, *Freely I Served*, pp.93-94. For details of the establishment of the Commando Training Centre, see Ladd, *Commandos and Rangers*, p.168
78 For details of these establishments see Chapter Seven above, note fourteen
79 Sosabowski, p.95; and AIR 29/512, CLE ORB, entry for 28/10/1940
80 AIR 29/512, CLE ORB, entry for 14/03/1941
81 *Ibid.*, CLE ORB, various entries between 14/04/1941 and 12/08/1941
82 Sosabowski, pp.90-92
83 Cholewczynski, pp.44-46; and Sosabowski, pp.93-95
84 Sosabowski, pp.96-97
85 Krzysztof Barbarki, '1st Polish Independent Parachute Brigade, 1941-47 (1)' *Military Illustrated Past and Present* No.12, April/May 1988, p.24
86 Sosabowski, p.97
87 AIR 29/512, CLE ORB, entry for 21/07/1941
88 AIR 39/7, doc. 87A, letter ' Polish Parachute Training School', from CLE to 70 Group, dated 29/08/1941; and doc. 91A, letter from 70 Group to CLE, dated 02/09/1941
89 *Ibid.*, doc. 81A, letter from ACC to 70 Group, dated 03/08/1941
90 *Ibid.*, doc. 78A, report 'Parachute Training School – Polish', from CLE to 70 Group & ACC, dated 27/07/1941; this improvised apparatus was also

mentioned by Colonel Jan Lorys during the interview in June 1998

91 AV 20/3, doc. 13, letter from Polish GS to WO, dated 24/01/1941

92 Cholewczynski cites 100 feet but a British report quotes a figure of sixty feet. Colonel Jan Lorys, who trained on the tower, commented upon its similarity to pre-war Polish civilian types during the PISM interview in June 1998. See Cholewczynski, p.49; and AIR 39/7, doc. 78A, report 'Parachute Training School – Polish', from CLE to 70 Group & ACC, dated 27/07/1941

93 Sosabowski, p.100; and Cholewczynski, p.49

94 AIR 29/512, PTS ORB, entry for 01/01/1942

95 AIR 39/7, doc. 78A, report 'Parachute Training School – Polish', from CLE to 70 Group & ACC, dated 27/07/1941

96 Harclerode, *Go To It*, pp.27-28

97 AIR 29/512, CLE ORB, entries for 02/04/1941 & 01/07/1941

98 The US Parachute Test Platoon used towers in August 1940, utilising two civilian towers constructed for the 1939 World Fair in August 1940. The American towers did not incorporate a platform, but hoisted the trainee up from the ground. Similar towers were built later at the US Army Airborne Training School at Fort Benning, Georgia; see Devlin, Paratrooper, pp.56-58

99 According to Harry Ward, Bruce Williams suggested a 350-foot tower, costing an estimated £30,000; see Ward, *The Yorkshire Birdman*, p.149

100 For details of the obstacles, see AIR 39/7, doc. 78A, report 'Parachute Training School – Polish', from CLE to 70 Group & ACC, dated 27/07/1941; and Cholewczynski, p.49

101 WO 32/9778, doc. 26A, 'Agenda for WO Meeting 23 July 1941 to Discuss Raising Two Parachute Battalions', dated 17/07/1941; and doc. 27A, 'Notes of Meeting at WO on 23 July 1941 to Consider Plan for Raising Additional Parachute Battalions', dated 26/07/1941

102 The four locations cited in the report were Largo House, Ludlin Links, Elie and Fort William. The first and last of these are on the eastern and western coasts of Scotland respectively; see AIR 39/7, doc. 78A, report 'Parachute Training School – Polish', from CLE to 70 Group & ACC, dated 27/07/1941

103 The Major's name is illegible; see AV 20/3, doc. 150, letter from Major WO to Sosabowski c/o Polish HQ SW1, dated 20/08/1941

104 WO 32/9778, doc. 24A, covering letter from Rock CLE to WO SD4, dated 07/07/1941; and doc. 24B, 'Formation of Further Parachute Battalions', n.d., *c.*07/07/1941

105 Sosabowski, pp.96-97

106 *Ibid.*, p.96

107 Cholewczynski, p.53

108 AV 20/3, doc. 13, letter from Polish GS to WO, dated 24/01/1941; and Sosabowski, p.97

109 AIR 29/512, CLE ORB, entry for 14/03/1941

110 See Garlinski, *Poland, SOE and the Allies*

111 The letter did include details of the alleged infractions; see AV 20/4, doc. 5, letter from Sosabowski to Mackworth Praed, OC STC, dated 02/01/1941

112 *Ibid.*, doc. 28, letter from O'Brien STC to Sosabowski, n.d., *c.*03/1941

113 *Ibid.*, doc. 83, Polish translation attached to copy of British Army Act, dated

25/02/1941; and doc. 84, letter from WO to Polish Independent [Parachute Brigade], dated 25/02/1942

114 Otway, p.39

115 Sosabowski, pp.105-106; and Cholewczynski, pp.50-51

116 Cholewczynski, p.53

117 Dover, *The Sky Generals*, pp.144-145

118 Middlebrook, *Arnhem 1944*, p.42

119 *Ibid.*, pp.414-416, 447-448

120 Otway, pp.147, 261, 271-283

121 AIR 2/7338, doc. 8A, 'Training and Organisation of Air Landing Troops' from Rock at the CLS, n.d., *c.*08/1940

122 WO 32/9778, doc. 25B, telegram from WO SD4 to 11 Battalion [*sic*], dated 15/07/1941

123 *Ibid.*, doc. 24B, 'Formation of Further Parachute Battalions', n.d., *c.*07/07/1941

124 Thompson, p.22

125 Curtis, *Churchill's Volunteer*, p.71

126 AIR 2/7338, doc. 8A, 'Training and Organisation of Air Landing Troops' from Rock CLS, n.d., *c.*08/1940

127 WO 32/9778, doc. 34A, 'Minutes of Meeting Held at Hobart House on August 26 1941 at 1500 to discuss Formation of Two New Air Battalions', paragraph headed 'Parachute Pay', dated 30/08/1941

128 Eighty-five per cent of the existing battalion chose to remain; see Thompson, p.22

129 Saunders, *The Red Beret*, pp.41-42

130 Curtis, p.83

131 Saunders, p.42

132 Otway, p.34; and Dover, pp.26-27

133 AIR 2/7574, doc. 19B, letter from WO MT 1 to CO 1 Para Brigade, dated 29/09/1941; according to Dover, Gale was asked if he wanted the command on 15 September, an unusual step in itself. Gale was at that time commanding a battalion of the Leicester Regiment, but the minutes of the 9 September conference clearly list him as 'Brigadier i/c 1 Para Brigade'; see Dover, pp.26-27; and AIR 39/7, doc. 107B

134 WO 32/9778, doc. 59A, letter from CIGS to C in C HoFor, dated 14/01/1942

135 Otway, pp.38-39

136 WO 32/9778, doc. 34A, 'Minutes of Meeting Held at Hobart House on August 26 1941 at 1500 to discuss Formation of Two New Air Battalions', paragraph headed 'Parachute Pay', dated 30/08/1941

137 PRO AIR 39/7 doc. 88B Appendix A, 'Formation of Parachute Brigade', from SD4 WO to DMC AM, n.d., *c.*27/08/1941

138 For details see Chapter Seven above

139 WO 32/9778, doc. 35A, 'Urgent Memo Re; Formation of 2 Additional Airborne Battalions', from WO AAG to all HoFor Commands, dated 28/08/1941

140 Thompson, p.26

141 *Ibid.*, pp.26-27

142 AIR 29/512, CLE ORB, entry for 15/10/1941

143 AIR 39/7, doc. 176A, covering letter from AFE to HQ 1 Para brigade, re: attached 'Standing Orders – Aircraft Drill parachuting', dated 24/10/1941

144 AIR 29/512, CLE ORB, entries for 01/11/1941 and 02/11/1941

145 AIR 39/7, doc. 197A, signal from AFE to RAF ACC, dated 15/11/1941

146 AIR 29/512, CLE ORB, entry for 12/11/1941

147 *Ibid.*, CLE ORB, entry for 15/11/1941

148 *Ibid.*, CLE ORB, entry for 18/11/1941; and AIR 39/7, doc. 203, signal from AFE to RAF ACC, dated 30/11/1941

149 AIR 29/512, CLE ORB, entry for 30/11/1941

150 AIR 39/7, doc. 203, signal from AFE to RAF ACC, dated 30/11/1941

151 AIR 29/512, CLE ORB, entry for 05/12/1941

152 *Ibid.*, CLE ORB, table at end of entry for 13/12/1941

153 *Ibid.*, CLE ORB, entry for 13/12/1941

154 *Ibid.*, CLE ORB, entries for 08/12/1941 & 11/12/1941

155 *Ibid.*, CLE ORB, entries for 17/12/1941 & 25/12/1941

156 *Ibid.*, CLE ORB, entry for 30/12/1941

157 *Ibid.*, CLE ORB, entry for 31/12/1941

158 *Ibid.*, CLE ORB, entry for 31/12/1941

159 *Ibid.*, doc. 232A, letter from AFE to RAF ACC 'Paratroop Training: Night Dropping', dated 10/01/1942

160 AIR 39/7, doc. 209A, letter from AFE to RAF ACC, n.d.; and doc. 219A, letter from RAF ACC to AFE, dated 16/12/1941

Appendices

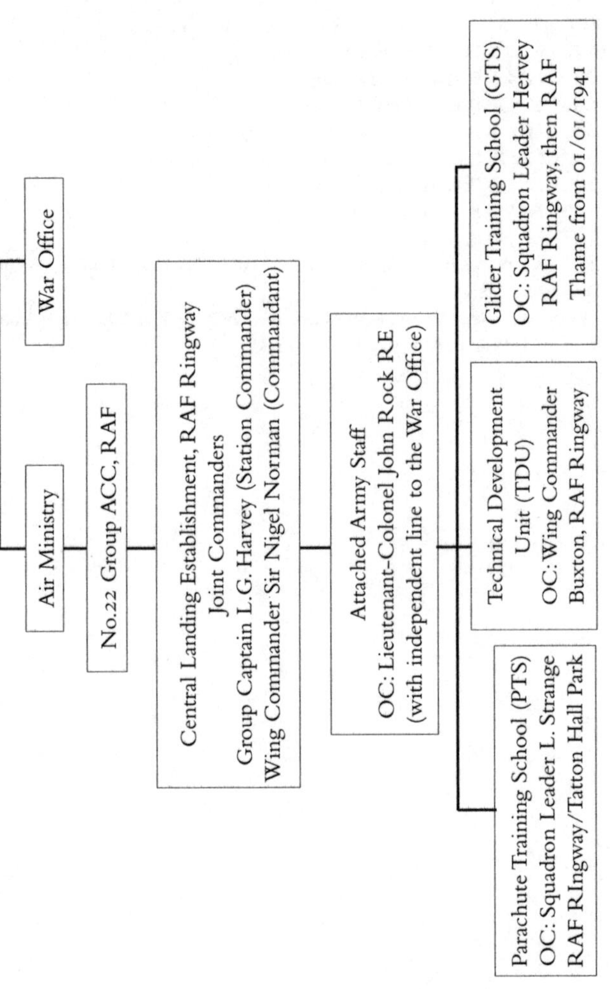

1 Central Landing Establishment with effect from 1 October 1940

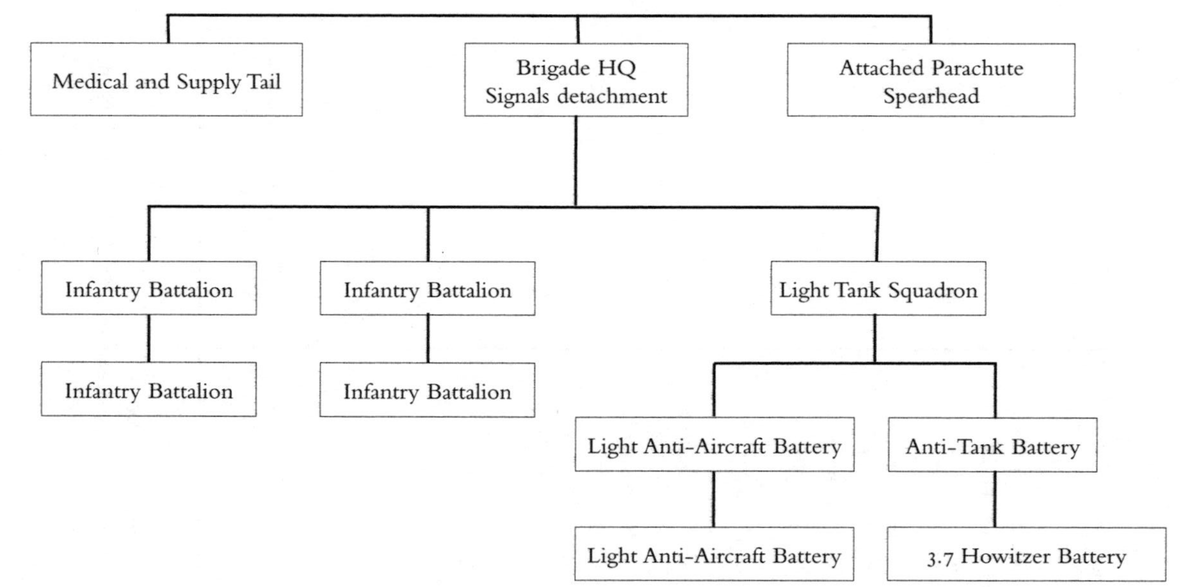

2 Proposed Army 'Invasion Corps', as detailed in WO Paper of 10 January 1941

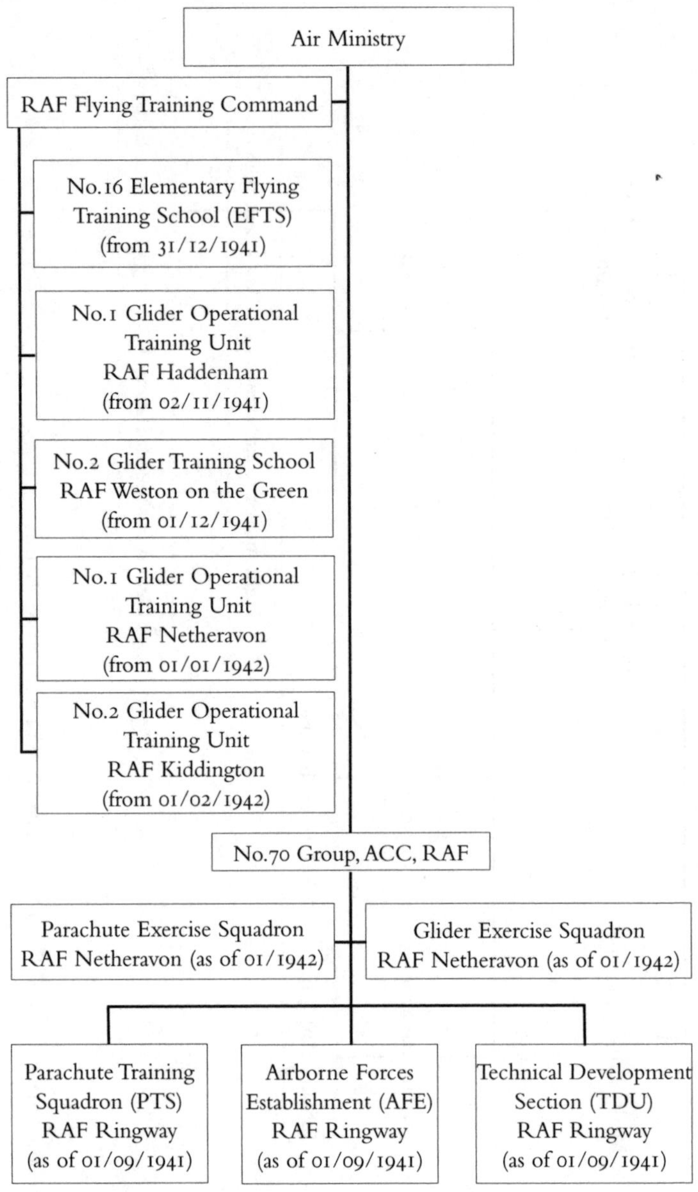

3 Airborne Forces Establishment and Glider Training Organisation, beginning 1 September 1941

Bibliography

UNPUBLISHED SOURCES

British National Archives, Kew

AIR Files:

AIR 2/3897: 1938 – Formation of Parachute Troops in Germany: Report from British Air Attaché, Berlin

AIR 2/4586: 1940–1941 Parachute Training Centre: Formation

AIR 2/7239: 1940–1942 Airborne Forces: Organisation

AIR 2/7338: 1940–1941 Airborne Forces: Provision of Aircraft and Gliders – Policy

AIR 2/7470: 1940–1943 Airborne Forces: Preparation of Papers for Chiefs of Staff

AIR 2/7574: 1941 Parachute Troops: Training

AIR 29/512: 1940 July–1944 July: Central Landing School, Ringway, later Central Landing Establishment, Airborne Forces Establishment, later AFEE, Sherburn in Elmet (Operational Record Books)

AIR 32/2: Provision of an Airborne Force

AIR 32/3: Provision of an Airborne Force: Part II

AIR 32/4: 1941 April–1942 February Role and Use of Parachute Troops

AIR 39/4: 1941 Feb–Nov Formation of Central landing Establishment, RAF Ringway

AIR 39/7: 1941 May–1942 Jan: Parachute Training Squadron

AIR 39/52: 1941 Nov–1942 Aug Airborne Forces – Role and Tactics – Investigation

and Development of Glider Tactics
Cabinet Files:
CAB 120/10: Prime Minister's Directives
CAB 120/262: 1940 June–1946 November: Airborne Forces
War Office Files:
WO 32/4723: Badges for Paratroops
WO 32/9778: 1940–1943 Airborne Forces: Policy and Requirements
WO 190/811: 1939 May 19 – Note Parachute Units in German Defence Forces
WO 193/27: 1940 Jun–1941 Jan Formation of Parachute and Glider Units
WO 193/38: 1941 Jan–Dec: Role of Polish Military Personnel in Allied Forces
WO 193/384: Combined Operations 2: Independent Companies 20 June 1940–December 1940
Polish Institute and Sikorski Museum Archive Files:
AV20/3
AV20/4
Theses:
Crang, Jeremy, *A Social History of the British Army 1939–45* (PhD Thesis, University of Edinburgh, 1992)
Harrison Place, Timothy, *Tactical Doctrine and Training in the Infantry and Armoured Arms of the British Army, 1940–1944* (PhD Thesis, University of Leeds, 1997)
Massam, David, *British Maritime Strategy and Amphibious Capability, 1900-1940* (PhD Thesis, Oxford University, 1995)

PUBLISHED SOURCES

Official Publications

Chatham, *The History of the Corps of Royal Engineers* (Chatham: The Institution of Royal Engineers, 1951)
Great Britain, Air Ministry, R*AF Airborne Forces Manual: The Official Air Publication* 3231, 1951 (London: Arms and Armour Press, 1979)
Otway, Lieutenant-Colonel T.B.H., DSO, *The Second World War 1939-1945 Army: Airborne Forces* (London: War Office, 1950: facsimile Imperial War Museum, 1990)
Parliamentary Debates, 5th Series, CCCLXI, 4 June 1940
War Office, *By Air to Battle: The Official Account of the British Airborne Divisions* (London: HMSO, 1945: reprint Cambridge: Patrick Stephens, 1978)
War Office, *Airborne/Airtransported Operations No.4:* Army/Air Operations Pamphlet No.4 (London: War Office, 1945)

Other Published Works

Allen, Louis, *Burma: the Longest War 1941–1945* (London: Dent, 1986)
Ambrose, Stephen, *Pegasus Bridge, 6 June 1944* (London: Pocket Books, 1994)
Arthur, Max, *Men of the Red Beret: British Airborne Forces 1940–1990* (London:

Hutchinson, 1990)

Asher, Michael, *Shoot To Kill: A Soldier's Journey Through Violence* (London: Penguin, 1991)

Barnes, C.H., *Handley Page Aircraft Since 1907* (London: Putnam, 1976)

Beachey, Ray, *The Warrior Mullah: The Horn Aflame 1892-1920* (London: Bellew Publishing, 1990)

Bekker, Cajus, *The Luftwaffe War Diaries* (New York: MacDonald, 1966)

Bialer, Uri, *The Shadow of the Bomber: The Fear of Air Attack and British Politics 1932–1939* (London: Royal Historical Society, 1980)

Blunt, Vernon, *The Use of Airpower* (London: Thorsons, 1942)

Bond, Brian, *British Military Policy Between the Two World Wars* (Oxford: Clarendon Press, 1980)

— (ed.), *Chief of Staff: The Diaries of Lieutenant-General Sir Henry Pownall, Volume One: 1933–1940* (London: Leo Cooper, 1972)

— *Victorian Military Campaigns* (London: Tom Donovan, 1994)

— 'Doctrine and Training in the British Cavalry, 1870–1914', in Michael Howard (ed.), *The Theory and Practice of War* (London: Cassell, 1965)

Bryant, Arthur, *Jackets of Green: A Study of the History, Philosophy and Character of the Rifle Brigade* (London: Collins, 1972)

— *The Turn of the Tide: A Study based on the Diaries and Autobiographical Notes of Field Marshal The Viscount Alanbrooke* (London: Collins, 1957)

Cholewczynski, George F., *Poles Apart: The Polish Airborne at the Battle of Arnhem* (London: Greenhill Books, 1993)

Cole, Christopher (ed.), *Royal Air Force Communiqués 1918* (London: Tom Donovan, 1990)

Connell, John, *Wavell: Soldier and Scholar* (London: Collins, 1964)

Cooper, Malcolm, *The Birth of Independent Air Power: British Air Policy in the First World War* (London: Allen & Unwin, 1986)

Coox, Alvin D., *Nomonhan: Japan Against Russia, 1939* (Stanford: California University Press, 1990)

Cuneo, John R., *Winged Mars*, Volume II (Harrisburg: Military Publishing Co., 1947)

Curtis, Reg, *Churchill's Volunteer: A Parachute Corporal's Story* (London: Avon Books, 1994)

Davis, Brian L., *British Army Uniforms & Insignia of World War Two* (London: Arms & Armour, 1992)

Devlin, Gerard M., *Paratrooper! The Saga of US Army and Marine Parachute and Glider Troops during World War II* (New York: St Martin's Press, 1979)

Dixon, Norman, *On the Psychology of Military Incompetence* (London: Futura, 1985)

Dover, Major Victor MC, *The Parachute Generals* (London: Cassell, 1981)

Edgerton, David, *England and the Aeroplane: An Essay on a Militant and Technological Nation* (Basingstoke: Macmillan Academic and Professional Ltd, 1991)

Ellis, Major L.F., CVO, CBE, DSO, MC, *The War In France and Flanders 1939–1940* (London: HMSO, 1953)

Foot, M.R.D., *SOE in France: An Account of the Work of the British Special Operations Executive in France, 1940–1944* (London: HMSO, 1966)

Foxall, Raymond, *The Guinea Pigs: Britain's First Paratroop Raid* (London: Hale, 1983)

Franks, Norman, *The Air Battle of Dunkirk* (London: Kimber, 1983)
Fraser, David, *Alanbrooke* (London: Harper Collins, 1997)
— *And We Shall Shock Them: The British Army in the Second World War* (London: Hodder & Stoughton, 1983)
French, David, *Raising Churchill's Army: The British Army and the War Against Germany 1919–1945* (Oxford: Oxford University Press, 2000)
Fuller, J.F.C., *Lectures on FSR III (Operations Between Mechanised Forces)* (London: Sifton Praed, 1932)
— *The Army In My Time* (London: Rich & Crown, 1935)
Gale, General Sir Richard, *Call To Arms: An Autobiography* (London: Hutchinson, 1968)
Garlinski, Jozef, *Poland, SOE and the Allies* (London: Allen & Unwin, 1969)
Gates, David, *The British Light Infantry Arm c.1790–1815* (London: Batsford, 1987)
Geraghty, Tony, *Who Dares Wins: The Story of the Special Air Service, 1950–1980* (London: Arms & Armour, 1980)
Gilbert, Martin, *The Churchill War Papers: Volume II: Never Surrender, May 1940–December 1940* (London: Heinemann, 1994)
— *Winston S. Churchill, Volume VI: Finest Hour, 1939-1941* (London: Heinemann, 1983)
Glantz, David M., *The History of Soviet Airborne Forces* (Essex: Frank Cass, 1994)
Gottman, Jean, 'Bugeaud, Gallieni, Lyautey: The Development of French Colonial Warfare', in Edward Meade Earle (ed.), *The Makers of Modern Strategy: Military Thought from Machiavelli to Hitler* (Princeton: Princeton University Press, 1943)
Grant, Roderick and Christopher Cole, *But Not In Anger: The RAF in the Transport Role* (London: Ian Allan, 1979)
Harclerode, Peter, *'Go To It': The Illustrated History of the 6th Airborne Division* (London: Bloomsbury, 1990)
Hearn, Peter, *Flying Rebel: The Story of Louis Strange* (London: HMSO, 1994)
— *Sky High Irvin: The Story of a Parachute Pioneer* (London: Robert Hale, 1983)
Hickey, Michael, *Out of the Sky: A History of Airborne Warfare* (London: Mills & Boon, 1979)
Jackson, A.S., *De Havilland Aircraft Since 1909* (London: Putnam, 1962)
Johnson, Franklyn Arthur, *Defence by Committee: The British Committee of Imperial Defence 1885–1959* (London: Oxford University Press, 1960)
Junger, Ernst, *The Storm of Steel: From the Diary of a German Storm-Troop Officer on the Western Front* (New York: H. Fertig, 1929)
Kennedy, Captain J.R., MC, RA, (Retd) *This, Our Army* (London: Hutchinson, 1935)
Kennedy, John, *The Business of War: The War Narrative of Major-General Sir John Kennedy* (London: Hutchinson, 1957)
Kennett, Lee, *The First Air War 1914-1918* (New York: The Free Press, 1991)
Kilduff, Peter, *Germany's First Air Force* (London: Arms & Armour Press, 1991)
Ladd, James D., *Commandos and Rangers of World War II* (London: BCA, 1978)
Laffin, John, *British Butchers and Bunglers of World War One* (Stroud: Alan Sutton, 1988)
Lamb, Richard, *Montgomery in Europe 1943–1945: Success or Failure* (London: Buchan & Enright, 1983)
Landau, Alan M. and Frieda W. Landau, *Airborne Rangers* (Wisconsin: Motor Books

International, 1992)

Layman, R.D., *Naval Aviation in the First World War: Its Impact and Influence* (London: Chatham Publishing, 1996)

Liddell Hart, Sir Basil, *The British Way in Warfare: Adaptability and Mobility* (Harmondsworth: Penguin, 1942)

— '[The Next Ten Years] In Warfare', in *The Spectator Booklet II: The Next Ten Years* (London: Methuen, 1934)

— *The Future of Infantry* (London: Faber & Faber, 1933)

— *Paris: Or, The Future of War* (London: Kegan Paul, 1925)

Lucas, James, *Storming Eagles: German Airborne Forces in World War Two* (London: Grafton, 1990)

— *Kommando: German Special Forces of World War Two* (London: Grafton, 1986)

MacDonald, Callum, *The Lost Battle: Crete 1941* (London: Papermac, 1995)

Mackenzie, S.P., *The Home Guard: A Military and Political History* (Oxford: Oxford University Press, 1995)

Martel, Lieutenant-General Sir Giffard, *An Outspoken Soldier: His Views and Memoirs* (London: Sifton Praed, 1949)

Mason, Francis K., *The British Bomber Since 1914* (Annapolis: Navy Institute Press, 1994)

McCue, Paul, *Operation Bulbasket: Behind the Lines in Occupied France, 1944* (London: Leo Cooper, 1996)

McLeod, Colonel Roderick and Dennis Kelly (eds), *The Ironside Diaries 1937-1940* (London: Constable 1962)

Messenger, Charles, *The Art of Blitzkrieg* (Surrey: Ian Allan, 1991)

— *The Commandos 1940-1946* (London: Kimber, 1985)

Middlebrook, Martin, *Arnhem 1944: The Airborne Battle* (London: Viking, 1994)

Miksche, F.O., *Paratroops: The History, Organisation and Tactical Use of Airborne Formations* (London: Faber, 1943)

Militargeschichtliches Forschungsamt, Freiburg (eds), *Germany and the Second World War, Volume II: Germany's Initial Conquests in Europe* (Oxford: Clarendon Press, 1991)

Morrow, John H. Jr, *The Great War in the Air: Military Aviation from 1909 to 1921* (London: Smithsonian Institute Press, 1993)

— *German Air Power in World War I* (London: University of Nebraska Press, 1982)

Newnham, Maurice, *Prelude to Glory: The Story of the Creation of Britain's Parachute Army* (London: Sampson Low, 1948)

Omissi, David, *Air Power and Colonial Control: The Royal Air Force, 1919-1939* (Manchester: Manchester University Press, 1990)

Quarrie, Bruce, *Airborne Assault: Parachute Forces in Action 1940-1991* (Sparkford: Patrick Stephens, 1991)

— *German Airborne Troops 1939-1945* (London: Osprey, 1983)

Raleigh, Sir Walter and H.A. Jones, *The War in the Air, Volume VI* (Oxford: Clarendon Press, 1935)

Regan, Geoffrey, *Someone Had Blundered* (London: Batsford, 1987)

— *The Guinness Book of Military Blunders* (London: Guinness, 1991)

Rezun, Miron, *Intrigue and War in Southwest Asia: The Struggle for Supremacy from Central Asia to Iraq* (London: Praeger, 1992)

Rowan-Robinson, Major-General H., *Imperial Defence: A Problem in Four Dimensions*

(London: Frederick Muller, 1938)

— *Security? A Study of Our Military Position* (London: Methuen, 1935)

— *The Infantry Experiment* (London: William Clowes, 1934)

— *Some Aspects of Mechanisation* (London: William Clowes, 1923)

Saunders, Hilary St George, *The Red Beret: The Story of the Parachute Regiment at War 1940–1945* (London: Michael Joseph, 1950)

Scott, H.F. and W.F. Scott (eds), *The Soviet Art of War: Doctrine, Strategy and Tactics* (Boulder: Westview Press, 1982)

Sempill, The Master of, '[The Next Ten Years] In Aviation' in *The Spectator Booklet II: The Next Ten Years* (London: Methuen, 1934)

Shannon, Kevin, *One Night in June: The Story of Operation Tonga, the Initial Phase of the Invasion of Normandy, 1944* (Shrewsbury: Airlife, 1994)

Simpkin, Richard, *Deep Battle: The Brainchild of Marshal Tukhachevskii* (London: Brassey's, 1987)

Sims, James, *Arnhem Spearhead: A Private Soldier's Story* (London: Imperial War Museum, 1978)

Slessor, Sir John, GCB, DSO, MC, *The Central Blue* (London: Cassell, 1956)

Smith, Claude, *The History of the Glider Pilot Regiment* (London: Leo Cooper, 1992)

Smith, Malcolm, *British Air Strategy between the Wars* (Oxford: Clarendon Press, 1984)

Sosabowski, Stanislaw, *Freely I Served* (London: Kimber, 1960)

Terraine, John, *The Right of the Line: The Royal Air Force in the European War 1939–1945* (London: Sceptre, 1988)

'The Counter-Raiders', *Blackwood Tales from the Outposts III: Tales of the Border* (London: William Blackwood & Son, 1934)

Thetford, Owen, *Aircraft of the Royal Air Force Since 1918* (London: Putnam, 1979)

Thompson, Julian, *Ready for Anything: The Parachute Regiment at War, 1940–1982* (London: Weidenfeld and Nicolson, 1989)

Towle, Philip, *Pilots and Rebels: The Use of Aircraft in Unconventional Warfare, 1918–1988* (London: Brassey's, 1989)

Townshend, C., 'Civilisation and Frightfulness: Air Control in the Middle East Between the Wars', in Chris Wrigley (ed.), *Warfare, Diplomacy and Politics* (London: Hamish Hamilton, 1986)

Tugwell, Maurice, *Airborne To Battle: A History of Airborne Warfare 1918–1971* (London: Kimber, 1971)

Turnbull, Patrick, *Dunkirk: Anatomy of a Disaster* (London: Batsford, 1978)

Ward, Harry with Peter Hearn, *The Yorkshire Birdman: Memoirs of a Pioneer Parachutist* (London: Robert Hale, 1990)

Warner, Philip, 'Auchinleck', in John Keegan (ed.), *Churchill's Generals* (London: Weidenfeld and Nicolson, 1991)

Wiggan, Richard, *Operation Freshman: The Rjukan Heavy Water Raid 1942* (London: Kimber, 1986)

Winton, Harold R., *To Change An Army: General Sir John Burnett-Stuart and British Armoured Doctrine, 1927–1938* (Kansas: University of Kansas Press, 1988)

Wood, Derek and Derek Dempster, *The Narrow Margin: The Battle of Britain and the Rise of Air Power 1930–1940* (London: Arrow, 1969)

Wright, Lawrence, *The Wooden Sword: The Untold Story of the Gliders in World War II* (London: Elek, 1967)

Wynn, Humphrey and the Air Historical Branch (RAF), Ministry of Defence, *Forged in War: A History of RAF Transport Command 1943–1967* (London: HMSO, 1996)

Zeidler, Manfred, *Reichswehr und Röte Armee 1920–1933: Wege und Stationen einer ungerwohnlichen Zusammenarbeit* (Oldenbourg: Beitrage zur Militärgeschichte, 1994)

Articles and Essays

Algazin, A., 'Aviatsiia v reide MMC', *Vestnik Vozdushnovo Flota* No.10-11, 1931

Barbarski, Krzysztof, '1st Polish Independent Parachute Brigade, 1941-47 (1)' *Military Illustrated Past and Present*, No.12, April/May 1988

Barthorp, Michael, 'The Mountain Gun', *Military Illustrated Past and Present*, No.78, November 1994

Bassett, Lieutenant-Colonel James A., 'Past Airborne Employment', *Journal of Military History*, Volume 12 No.4 (Winter 1948)

Borisov, A., '*Desant* onto the Sand in Aircraft', *Vestnik Vozdushnovo Flota* (January 1929)

Broad, Captain H.S., 'If It Happened To-day! War From The Air', *The Army, Navy and Air Force Gazette*, Volume LXXVII (30 July 1936)

Campbell, John P., 'Facing the German Airborne Threat to the United Kingdom, 1939–1942', *War In History*, Volume 4, No.4 (1997)

Cox, Jafna L., 'A Splendid Training Ground: The Importance to the Royal Air Force of its Role in Iraq, 1919-32', *The Journal of Imperial and Commonwealth History*, Volume 13 No.1 (October 1984)

Dean, D.J., 'Air Power In Small Wars: The British Air Control Experience', *Air University Review*, Volume 34 No.5 (1983)

Decurion, 'The Recruiting Problems of the British Army', *The Army Quarterly*, Volume 33

Fletcher, David, 'Steam Sappers: Steam Engines in the Boer War', *Military Illustrated Past and Present*, No.47, July 1994

Fuller, Major-General J.F.C., 'Our Recruiting Problem, and a Solution', *The Army Quarterly*, Volume 33

Fuller, Major-General J.F.C., 'Airpower: The Keystone in our Defence Problem', *The Army, Navy and Air Force Gazette*, Volume LXXVII (10 September 1936)

Godfrey, Major J.T., 'Winged Armies', *The RUSI Journal* (August 1935)

LVSB, 'Three Infantries Not One Infantry', *The Army, Navy and Air Force Gazette*, Volume LXXVII (14 May 1936)

Maclennan, I.A.M., 'Recruiting Stagnation: A Younger View', *The Army Quarterly*, Volume 33

MacNamara, Captain J.R.J., MP, 'Army Methods of Training: Approach of the Modern Reorganised Infantry Toward the Enemy', *The United Services Review* (26 August 1937)

Margry, Karel, 'Tragino 1941: Britain's First Paratroop Raid', *After the Battle*, No.81, 1993

Minov, L., 'Obuchenie Parashiutnum Prizkham', *Vestnik Vozdushnovo Flota* No.2, 1931

Moreman, T.R., 'The British and Indian Armies and North-West Frontier Warfare, 1846–1914', *Journal of Imperial and Commonwealth Studies*, Volume 20 No.1 (1992)

Ramanichev, Colonel N., 'The Development of the Theory and Practice of the Combat Use of Airlanding Forces in the Inter-War Period', *Military-History Journal*, No.10 (October 1982)

Rowan-Robinson, Major-General H., 'Air Infantry: How Can This Development Assist Great Britain?', *The United Services Review*, (17 December 1936)

Ryan, W. Michael, 'The Influence of the Imperial Frontier on British Doctrines of Mechanised Warfare', Albion, Volume 15, No.2 (1983)

Seton Hutchinson, Lieutenant-Colonel Graham, 'The Army of Tomorrow: How to Make it a Corps D'elite', The Army Quarterly, Volume 30

—, 'Recruiting: The Real Problem and Its Solution', The Army Quarterly, Volume 33

Spiers, Edward M., 'The British Cavalry, 1902–1914', *Journal of the Society for Army Historical Research*, Volume 57 (1979)

Stevens, Andrew and Peter Amodio, 'British Airborne Forces, 1940–42', *Military Illustrated Past and Present*, No.54 (November 1992)

Telfer, Captain R.L., 'The Army of Today', *The Army Quarterly*, Volume 30

Thorburn, Captain R.G., 'The Operation in South Kurdistan, March–May 1923', *The Army Quarterly*, Volume 31 (October 1935–January 1936)

Wilberforce, Lieutenant-Colonel W., DSO, MC, 'The Infantry of the Future', *The United Services Review* (22 April 1937)

Periodicals and Newspapers

The Army, Navy and Air Force Gazette

'Notes of the Week', Volume LXXVII (March 12 1936)

'Soviet Film of Kiev Manoeuvres', Volume LXXVII (September 17 1936)

The Army Quarterly

'The New Warrior', January 1934

The United Services Review

'Notes of the Week', (10 December 1936)

'Notes of the Week', (16 June 1938)

'Wings of the German Air Force' (Photo essay), (13 October 1938)

'Empire Day Thrills' (Photo essay), (10 June 1937)

The Sheffield Telegraph and Independent, as footnoted

The Times, as footnoted

Index

TEMPUS – REVEALING HISTORY

D-Day The First 72 Hours

WILLIAM F. BUCKINGHAM

'A compelling narrative' ***The Observer***

A ***BBC History Magazine*** Book of the Year 2004

£9.99 0 7524 2842 X

The London Monster

Terror on the Streets in 1790

JAN BONDESON

'Gripping' ***The Guardian***

'Excellent... monster-mania brought a reign of terror to the ill-lit streets of the capital' ***The Independent***

£9.99 0 7524 3327 X

London

A Historical Companion

KENNETH PANTON

'A readable and reliable work of reference that deserves a place on every Londoner's bookshelf' ***Stephen Inwood***

£20 0 7524 3434 9

M: MI5's First Spymaster

ANDREW COOK

'Serious spook history' ***Andrew Roberts***

'Groundbreaking' ***The Sunday Telegraph***

'Brilliantly researched' ***Dame Stella Rimington***

£9.99 978 07524 3949 9

Agincourt

A New History

ANNE CURRY

'A highly distinguished and convincing account' ***Christopher Hibbert***

'A *tour de force*' ***Alison Weir***

'*The* book on the battle' ***Richard Holmes***

A ***BBC History Magazine*** Book of the Year 2005

£12.99 0 7524 3813 1

Battle of the Atlantic

MARC MILNER

'The most comprehensive short survey of the U-boat battles' ***Sir John Keegan***

'Some events are fortunate in their historian, none more so than the Battle of the Atlantic. Marc Milner is *the* historian of the Atlantic campaign... a compelling narrative' ***Andrew Lambert***

£12.99 0 7524 3332 6

The English Resistance

The Underground War Against the Normans

PETER REX

'An invaluable rehabilitation of an ignored resistance movement' ***The Sunday Times***

'Peter Rex's scholarship is remarkable' ***The Sunday Express***

£12.99 0 7524 3733 X

Elizabeth Wydeville: England's Slandered Queen

ARLENE OKERLUND

'A penetrating, thorough and wholly convincing vindication of this unlucky queen' ***Sarah Gristwood***

'A gripping tale of lust, loss and tragedy' ***Alison Weir***

A ***BBC History Magazine*** Book of the Year 2005

£9.99 978 07524 3807 8

If you are interested in purchasing other books published by Tempus, or in case you have difficulty finding any Tempus books in your local bookshop, you can also place orders directly through our website

www.tempus-publishing.com

TEMPUS – REVEALING HISTORY

The Defence and Fall of Singapore

1940-42

BRIAN FARRELL

'A multi-pronged attack on those who made the defence of Malaya and Singapore their duty... [an] exhaustive account of the clash between Japanese and British Empire forces' ***BBC History Magazine***

'An original and provocative new history of the battle' ***Hew Strachan***

£13.99 0 7524 3768 2

Zulu!

The Battle for Rorke's Drift 1879

EDMUND YORKE

'A clear, detailed exposition... a very good read' ***Journal of the Royal United Service Institute for Defence Studies***

£12.99 0 7524 3502 7

Paras

The Birth of British Airborne Forces from Churchill's Raiders to 1st Parachute Brigade

WILLIAM F. BUCKINGHAM

£17.99 0 7524 3530 2

Voices from the Trenches

Life & Death on the Western Front

ANDY SIMPSON AND TOM DONOVAN

'A vivid picture of life on the Western Front... compelling reading' ***The Daily Telegraph***

'Offers the reader a wealth of fine writing by soldiers of the Great War whose slim volumes were published so long ago or under such obscure imprints that they have all but disappeared from sight like paintings lost under the grime of ages' ***Malcolm Brown***

£12.99 0 7524 3905 7

Loos 1915

NICK LLOYD

'A revealing new account based on meticulous documentary research... I warmly commend this book to all who are interested in history and the Great War' ***Corelli Barnett***

'Should finally consign Alan Clarke's farrago, *The Donkeys*, to the waste paper basket' ***Hew Strachan***

£25 0 7524 3937 5

The Last Nazis

SS Werewolf Guerilla Resistance in Europe 1944-47

PERRY BIDDISCOMBE

'Detailed, meticulously researched and highly readable... a must for all interested in the end of the Second World War' ***Military Illustrated***

£12.99 0 7524 2342 8

Omaha Beach A Flawed Victory

ADRIAN LEWIS

'A damning book' ***BBC History Magazine***

£12.99 0 7524 2975 2

The English Civil War

A Historical Companion

MARTYN BENNETT

'Martyn Bennett knows more about the nuts and bolts of the English Civil War than anybody else alive' ***Ronald Hutton***

'A most useful and entertaining book – giving us all precise detail about the events, the places, the people and the things that we half-know about the civil war and many more things that we did not know at all' ***John Morrill***

£25 0 7524 3186 2

If you are interested in purchasing other books published by Tempus, or in case you have difficulty finding any Tempus books in your local bookshop, you can also place orders directly through our website

www.tempus-publishing.com

TEMPUS – REVEALING HISTORY

R.J.Mitchell
Schooldays to Spitfire
GORDON MITCHELL
'[A] readable and poignant story'
The Sunday Telegraph
£12.99   0 7524 3727 5

Forgotten Soldiers of the First World War
Lost Voices from the Middle Eastern Front
DAVID WOODWARD
'A brilliant new book of hitherto unheard voices from a haunting theatre of the First World War' ***Malcolm Brown***
£12.99   978 07524 4307 2

1690 Battle of the Boyne
PÁDRAIG LENIHAN
'An almost impeccably impartial account of the most controversial military engagement in British history' ***The Daily Mail***
£12.99   0 7524 3304 0

Hell at the Front
Combat Voices from the First World War
TOM DONOVAN
'Fifty powerful personal accounts, each vividly portraying the brutalising reality of the Great War… a remarkable book' ***Max Arthur***
£12.99   0 7524 3940 5

Amiens 1918
JAMES MCWILLIAMS & R. JAMES STEEL
'A masterly portrayal of this pivotal battle'
Soldier: The Magazine of the British Army
£25   0 7524 2860 8

Before Stalingrad
Hitler's Invasion of Russia 1941
DAVID GLANTZ
'Another fine addition to Hew Strachan's excellent *Battles and Campaigns* series'
BBC History Magazine
£9.99   0 7524 2692 3

The SS
A History 1919-45
ROBERT LEWIS KOEHL
'Reveals the role of the SS in the mass murder of the Jews, homosexuals and gypsies and its organisation of death squads throughout occupied Europe' ***The Sunday Telegraph***
£9.99   0 7524 2559 5

Arnhem 1944
WILLIAM BUCKINGHAM
'Reveals the real reason why the daring attack failed' ***The Daily Express***
£10.99   0 7524 3187 0

If you are interested in purchasing other books published by Tempus, or in case you have difficulty finding any Tempus books in your local bookshop, you can also place orders directly through our website

www.tempus-publishing.com